CREATING AND SUSTAINING
COMPANY GROWTH

An Entrepreneurial Perspective
for Established Companies

CREATING AND SUSTAINING COMPANY GROWTH

An Entrepreneurial Perspective
for Established Companies

James B. Hangstefer

BURTON-MERRILL COMPANY

Creating and Sustaining Company Growth:
An Entrepreneurial Perspective for Established Companies

Published by Burton-Merrill Company, Waltham, MA 02154

Copyright © 1997 by James B. Hangstefer.

The paper used in this book meets the requirements of the American National Standard for Permanence of Paper for Printed Library Materials Z39.48-1984.

This book is distributed by: Burton-Merrill Company, 318 Bear Hill Road, Suite 3, Waltham, MA 02154. Telephone: 1-800-293-4299.

Book design by Deborah Rust

Publisher's Cataloging in Publication
(Prepared by Quality Books Inc)

Hangstefer, James B.

Creating and Sustaining Company Growth: An Entrepreneurial
Perspective for Established Companies
p. cm.
Includes index
ISBN 0-9656067-0-8.

1. Strategic planning.   2. Organizational change.   3. Management.
I. Title.

HD30.28.H36 1997   658.4'012
                                                         QBI96-40805

First Edition
Manufactured in the United States of America
1 2 3 4 5 6 7 8 9 / 05 04 03 02 01 00 99 98 97

This book is dedicated to my wife, Lucie, for her love, support, and friendship over the past twenty-five years. I have been very fortunate to have her as a partner in our business ventures as well as in sharing the many life experiences we have enjoyed together.

ACKNOWLEDGMENTS

Many articles and books on management, cited throughout the text, have been helpful to me over the years, but the seminal thoughts of Peter F. Drucker, starting with his 1953 book *The Practice of Management*, have set the foundation for my views on management. His influence is apparent in what follows.

Two people deserve special recognition for their help in the evolution of this book, my wife, Lucie, and my stepson, Dr. Peter Hainer, professor of anthropology at Curry College in Milton, Mass. Lucie has spent countless hours reading drafts of every page and offering many, many helpful thoughts and editorial corrections. Her contributions have been invaluable. Peter, who saw from the start the intrinsic merit in momentum as an organizing theme for a management strategy, has carefully read each draft. His thoughts about the book's content and structure have materially improved the final product.

I would also like to acknowledge the support I have received from Boruch (Bill) Frusztajer, founder, president, and CEO of BBF Corporation, Waltham, Mass. After reading an early draft, he responded with enthusiasm and encouraged me by telling me he had already put some of my ideas into practice in his own company.

The book has been edited by Sara Blackburn, who crafted the last draft of the manuscript into its final form. She is a true professional with great insight into the subtleties of business.

CONTENTS

PREFACE

S ince World War II, the job of top management has been viewed as two-dimensional: setting business strategy and executing that strategy. The approach to company management usually has taken the form of "command and control." In today's business environment, this model is obsolete for companies seeking significant continuous growth.

The alternative management techniques proposed over the past several decades—strategic management, total quality (TQM), time-based competition, and others—have shown significant limitations in the light of real-world situations. Each is interesting and potentially useful, but none succeeds in encompassing the entire scope of actual company needs that top management must consider to build a growing business in an aggressively competitive marketplace. This book lays out a vigorous, all-encompassing strategy, Three Dimensional Management, for achieving superiority in the management of any company.

Three Dimensional Management (TDM) incorporates momentum building as a third dimension of managerial responsibility. Once momentum joins the traditional dimensions of strategy and execution, the approach to management changes, and the new focus becomes company strengthening within a time frame that provides consistent growth in stakeholder value. TDM integrates the kind of entrepreneurial thinking that will stimulate growth in any company. In a vital atmosphere that nurtures astute strategy, unique competencies, creativity, and continual momentum-building, entrepreneurial achievement flourishes and is sustained over time.

The importance of momentum building became apparent to me in my first position as a CEO, and Three Dimensional Management is the result of many years of experience since then. I have tried to make this the kind of book I wish I had had early in my own career.

I have seen many businesses with considerable potential never achieve that potential. Occasionally, they made splashes with new products, but usually they were so entangled in the seaweed of mediocre management that their competitors moved forward at a faster rate. Some faced and solved their management problems and moved forward. The others might have succeeded if they had understood that superior company management is the foundation for company strength, and had sought out the principles by which to achieve it.

The guidelines in this book are useful for any company of any size, whether manufacturing, distribution, or service. The particular emphasis here, however, is on the needs of established small- to medium-sized, $5 to $200 million sales, stand-alone, product manufacturing businesses. These include independent companies as well as subsidiaries, divisions, or business units of larger multibusiness corporations.

Developing the material for this book has caused me to rethink management terminology, and I have sought to clarify some managerial language and make it more precise. A few new words have been coined to help communicate new ideas. Appendix A provides a glossary of terms.

Because Three Dimensional Management is a newly proposed strategy and not in current use, I have created a hypothetical medium-sized product company, Multi-Med, Inc., which is referred to from time to time as an example to elaborate on particular points. The characteristics of this company are an amalgam of successful management practices that have been a part of my own business experiences or those I have observed. A company profile of Multi-Med is found in Appendix B.

Creating and Sustaining Company Growth distills my experience as a practitioner of entrepreneurship and management, a CEO and director of a variety of different businesses, an investor in private companies, and, throughout, a self-taught student of management. Active participation as a trustee and officer in several not-for-profit cultural corporations has added still another dimension to my perspective.

Although I have gained many useful ideas from others, my most fruitful source for understanding the intricacies of management and managing has been in the laboratory of the real world. During my career, I have been the CEO of two small businesses, one in semiconductor technology, the other in retailing and wholesaling consumer products (fine wine), and a member of the boards of directors of both private and public product companies. Being an investor in a variety of company startups and growing young companies has given me another vantage point from which to understand what contributes to both failure and success in business undertakings.

My thoughts about the importance of momentum in business began in 1958, when several associates and I started a semiconductor company to develop, produce, and sell thyristor switching devices for military and aerospace applications. No market then existed for these products, and even before the products could be made, the essential technology needed considerable development. Wearing both CEO and sales manager hats, I set out to bring the company to the point of initial profitability with a fixed amount of venture capital. One of our investors characterized the venture capital as a block of ice in the sun; my job was to get the company established before the ice was fully melted. Fortunately this was accomplished, and the company went on to become a successful niche business that was sold, in 1967, to a publicly traded company.

My management perspective was further broadened when in 1963 I joined the board of directors of Dynatech Corporation, then a very small, technology-based research and development consulting company. In 1967, Dynatech began in earnest a program to acquire promising technology-based product companies. One early acquisition was highly successful, and Dynatech continued a profitable growth program, through both internal development and acquisition, reaching nearly $500 million sales by 1993. More than seventy small businesses were acquired. At that point, it became clear that the company's growth strategy was no longer working.

A new, more narrowly focused market strategy was established based on Dynatech's existing strengths in several sectors of the communications industry. The company was then reorganized to concentrate its resources within that strategy, and nonstrategic companies were divested.

In 1972, my wife, Lucie, and I decided to turn an interest in fine wines into a serious business in the greater Boston area. Our approach was to start a new entity, concentrate only on fine wine, and become a vertically integrated importer, wholesaler, and retailer. As we had no previous experience in the wine industry, we faced a major learning task. My transition from technology-based products for military, NASA, industrial, and computer use to a distribution business in upscale consumer products forced me to look closely at those management principles that were universal and transferable and to sort out and tailor the related fundamental issues in management to still another venue. Our wine company grew steadily, and always profitably, to a prominent marketplace position; we sold the corporation in 1990 to a private partnership.

In 1989, I joined the board of directors of Aerovox, Incorporated, when it became a public company listed for trading on the NASDAQ. This $120 million-plus company, founded in 1924, manufactures capacitors for the electric and electronic equipment markets. Revenue margins are low in this mature business, and the company competes on product performance, quality, low manufacturing costs, and company reputation. Large investments have been made to strengthen both products and productivity. Acquisitions have allowed Aerovox to expand into market niches related to its core technologies and marketing competencies.

Since 1969, I have maintained a management consulting business, Cordel Associates, Inc., as a part of my business activity. Through Cordel I have engaged in projects involving startup companies, venture capital investment, troubled companies, and acquisitions and divestitures.

The theme of building momentum resonates through all these experiences. I consider it the indispensable activity that clears the way to achieving and sustaining growth.

James B. Hangstefer
Waltham, Mass.
January 1997

## CHAPTER 1

Three Dimensional Management
An Overarching Strategy

INTRODUCTION

Many company managements can deliver growth in value to key stake-holders—customers, employees, and shareholders—when market conditions are favorable; few can deliver it during economic down-turns or when new competitors or technology redefine the nature of market demand. Only *superior* performance by top management can provide the sound foundation necessary for sustained growth year after year. Even "shooting star" companies normally diminish in brilliance over time unless they find the path to superior management.

To perform at a superior level, providing value to customers has to be management's first priority. Otherwise, the company will lack sufficient revenue margin to deliver growth in value for employees and shareholders. If employees are slighted because there is not enough revenue margin, organizational vitality will suffer, holding down the rate of company achievement. Productivity will also be limited, which limits operating profit. Growth in earnings per share and cash flow will be modest or nonexistent, thereby keeping down both the company's price-to-earnings ratio and share price.

This discouraging pattern will occasionally be interrupted when new products, new customers, geographic expansions, or economic upturns produce a spurt in growth. Usually, however, the previous pattern ultimately returns. Without sustained growth in value for all three stakeholders, the company will be on a performance roller coaster with many ups and downs over time. The only way to avoid this roller-coaster ride is for top management to succeed year after year in producing continuous and concurrent growth in value for the key stakeholders.

This book describes an overarching, pragmatic strategy, Three Dimensional Management, that brings together proven management fundamentals that can lead to superiority in management both today and in the knowledge-driven, rapidly changing marketplace of the future. The important fundamentals of management are timeless and have been known for decades. But this is the first concise strategy that integrates the essential fundamentals into a dynamic and practical guide for achieving sustained company growth.

In its 1969 publication *The Chief Executive and His Job*, The Conference Board made a cogent and durable statement. It said the CEO's ultimate accountability to the company's stakeholders is for company *growth*, as evidenced primarily by financial performance; *character*, as evidenced by the favorable reputation the company has earned; and *perpetuation*, as evidenced by the company's capacity for self-renewal and sustained momentum.[1]

Three Dimensional Management provides a compass for staying off the roller coaster of company performance and staying on the unending road on which self-renewal and sustained momentum take place. This strategy seeks to build the many characteristics which distinguish a company that is consistently able to deliver growth in stakeholder value. These characteristics include:

- Growth, year to year, in financial performance that is driven by organizational vitality
- Employees' trust in the company and enthusiasm in being a part of it
- A unity of cause that is known and felt by everyone
- A sense of accountability that is company wide and viewed as a personal opportunity
- Widespread innovation and risk taking
- The expectation that external competition will be intense
- A sense of urgency to move forward and accomplish more
- Care and concern for doing things right, even the little things

Why momentum as the basis of a strategy for management? Because there is a vital interdependent link between a company's momentum and its long-term growth in operating profit. Virtually everything done by every company involves a time dimension. Cycle times in manufacturing, selling, product development, administration, and management all have an impact on company results. Finding ways to get the most done in the least time is always important and in many instances critical. Making time per se a principal priority, however, is usually counterproductive; often faster is slower.

Building momentum depends on much more than an emphasis on time. Nurturing ideas, vitality, and competency to achieve and sustain exceptional accomplishments are the more important priorities. When growth is derived from these sources relative to time, then company momentum emerges as the *seminal force* that drives growth in value for the key stakeholders.

Every company, at any time, experiences one of four situations: crisis; low or no growth; high growth; optimum growth. Each of these can be characterized by the level of company momentum in market-position strength and internal operations. A crisis situation exists when the company's financial performance is unsatisfactory because of weakness in both its market position and its internal operations. Low or no growth maintains when financial performance is mediocre and the company is not adequately moving forward; usually, there is a combination of problems in both market position and internal operations. High growth exists when the company is achieving exceptional success in the marketplace, even though marketplace success may be masking serious internal problems. Optimum growth occurs only when market position and operations are being sufficiently strengthened, a process that continues over time.

If a company's long-term financial performance is below expectations, the probable cause is too little company momentum. How much company momentum is necessary to identify the presence of superior management? There is "enough" momentum when the company remains strong and consistent in providing value to the marketplace as conditions in that marketplace change and evolve. Simply put, momentum is sufficient when a business has as many customers as it wants, is able to eliminate "undesirable customers," and has a growing revenue-margin level that permits continuing long-term investment in momentum-building projects. In essence, management must be able to continuously redefine the needs for competitive success in its chosen marketplace(s). At the same time, it must establish and maintain the performance capability to profitably exploit its marketplace opportunities. Because what determines company performance over the long term are the decisions and actions of top management, a central focus on company momentum provides the basis for a meaningful and objective way of evaluating and guiding management performance.

There are no "silver bullet" easy answers to attaining superior management. Nevertheless, an explicit strategy for management can provide the focus from which imaginative, competent, conscientious people can maintain a broad perspective and achieve a superior result.

New in this book is the concept of momentum building as an essential responsibility of managers, buttressed by the introduction of anchorpoint objectives, momentum indicators, and momentum drivers. These are brought together within a comprehensive, concise perspective on management accountability that is also new. Applied in concert, they provide an accurate and impartial basis for evaluating managerial performance, a method that uses momentum indicators to supersede traditional performance appraisal processes.

THE MOMENTUM ERA

Until the dawn of the information revolution, which began with the advent of radio and the telephone at the start of the 20th century, most businesses were local. As communications, including voice, data, and video, became more widespread, so did the scope of business interests, which also expanded accordingly with the ease of face-to-face communications afforded by air travel.

The invention of the transistor in 1948, followed by the invention of integrated circuits in 1959, radically altered the marketplace. These tiny semiconductor chips made possible dramatic improvements in computer, communications, and other products. By 1980 there was instantaneous worldwide communication by satellite; the following decade produced flat-screen displays, multimedia communications, expert systems, and neural networks. By the early 1990s, most consumer and industrial products drew on semiconductor-based hardware and computer software. Many electronic, electrical, and electromechanical products were redesigned to incorporate the new technologies because they provided opportunities to substantially improve product performance, quality, size, and value. The process continues.

Along with the marketplace impact of semiconductor- and software-based products, another revolutionary change was underway. At a conference in Stockholm in 1966, Joseph M. Juran warned: "The Japanese are headed for world quality leadership and will attain it in the next two decades because no one else is moving there at the same pace."[2] In the early 1970s, a few Japanese companies launched a new industrial era that redefined the nature of competition in many important worldwide product-based industries. By concentrating on very high levels of product performance, quality, and value, they began to take market share from traditional producers. Most established companies in the United States and Western Europe were slow to recognize the change, which provided a lasting opportunity to aggressive Pacific Rim companies. Makers of consumer products, copiers, personal computers, semiconductors, machine tools, and other such products conceded significant share to these new competitors before the affected companies sat down to serious introspection and redirection. I call this period the Re-vision Era because top management of these companies had to alter their vision of their companies' future before they could take meaningful steps to strengthen their market position and performance capability.

Juran's 1966 warning that the Japanese were moving faster in building strength in some product markets than businesses in the West went largely unheeded until the result of superior competitor performance showed up years later as severe marketplace pain. Apparently his insight was ignored because of a blinding overconfidence in the top executives of the companies that would be seriously damaged by these profound marketplace changes. Even today, after a multitude of vivid examples of company trauma in many different industries, companies that are now far more sensitive to quality still find it difficult to keep their rate of strengthening at a high enough level to attain value leadership in the changing marketplace.

Propelled by technology-driven, product-performance improvements and by the higher value and quality standards set in the Re-vision Era, the pace of change in the marketplace continues to accelerate steadily. Individual product life expectancy has been cut in half or less in many instances, not because of wear-out, but as a result of market obsolescence, and there is no end in sight for these rapid market changes. In the struggle to be more competitive, most companies are improving their customer services and productivity as well as their products, and they now look not just to their own countries as their marketplace but to the entire world.

Companies of every size that are unwilling or unable to change sufficiently will face severe problems and probably failure. What is being done today simply is not going to be good enough tomorrow, and the time span between today and tomorrow is growing shorter.

I call the era beyond Re-vision the Momentum Era. In the Momentum Era, I believe the level and continuity of company momentum will be *the primary indicator* of management acuity and effectiveness.

MOMENTUM BUILDING: A CENTRAL THEME

Momentum building provides a clear, simple, and permanent unity of cause for every employee, both managers and nonmanagers. It is necessary for a variety of reasons:

- Profit is reduced by product/market maturity and must be renewed
- Changes in the marketplace, technology, the company, and in the operating environment continuously redefine the required company capabilities and competencies essential to retain market-position strength
- Product performance, value, quality, configuration, and availability must all be routinely improved
- Technology advances have to be incorporated into products and processes
- Company competencies have to be restored when employees are transferred or leave
- Changing company goals require new competencies and capabilities

Without sufficient momentum, no company will remain strong, and its financial performance will become mediocre or unsatisfactory even if it has a sound market strategy, good people, and efficient business processes and operational plans. All these must be shaped and reshaped as needed into a unified force that produces superior company performance in changing external and internal environments. This continual shaping is the role of top management.

To accomplish the desired results, management, interactively with operating people, must:

■ Define necessary improvements—structural and continuous—in company market-position and in performance capability. Structural and continuous improvement do not simply mean incremental gain; both also imply step-function jumps ahead that produce new, higher levels of performance

■ Set priorities for undertaking improvement programs based on their importance in providing market-position advantages

■ Obtain the improved results within a time frame defined by market conditions

When we perceive that the right actions are being taken in the right way and at the right time, we can sense that momentum exists, a phenomenon well illustrated in sports, where momentum is the key to winning. Building momentum puts a much higher priority on getting things right rather than just getting them done in the shortest possible time; doing something faster does not necessarily produce higher momentum and in fact may retard it if too little care and concern about how well things are done produces poor results. As noted, it is strengthening, not time per se, that is the primary factor in momentum building. Taking time before proceeding to determine where, why, what, when, and how to strengthen raises the probability of doing the right thing and normally minimizes the time and cost for completing an action.

Max De Pree has lucidly expressed the importance of company momentum:

> Leaders are obligated to provide and maintain momentum. Momentum in a vital company is palpable. It is not abstract or mysterious. It is the feeling among a group of people that their lives and work are intertwined and moving toward a recognizable and legitimate goal. It begins with leadership and a management team strongly dedicated to aggressive managerial development and opportunities. The team's job is to provide an environment that allows momentum to gather. Momentum comes from a clear vision of what the corporation ought to be, from a well-thought-out strategy to achieve that vision and from carefully conceived and communicated directions and plans that enable everyone to participate and be publicly accountable in achieving those plans.[3]

As the areas in a company that need strengthening are continuously changing, so too is the necessary rate at which strengthening has to take place. There is no endpoint for momentum building, only milestones on a path that can have frequent changes in direction.

The ongoing need to adapt a company to its changing environment was arrestingly addressed by Henry Ford in a 1922 autobiography:

> I saw great businesses become but the ghost of a name because someone thought they could be managed just as they were always managed, and though the management may have been most excellent in its day, its excellence consisted in its alertness to its day, and not in its slavishly following of its yesterdays. Life, as I see it, is not a location but a journey. Even the man who most feels himself `settled' is not settled—he is probably sagging back. Everything is in flux, and was meant to be. Life flows.[4]

It would be difficult to find a better description of business or, indeed, life. Those leaders who keep these elusive qualities in mind set a constantly improving standard for marketplace performance. They are generally very much aware of the necessity to run scared and to work continuously toward upholding company strengths while building new ones. They take the best ideas, from whatever source, and adapt them for their needs. Their business is a body in motion, and its momentum comes from the force of innovation and energy. If their competitors do not find ways to move ahead, or at least to catch up in a marketplace-defined time frame, they lose market share, profit, or both, as their only alternative for obtaining customer orders is usually some form of price cutting.

ENSURING OPTIMIZED PROFIT GROWTH

The basic premise of TDM is that optimized long-term profit growth occurs only when there is sufficient company momentum to provide continuous strengthening of the company's market position and its performance capability. Sufficient momentum usually exists, although not always, when a company's market position is improving more rapidly than that of its competitors.

Figure 1-1 shows the interdependence of operating profit and momentum-building in a company's value flow chain. The value flow begins with customers who provide opportunities for orders. The company's market position strength determines the nature and volume of its orders. When shipped, the orders provide revenue margin, which pays for all nonrevenue generation expense and the expense involved in momentum building. What remains is operating profit. If investment in momentum building adds sufficiently to the company's market-position strength, then revenue margin increases, and this increases operating profit. The lowest investment expense normally occurs when strengthening initiatives are taken before competitor action or market change *requires* a response. The key questions are: How do we keep our present momentum? and How do we get more?

Although there is invariably a "front end" expense involved in company strengthening, the return on investment can be quite high when sufficient market-position momentum is achieved. When enough of a company's *revenue margin* is effectively and regularly reinvested in momentum building, a positive feedback loop can be created that will produce increasing revenue margin.*

Rubbermaid Inc., a housewares company in Wooster, Ohio, understood clearly the need to invest revenue margin to strengthen its market position. *Fortune* reported that over the ten-year period 1983 to 1993, Rubbermaid achieved a 23.4 percent annual rate of return to investors, and, based on *Fortune*'s survey, headed the list of America's most admired companies. Sales were $1.9 billion with earnings of $211 million in 1993. "Famous for fecundity, Rubbermaid is known as a new-product machine," *Fortune* observed. "Last year it churned out new (not just improved) products at the rate of one a day. No one would admire that, of course, if the products bombed. Few do....The company habitually pumps 14 percent of profit into R&D. Admits a competitor in the cookware business: `They are in a class by themselves.'"

Fortune further reported: "Most [Rubbermaid] ideas flow from a single source: teams. Twenty teams, each made up of five to seven people (one each from marketing, manufacturing, R&D, finance, and other departments), focus on specific product lines, such as bathroom accessories. So successful has been the team approach to innovation that Dick Gates [head of business development] fears to contemplate a world without it."[5]

Rubbermaid's 1994 goals, under president Wolfgang Schmitt, included entering a new product area every twelve to eighteen months, getting 33 percent of sales from products introduced in the past five years, and by the year 2000 obtaining 25 percent of revenues, up from 18 percent, from markets outside the United States. Rubbermaid remained number one in *Fortune*'s listing of America's most admired companies in 1994, and was number three on the list in 1995.

On the other hand, declining market-position strength reduces market opportunities. This translates directly into declining revenue margin. An example of this is Wang Laboratories, Inc., as it was described in a *Boston Globe* article by Charles Stein on November 26, 1989: "The recent past has not been kind to Wang Laboratories. Since its peak in 1984, the company has lost money as often as it has made a profit. Its stock price has tumbled from a high of $41 a share to under $5....Its work force has been cut from 30,000 to 23,000 in the past year, with no guarantee that the cutting is over....The red ink put the company in vio-

---

* *Revenue margin* (REM), a new term introduced here, is revenue less all costs of goods sold and all costs of sales normally included in the SG&A line item on an income statement. REM is the profit obtained from a company's revenue-generation activities. It is a more useful performance measure than gross margin. Chapter 3 considers further the concept of REM as a means of measuring market-position momentum.

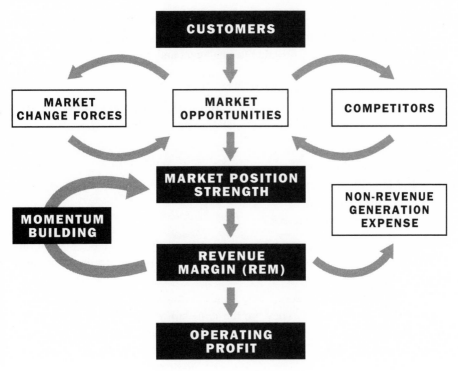

Figure 1-1: Value Flow Chain

lation of its loan agreements." Wang filed for bankruptcy in August 1992.

Every month, every business makes dozens of major and thousands of lesser decisions and takes countless actions. Their collective impact determines a company's performance. How decisions and actions, by both managers and nonmanagers, mesh together and contribute to company-wide momentum determines the company's overall success level.

If a company's momentum trend is down, or even if it is up but not by enough, the company is in for future financial trouble. Adverse business conditions can sometimes cause a temporary loss of market-position momentum that is not of long-term concern, but in the absence of a specific reason that will be self-clearing, too little momentum is a serious danger sign. Far too many managements blame external market conditions for their weak performance when the real problem is a lack of internal accomplishments that will assure a strengthening position in their marketplace. All managements face the issue of understanding the forces that are adversely affecting company momentum, then identifying solutions, setting priorities for actions, and seeing that effective actions are taken in a timely way.

Momentum building might be considered a business's health fitness program. Its purpose is to make and keep the company alert, creative, lean, strong, and profitable. Sustained, long-term market-position momentum is the only employment security available to managers and nonmanagers alike.

ANCHORPOINT OBJECTIVES

The word *anchorpoint*, a new managerial term, is used to describe the five central needs, shown below, of every stand-alone company.

- Astute core strategy
- Organizational vitality
- Market-position strength
- Productivity gain
- Financial performance

These are called anchorpoints because collectively these five universal objectives define, or tie down, the performance areas that determine long-term company strength.*

The five anchorpoints are the exigent areas that must have sufficient ongoing company achievement. They are the *universal critical success factors* for every business. Distinct goals set under each of these anchorpoints are the company-specific critical success factors that guide the company's direction and priorities. The results—quantitative and qualitative—achieved under these goals indicate company performance, and their trends indicate company momentum. The goals have to be adjusted as often as conditions change in a company's marketplace and internal operations, or when top management wants to reset company direction. Management performance is measured by the results achieved in the anchorpoint areas.

Net income is the first thought that comes to mind when a company's financial performance is mentioned, but a business cannot, in the long term, be managed for profit per se. Profit is an outcome of management's collective decisions and actions in their three areas of essential responsibility: strategic positioning, performance-capability positioning, and momentum building. These decisions and actions set the level of result achieved in the anchorpoint objectives.

The interdependency of the anchorpoints is illustrated in Figure 1-2.

Financial performance is directly dependent on the company's *market-position strength* and on its capability to achieve *productivity gain* regularly.

---

* One use of the word *anchorpoint* is defined by Webster's Third International Dictionary as "A point in an archer's face (as the chin) up to which he brings his drawing hand in order to stabilize his aim before release of the arrow." In business, anchorpoints are the references that aim managerial actions toward momentum building.

These two in turn are dependent on *organizational vitality* and *astute core strategy*. Only when results in the nonfinancial anchorpoints are present in sufficient measure will there be optimized financial performance. When performance in any of these anchorpoints wanes, relative to customer need or competitor action, problems soon develop that adversely affect profit.

The awareness that four nonfinancial bottom lines exist leads to the understanding that the critical long-term factor which underlies profit is the contribution from people. This is neither a new nor a surprising revelation, because all successful business endeavors count on a combination of ideas, abilities, and persistence to fuel their financial performance. Everyone in the company has to contribute to strengthening company anchorpoint performance. Paying careful attention to the company's people and encouraging and thereby obtaining accountability, involvement, imagination, ingenuity, and timely result are the management actions that can make the most difference in achieving a high level of desired financial performance. Explaining and demonstrating the importance of the anchorpoint objectives to everyone in the company and embedding them into the company culture is an ongoing process that is essential in managerial momentum-building.

The anchorpoint objectives can be likened to the markers on an endless trail through challenging terrain. They are critical success factors because they mark the only route that avoids ravines and other dangers. Company-specific goals under each anchorpoint are the milestones that mark progress on the journey. Momentum is the force for moving forward, and measuring momentum will indicate the pace of progress. While there is no end to the trail, those

Figure 1-2: Interdependency of Anchorpoint Objectives

who take the journey can experience deep satisfaction from witnessing its vistas and meeting its many challenges.

THREE DIMENSIONAL MANAGEMENT

In spite of the rapid marketplace changes, the two-dimensional management approach from the past remains in common use today in many, perhaps most, companies. To succeed in the business environment of today and tomorrow, however, top management must synergistically tie together company strategy, performance capability, and operational dynamics. The weak element in most companies has been operational dynamics, which I call company momentum.

To build company momentum, core business strategy has to be right, performance capability has to be right, and the strategy for and conduct of company management has to be right. Three Dimensional Management adds momentum-building to strategy and execution and ties together these elements. TDM replaces the traditional terms of strategy and execution with *strategic positioning* and *performance-capability positioning*. A company's current revenue stream, which produces today's profit, is determined by its existing strategic and performance-capability positioning. Its future revenue stream will be determined by momentum building today that strengthens both the company's market position and performance capability. All three dimensions of responsibility are essential for management to become superior. They form the core of every policy management job.

Strategic positioning means defining and redefining, as needed, the company's specific core strategy for achieving essential market position and operations strength. The aim is to set and communicate, clearly and concisely, the long-term view of where the company is going and how it will get there.

Performance-capability positioning means putting in place the right people and infrastructure to effectively conduct the affairs of the company. This involves establishment, oversight, guidance, and support of essential operating activities, but not routine supervision or direction of daily affairs by top management except in exceptional circumstances.

Momentum building means enhancing the rate of company strengthening. This takes place through the decisions and actions that change the company from its existing strategic and performance-capability positioning to its envisioned future positioning. Momentum level is the rate of movement into that defined future. Market-position momentum is the rate at which market-position strengthening is taking place; operations momentum is the rate at which performance-capability strengthening is taking place.

For Three Dimensional Management, the primary responsibility of management is defined as follows:

Management's primary responsibility, as a team under CEO leadership, is to establish the company's core business strategies and relevant performance capabilities, and to build and hold the company's marketplace and operations momentum to a level that ensures lasting company strength.

TDM is not a how-to manage methodology but a strategic frame of reference, a perspective and guideline from which managers and all other employees are encouraged to apply their own ideas and abilities. Its open architecture can easily accommodate the useful concepts of earlier management pioneers, like Peter Drucker, along with current insights such as organizational learning and total quality, while keeping the central focus for executives on the need to achieve lasting company strength by building company momentum.

LASTING COMPANY STRENGTH

Although maximizing shareholder value is commonly regarded as the ultimate aim for management, I believe it is the wrong aim, as it puts the cart before the horse. A shareholder-value emphasis often encourages management actions that might satisfy some shareholders in the short term but could be unwise uses of resources for long-term company growth. Focusing chiefly on shareholder value also stimulates a negative reaction from most nonshareholder employees, and properly so; their interest is in improving their own and the company's well-being, not in creating shareholder wealth.

As it is the intellectual power, motivation, and energy of all employees that is the driving force for company financial performance, I believe the ultimate aim of management must be to produce and sustain lasting company strength.

With this said, long-term growth in shareholder value is nevertheless an important outcome. The only ways to achieve continuing growth in shareholder value are to maintain a high level of value to customers and provide opportunity for employees to grow in capability and share in the company's financial gains. If management is successful in its quest for lasting company strength by having created sufficient value for customers and employees, in the process the shareholders will normally achieve both significant long-term growth in the value of their investment and a much lower downside risk. Pursuing lasting company strength is the only way to maximize shareholder value. Nothing else works for very long.

One company that has demonstrated the potential for lasting company strength and has created substantial value is Compaq Computer Corporation. After a long period of market leadership and growth, in 1991 it experienced brutal competition from new competitors who were offering comparable product performance and services at much lower prices. Compaq's earlier strategy of competing on technical innovation, quality, and size was no longer working. After a period of faltering, the CEO was replaced and the company's core strategy was broadened to include high productivity and low cost. The company also adopted activity-based accounting (ABC) to clearly define product costs. The new market strategy was to become the lowest-cost producer while retaining technical innovation leadership in the company's chosen market areas. Referring to the company's need to redefine and transform itself from a traditional mindset to that of a market leader in a market in which price was a critical factor, Compaq's then-new CEO Eckhard Pfeiffer commented,

> "We embraced customer satisfaction as our leading business goal....With speed as a crucial piece of our renewal strategy, we directed the whole organization to discover new market opportunities, to build new manufacturing capabilities....In nine months we met our goals." He advised: "Stay ahead of change by noting early signals. Welcome change, even if it means making hard decisions with painful effects. To reinvent your business, break away from the old mold. And most important, move fast."[6]

THE PRINCIPLES AND PATHS
OF THREE DIMENSIONAL MANAGEMENT

When Ralph Waldo Emerson wrote, "There is, at the surface, infinite variety of things; at the center there is simplicity and unity of cause," he was certainly not thinking of business, yet the thought is pertinent here. The "surface" for a company is where people spend most of their time, yet they rarely have a "center" that offers them simplicity and unity of cause. For most companies, such a center has not been established.

Emerson's wisdom has provided inspiration for the principles and paths of TDM that are intended to define that center. TDM's first guiding principle, *lasting company strength*, sets the core aim for management. The means for accomplishing that aim reside in its second guiding principle, *momentum building*. The unity of cause is *company strengthening through momentum building*, which takes place through five paths: accountability, anchorpoint objectives, momentum indicators, momentum drivers, and company infrastructure. These principles and paths form a simple yet comprehensive overview for a sound approach to consistent growth in company performance.

The perspective for management from Emerson's "center" is shown in Figure 1-3.

Managers, acting under their three dimensions of responsibility, set the direction for company operations. Organizational vitality is channeled through the company's unity of cause, which guides the company's people toward the five paths. Accountability is the foundation for superior performance. The anchorpoint objectives define the basic company needs. Momentum indicators are the quantitative and qualitative metrics that measure company performance. Momentum drivers are catalysts for company strengthening and

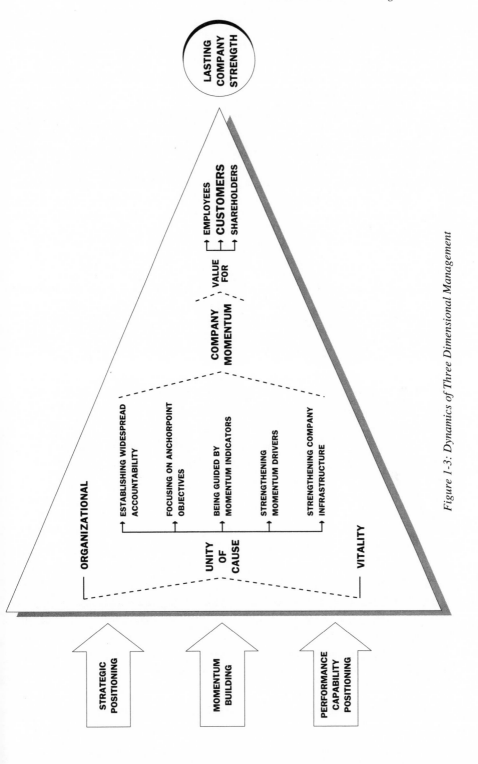

Figure 1-3: Dynamics of Three Dimensional Management

growth. Strengthening the company infrastructure—all the nonhuman assets and resources that provide the capability for operational performance—needs ongoing effort to keep performance capability at a high level. With sufficient sustained momentum, enough stakeholder value is created to keep the company moving toward lasting strength.

Three Dimensional Management places particular emphasis on management's accountability, as their model sets the stage for accountability throughout the company. Once management accountability is clearly set forth and managerial performance is evaluated objectively and impartially, each manager can clearly judge his or her own performance; higher-level managers can fairly judge the performance of others; and the board of directors can better judge CEO performance.

THE TRANSITION
TO INVOLVEMENT-ORIENTED OPERATIONS

While a certain amount of company strengthening takes place within a traditional two-dimensional management approach, the action is often inadequate and slow to occur because emphasis is on running current operations. In part, the lack of success is due to the way policy managers view their responsibility. The CEO's role is usually seen as that of leader and chief whip, whereas the functional managers' roles are to direct and manage their parts of the company; they are expected to be in control of everything that happens in their functional area. This arrangement breeds interface and "turf" problems, delays, excuses, and lots of finger pointing.

Under the traditional two-dimensional approach, decision making is centralized and control oriented so that policy managers' time is often preempted by daily operational demands. Their own involvement in daily operations also takes time away from the front-line people who are responsible for providing frequent reports and situational briefings to policy managers. Much of the time demanded by these vertically structured activities is wasted. Direct, frequent involvement by policy managers in operations leaves them with little managerial time for considering the core issues that really will lead to better company performance.*

With a Three Dimensional Management approach, the policy manager's job changes. The focus shifts from *running* a function to *strengthening* the company. This shift is both a reversal of the traditional priorities that prevail in two-dimensional management and a substantial widening of perspective from the function view to the much broader company-wide view. Although policy managers remain in an oversight role for particular parts of the company's performance capabili-

---

* To distinguish different roles within a company, I define three groups—management, professional, and associate— which together encompass all employees of every company.

ties, they no longer spend most of their time in hands-on operational direction.

In practice, TDM flattens a company's organizational structure and minimizes its authority-based hierarchy. All employees are expected to be more fully involved in the company and to deepen their sense of accountability to it. Front-line people become accountable for handling all matters central to recurring daily activities, communicating and acting in a horizontally structured way, so that policy managers are no longer on-site bosses.

Thus, making the transition from running to strengthening means reducing involvement in most daily recurring operational activities while remaining accountable for performance results. Once policy managers can devote most of their time to matters of strategy, performance capability, and strengthening, both managerial and operational effectiveness will significantly increase. Policy managers have a threefold undertaking:

- Setting the stage for operating people to do the daily recurring work in an environment that encourages superior performance
- Eliminating or minimizing problems and barriers that may get in their way
- Establishing communicating paths and measures for performance results

The company's *capability centers* are expected to run cooperatively most of the daily activities, including most problem-solving, with relatively little upper management supervision. These centers rely on leadership within their own group, based on competency and leadership authority as opposed to hierarchical authority, and on a high degree of individual accountability by each member of the group for his or her own performance.*

Policy managers do not micromanage daily activities. They do keep in close touch with those responsible and *accountable* for daily activity performance; understand their problems; and try to be certain that deterrents to their efforts are carefully addressed. To provide operating people as well as policy managers with information on what is working well and what is not, sensitive indicators of performance—financial and nonfinancial—need to be in place and routinely used. This ongoing real-time awareness of situational needs should ensure prompt actions without managerial intervention. Ear-to-the-ground, eyes-wide-open, and lots of communication and help is the routine managerial mode, not direct supervision or involvement in operational activity. This requires not simply practice, but trust and generous support.

---

* *Capability centers* refers to the specific work centers where operational activity takes place. Chapter 7, Operations Strategy, describes how these centers function within a horizontal organizational structure.

Edward E. Lawler has pointed out the distinctions between control-oriented and involvement-oriented management and suggests that for most businesses, more involvement by all employees and less control by management is not just a good idea but an economic necessity. Lawler believes the ultimate competitive advantage in many industries in the future will be management's ability to organize and manage people. In an interview with A.J. Vogl, he observes that the ultimate business organization is one in which people who are directly producing the product or directly serving the customer understand the business and have information about how it is performing, make decisions on how they do their jobs, and receive rewards contingent on business results.[7]

The role of a manager in an involvement-oriented company was described this way by Robert Haas, chairman and CEO of Levi Strauss & Co.:

> If people on the front line really are the keys to our success, then the manager's job is to help those people and the people that they serve....In the past, a manager was expected to know everything that was going on and to be deeply involved in subordinates' activities....In reality, the more you establish parameters and encourage people to take initiatives within those boundaries, the more you multiply your own effectiveness by the effectiveness of other people.[8]

The concept of an involvement-oriented company is critically important for Three Dimensional Management. Policy managers have to balance the tension between control and noninvolvement in a way that maximizes operational performance and productivity; they need to know when to intervene constructively and when to stay back. Once each operating person becomes accountable for her or his performance, the need for control is greatly reduced. It goes without saying that employees involved in daily operations must be highly competent.

SUPERIOR MANAGEMENT

There are only two routes to long-term profit growth in business. One is gaining and holding market strength by way of an economic franchise, the other is doing it through ongoing superior management.*[9]

An economic franchise is created when an important new or improved product is brought to market, or better processes for manufacturing, marketing, or distribution are introduced at a time when no other company is either able or willing to compete effectively with the innovator.

Many companies achieve an economic franchise briefly, but only a few can hold it for long because their momentum is too low. A high-demand product or service that has high revenue margin because of its singularity and utility

---

* Warren Buffett, chairman of Berkshire Hathaway Inc., calls an "economic franchise" a situation in which a product or service is needed or desired, is thought by its customers to have no close substitute, and is not subject to price regulation.

can temporarily reduce the need for superior management. In this sense, the observation that an advantageous market position can compensate for weak management remains true. Nevertheless, markets mature and change with the passage of time, and inevitably aggressive competitors will arrive. Creating follow-on market-dominating products or unique operations or marketing strategies is not easily done. Even a successful marketplace leader needs to look objectively, carefully, and continuously at its management effectiveness if it expects to succeed over the long term.

While TDM provides a solid foundation for achieving superior management, simply adopting such a strategy is, of course, not enough. The second vital element is how management is actually conducted—whether the decisions and actions taken apply and reinforce the strategy or undermine it. The third crucial element is constantly increasing the degree of company competency in the unique technical aspects of its chosen field(s) of endeavor.

When either an inadequate strategy or no strategy for management is in place, company success depends entirely on the latter two elements. The continuing presence of sufficient competency and creativity in these two areas is much less likely, however, when there is no overarching management strategy. Such a situation usually produces the kind of annual company performance that looks and feels like riding a roller coaster.

For all these reasons, the only sustainable competitive advantage for any company is superiority of management. And the ultimate test of management superiority, for the CEO and his or her team, is their ability to consistently and concurrently produce growing value for the company's customers, employees, and shareholders. The remainder of this book explores in more detail the principles and paths of Three Dimensional Management.

NOTES

1. *The Chief Executive and His Job.* New York: The Conference Board, 1969.

2. Joseph M. Juran, "Made in U.S.A.: A Renaissance in Quality," *Harvard Business Review,* July-August 1993.

3. Max De Pree, *Leadership Is an Art.* New York: Dell Publishing, 1989, p. 17.

4. Henry Ford with Samuel Crowther, *My Life and Work.* New York: Doubleday, 1922, p. 22.

5. "America's Most Admired Company," *Fortune,* February 7, 1994.

6. Comments made at the 1992 *Business Week* Symposium of CEOs.

7. Edward E. Lawler III, *The Ultimate Advantage.* San Francisco: Jossey-Bass, 1992, p. 25; A.J. Vogl, editor of The Conference Board's publication *Across the Board,* March 1993.

8. Robert Howard, "Values Make the Company: An Interview with Robert Haas," *Harvard Business Review,* September-October 1990.

9. Robert Metz, "Bullet-proof media franchises just a memory, Buffett says," *Boston Globe,* July 14, 1992.

CHAPTER 2

Managerial Accountability

The Foundation for Achievement

A s context for looking at managerial accountability, as well as other aspects of management, it is helpful to envision the operating structure of a company as depicted in Figure 2-1.

Every business is a singular social system within which there are four operations-based systems tied into a central information and control (cencon) system. A company-wide informal communication network permeates these systems. Peter F. Drucker has defined business as a process that converts a resource, distinct knowledge, into a contribution of economic value in the marketplace.[1] The structure in Figure 2-1 shows the means by which this conversion takes place.

The systems: Revenue Generation, Value Creation, Administration, Top Management, and Cencon provide the basis for the company's performance capability to operate as an economically viable unit. All systems are both interrelated and interactive, and each encompasses many specific processes, both formal and informal. The ongoing source of funds that support a company and its people is customers placing orders, receiving products and services, and paying for the value received. Company activity is of two basic kinds: conformance and innovation. Both are essential and take place in all systems. Conformance in

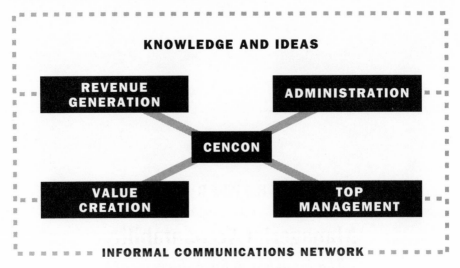

Figure 2-1: The Operating Structure of Every Business

performing recurring tasks is necessary for achieving consistent results; innovation is vital to achieve new, higher levels of performance. The external environment within which every company operates includes markets, competitors, suppliers, resources, laws, and a variety of outside organizations.

The purpose of every business enterprise is to produce value, both financial and psychological, for its customers, employees, and owners. The degree of satisfaction the company achieves for these three key stakeholders creates the perception of its psychological value. Producing value for customers, as they perceive it, is essential to obtain their orders. Producing value for employees is essential to maintain the highest level of company innovation and productivity. Producing value for shareholders is essential to attract new capital whenever it is needed, and because shareholders are the owners of the business.

All company employees are expected to contribute to adding and creating financial value in the normal course of performing their jobs. Financial *value added* describes revenue margin (REM) derived from existing operations. *Value created* refers to the establishment of new sources of revenue margin and the achievement of productivity gains. *Value produced* is the combination of value added and value created.

A company's revenue generation system encompasses sales, manufacturing, and the related support activities that deliver the revenue margin necessary to pay for all the company's activities. Continuous growth in the amount of REM is essential for long-term company growth. The value-creation system is company wide. The most visible parts of it are those activities involved in product, process, and customer development, and the company's formal education and training activities. Less obvious parts are the activities and actions taken throughout the company that raise the contribution level of its people.

Administration includes all centralized financial, accounting, legal, human relations, and other similar activities. This system contains the company's internal control processes that provide for the accuracy and trustworthiness of all internal data and information and for safeguarding company resources. The administrative people provide logistical and infrastructure support for the cencon system.

Cencon (central information and control) is a new term for the many company-wide processes for information acquisition, dissemination, and operations control that exist within every business organization. All the formal processes by which people—managers and nonmanagers—interact, communicate, and coordinate fall within this system. In most businesses today, cencon is a patchwork quilt of information systems, policy and practices manuals, reports, meetings, and personal correspondence. The company's management information system is part of cencon. The computer-based information-processing part of cencon may be a large mainframe or centralized information files and databases tied into a networked group of terminals with Internet and e-mail access.

The means by which the company's people routinely seek and give information is its informal communications network. Although the network is *amorphous*, it is nonetheless a vital link between people; people interacting, individually and in groups, all with a unique perspective, sharpen the company's focus on opportunities, needs, problems, and priorities. The information moving through the network is not always constructive. Rumors, judgments on management decisions and action, and attitudes that shape behavior are routinely disseminated, and negative or destructive elements in the communications loop are not usually passed on to top managers. This informal network is a powerful and useful means of obtaining and conveying information as well as influencing attitudes and behavior.

Top management conducts its activities through a variety of processes, both formal and informal, that in practice constitute its own system. These processes evolve from management's purpose and role as described in the following sections.*

---

* *Top management*, alternately called *policy management*, refers to the chief executive officer and those managers who report directly to the CEO. All others are called *operating managers*. When used alone, *management* refers to all levels of managers. The word *executive* refers to any top-level manager.

MANAGEMENT'S PURPOSE,
ROLE, AND RESPONSIBILITY

Where open-market competition exists, the nature of business management is the same throughout the world. Government policies, protectionism, and a range of cultural factors may provide advantages or disadvantages to some businesses, but these factors do not substantially alter the purpose, role, and responsibility of management.

> *Management's purpose is to provide leadership, oversight, clarity, coherence, and control so that all company operations work interactively and synergistically together to add and create value for the company's key stakeholders. The essential role of managers is to bring together ideas, people, competencies, and resources and shape them into a unified creative force that will achieve the company's anchorpoint objectives.*

> *Management's primary responsibility, as a team under CEO leadership, is to establish the company's core business strategies and relevant performance capabilities and to build and hold marketplace and operational momentum to a level that will ensure lasting company strength.* *

The company's people, its internal systems and processes, and all the external factors and forces influencing the company's operations are interrelated and interactive in complex and often subtle ways. Many constantly changing forces, some rapid, others slow moving, exist internally and externally and create ever-changing situations and challenges for the enterprise and its people. Managers are responsible for being aware of these factors and forces and for stimulating company performance short- and long-term to achieve consistent growth and sufficient profit. A company's performance is directly tied to its policy managers' foresight and abilities, and to the timeliness of their decisions and actions. Drucker has noted: "Managing a business must be a creative rather than an adaptive task. The more a management creates economic conditions or changes them rather than passively adapts to them, the more they manage the business."[2]

THE WORK OF MANAGING

In a general sense, management refers to handling or controlling something. Usually it means the group of people—managers—in charge of and with the authority to direct the affairs of a business. Another meaning refers to the process of managing, by which managers carry out their responsibilities. *Managing* describes the things done by managers while they are at work performing their managerial tasks. Both situations and people are man-

---

* This definition of management's primary responsibility was first set forth in chapter 1.

aged, although managing does not necessarily mean the direct supervision of people. The nature of each manager's job responsibilities, authority, and accountability for performance requires individual definition. Some nonmanagerial tasks, often not even mentioned in a job description, are also normally involved.

Individually and collectively, managers carry out their three essential responsibilities—strategic positioning, performance-capability positioning, and momentum building—by performing many *managerial tasks*. The most important of these tasks are:

- Learning about matters essential to the company
- Translating information into useful knowledge
- Communicating essential knowledge to others
- Defining values, objectives, strategies, goals, and priorities
- Establishing policies, processes, and organization structure
- Initiating plans and actions, and obtaining required resources
- Defining jobs, hiring, delegating authority, and involving people
- Evaluating individual performance, promoting employees, and terminating employment
- Building relationships and fostering communications and cooperation
- Building group synergy and leveraging resources
- Developing organizational and people competency
- Maintaining operational control
- Reviewing company performance and making changes for improvement

Certain *universal competencies* are necessary to perform successfully these managerial tasks. These include competency in:

- Situation analysis
- Communicating and negotiating
- Risk assessment
- Planning and organizing
- Evaluating and judging
- Building team effectiveness
- Problem solving
- Mentoring and helping

Underpinning both task performance and competency are some *essential traits* that are necessary for a superior outcome of the managing process. These include:

- Integrity
- Realism with idealism
- Sound judgment
- Commitment and persistence
- Insight and ingenuity
- Energy and concentration
- Mental agility
- Self-confidence

Interacting with others in a way that is both performance focused *and* sensitive to individual needs involves some *behavioral attributes* that apply at different times in interpersonal relationships. These are:

- Fairness
- Toughness
- Openness

- Empathy
- Supportiveness
- Compassion

For all managers, the actual process of managing is crucial, as distinct from competency as a specialist in technology, sales, accounting, manufacturing, and so forth. Many specialists are promoted into management roles on the basis of their talents in a specialty, not on the basis of their managerial competency. When this happens, it is urgent that they concentrate on gaining competency in management and managing.

THE MANAGING PROCESS

Every manager uses the same general process for performing the many tasks involved in his or her job. The process, shown in Figure 2-2, is a closed loop of making decisions, taking actions, solving problems, and analyzing results. Each step is facilitated by communicating, involvement with others, and most essential, learning. At each step, interaction with those who can contribute knowledge and insight helps shape a more perceptive conclusion. If the manager engages in too little learning, and not enough or the wrong kind of communication or involvement, the decisions and actions taken will be less effective.

The process of managing is performed repeatedly, usually subconsciously, in many different situations, each requiring different kinds of specific knowledge. Because needs within a company are frequently in conflict, it is often necessary to make compromises in decisions and actions, normally with infor-

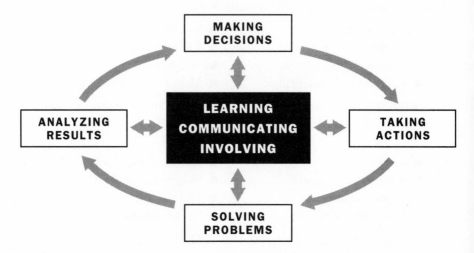

Figure 2-2: The Managing Process

mation that is sparse, biased, or downright wrong. Although the outcomes cannot always be predicted, decisions and actions have to be taken nevertheless. The issues of individual and group performance, as well as interactions between people, costs, schedules, quality, and workmanship, are usually present in many different shapes and sizes, and all need to be routinely addressed, sometimes urgently. The process requires sound intuition and critical judgment, the ability to anticipate how external factors and internal situations will affect actions, and an instinct for sensing the right thing to do and knowing when things are not being done well enough by others. Essential here is the capacity to deal simultaneously with many different matters without unduly neglecting, delaying, or compromising any of them.

If they are to function at a superior level, managers need a mental model that relates everyday decisions and actions to the degree of their importance in meeting company anchorpoint objectives and to momentum building.

Each manager carries out the managing process in her or his own manner. No "right" way has yet been found that will ensure success. Most managers find that in spite of studying techniques and diligently reading a vast number of how-to-manage publications, the actual process of managing is a complex and highly individual art. Managerial effectiveness is not as dependent on style, techniques, and methodology as it is on relationships based on trust and mutual respect. This trust and respect, combined with the competencies, traits, and behavioral attributes noted earlier, are the ingredients that add up to managerial stature. Because of the many subtle and personal issues involved, the right balance of these qualities is elusive, and managerial stature is not easily learned. Some people never develop enough of it to become effective managers, whereas others find it intuitive. Nevertheless, one's degree of interest and effort toward self-education and introspection is a key aspect of acquiring the essential qualities that underpin this expertise.

Figure 2-3 shows an overall perspective on the nature of the managerial job. It is intended to provide a framework for managerial performance evaluation.

While mastery of the work of managing and possessing a high degree of managerial stature are an essential base, the managerial success factors are the ultimate variables that determine the level of achievement of each manager. Leadership, strategy for management, imaginative decision-making, and accountability are at the heart of the long-term business success achieved by policy managers, both individually and as a team.

LEADERSHIP

Leadership is the most intangible of the four managerial success factors. In management, leadership refers to the actions taken by an individual and his or her personal qualities that build trust and respect. Raw exercise of authority is

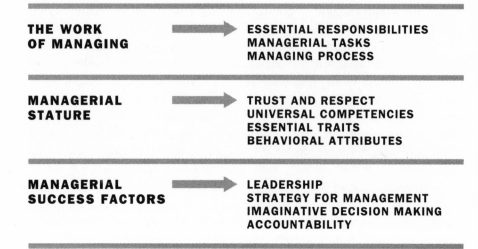

Figure 2-3: The Nature of the Managerial Job

not leadership. People with enough intellect, managerial stature, and commitment to performance have the potential for personal leadership, but successful leaders must be able to concisely articulate a convincing view of the future that the leader wants to bring about. Employees want to know, in plain, simple, and believable language, where they are going, what they have to do, and what it is going to be like when they get there. A leader has the ability to persuade others to follow a particular path for reasons other than the advocate's own authority. The credibility of the cause is also important, for this determines the willingness of the followers to believe in what the leader has to say. Charisma is not essential. A leader strengthens organizations, delegates authority, involves others, and builds their self-confidence. Effective leaders have the capacity to instill in others a belief in and enthusiasm for a cause and to inspire the kind of action that brings their vision to reality.

Leadership is also about facing uncertainty and difficult issues and having the strength of character to press forward in spite of obstacles and criticism. Making decisions that involve significant risk for the company as a whole, for the decision-maker personally, or for others are also key aspects of leadership, as are intellectual honesty, idealism, and the flexibility for change. John W. Gardner has observed:

> Leadership is not a mysterious activity. It is possible to describe the tasks that leaders perform. And the capacity to perform those tasks is widely distributed in the population....Leadership is the process of persuasion or example by which an individual (or leadership team) induces a group to pursue objectives held by the leader and his or her followers....

We must not confuse leadership with status. Even in large corporations and government agencies, the ranking person may simply be bureaucrat number 1....It does not follow that status is irrelevant to leadership. Most positions of high status carry with them symbolic values and traditions that enhance the possibility of leadership....Similarly, we must not confuse leadership with power. Leaders always have some measure of power, rooted in their capacity to persuade, but many people with power are without leadership gifts....Leadership requires major expenditures of effort and energy, more than most people care to make.[3]

John P. Kotter described an important aspect of executive leadership in this way:

Too often, I fear, we fall into the romantic trap of believing that great vision comes from magic or divine grace. In the business world, it rarely (if ever) does. Great vision emerges when a powerful mind, working long and hard on massive amounts of information, is able to see (or recognize in suggestions from others) interesting patterns and new possibilities.[4]

The essence of managerial leadership is being credible, formulating and communicating an insightful view of the future, making difficult decisions under uncertain conditions, getting the support of others, and then meeting the challenges necessary to make the future view become a reality.

SETTING A STRATEGY FOR MANAGEMENT

Defining a specific, cohesive, and comprehensive strategy for management has been largely a neglected area for most businesses. Although this is now gradually changing, nearly all managers have used a personally adapted version of the command-and-control approach that has been typical of most management education programs. Some companies, including Levi Strauss, mentioned earlier, have now learned that articulating a management strategy is vital to sustaining company growth.

Companies, small, medium, and large, have normally been run by their CEOs without any articulated comprehensive strategy for company management beyond the boss's personal approach, interests, and beliefs. Once in place, an established mode of management is unlikely to change until a company runs into hard times. Then the CEO is usually replaced, as this is the primary option available to a board of directors for redirecting a company.

As a company expands, its first significant management challenge occurs when it reaches a revenue level that requires the addition of policy managers. This point usually occurs at some level under $15 million in revenue. If seamless growth is to occur that will take the company past the $100 million revenue level, this is the time for serious thinking about a strategy for management. At some point above this level, the strategy should be further considered so that additional managers can be readily integrated into the management team in anticipation of growth toward the next revenue milestone.

Setting a management strategy means exploring the following questions: What approach will we take to company management, and what is expected of our managers? How can we work as a synergistic team? What do we mean by accountability and "performance focused?" How do we nurture creative innovation and ideas in all our people? How do we keep everyone in the company learning and growing in competency? These and related questions all point to the basic question: How do we keep the company off a performance roller coaster and on the road to self-renewal and sustained momentum?

Most successful managers know intellectually the fundamentals of sound management. Yet in day-to-day decisions and actions, the fundamentals usually become submerged because they have not been distilled into a simple conceptual structure that managers can always apply to the situation at hand. Unless these fundamentals become part of an intuitive mindset that guides all activities, "knowing" is not meaningful in practice; the gap between knowing and "doing" has to be routinely bridged for the fundamentals to be of value. What has been missing in most situations that later become troublesome is a universal, overarching strategy for management within which all managers, including the CEO, can see clearly their overall role, responsibilities, and accountability—a strategy that can be readily transformed into a mindset.

Although the issues continuously facing every management will always pose considerable complexity and risk, management efforts can be enhanced if they are guided by a strategy based on straightforward, uncomplicated, performance-focused fundamentals. Company performance will be stimulated and future troubles largely averted if the company explicitly pursues management superiority as its ultimate competitive advantage.

IMAGINATIVE DECISION-MAKING

Perhaps nothing is more difficult in the spectrum of managerial challenges than finding the single, elegant answer to an important opportunity or problem. Most everyday decisions do not need to be imaginative. They flow normally from a process that blends logical analysis, experience, and intuition. Where imaginative decision-making *is* needed are in those few critically important situations that will have a major impact on results. Every company needs imaginative decisions. They can range from deciding on what markets and products to pursue and how a company is organized, to selecting employees and setting operational policies.

Imaginative decision-making emerges from the deep desire to identify opportunities, externally and internally, and the willingness to pursue them. As Kotter points out, the capacity for logical analysis plays an important role, but creativity is also essential to finding a direction that offers important possibili-

ties. Chapter 4 further explores the matter of creativity and the other factors
that underpin imaginative decision-making.

ESTABLISHING MANAGERIAL ACCOUNTABILITY

To achieve management superiority, managers must function at the highest
level of accountability for their personal and company performance. Figure 2-
4 provides a working perspective on the responsibilities of policy management's job and the nature of this accountability. The principles and paths of
Three Dimensional Management are an integral part of this perspective.

For policy managers, being accountable means being answerable for all results and situations that may develop, whether good or bad, within their scope
of involvement. Accountability applies to actions, or lack of action, both by
the manager and by all others reporting to him or her. It means being both
proactive and reactive as appropriate to prevent or solve problems and take advantage of opportunities. Although extenuating circumstances can occur, few
if any reasons can justify the avoidance of accountability by any policy manager. A manager's ethical behavior in achieving results is taken for granted.
The actuality of an executive's own accountability is essential if he or she expects to obtain accountability from others.

The policy management team performs its essential role when it is meeting
important goals under each of the seven areas of managerial accountability.
These areas of accountability are universal and apply to every company and
every person in top management. An integral part of the goals is achieving
sufficient company momentum levels, in which managers can be guided by
utilizing the momentum indicators considered in chapter 3.

The Presidents Association, the CEO Division of the American Management Association, employs six elements of management in its educational program, the Management Course for Presidents: leadership, culture and climate,
developing people, planning, organizing, and controlling and implementing.
These elements, of course, are important aspects of managerial involvement,
but they are not performance focused. To achieve lasting company strength,
policy management's performance has to be defined and evaluated not in
terms of competency or tasks, but in terms of results. Under TDM, policy-level managers are expected to know what they have to do and to develop the
competency necessary to get it done effectively and consistently over time.

SHAPING AN ASTUTE CORE STRATEGY

Operations and market strategy are the guides for company operations. Together with a compatible financial strategy, they form a company's core business strategy. If the strategies are to lead to important company accomplishment, it is essential for them to be developed with wisdom and imagination.

PERSPECTIVE ON MANAGEMENT ACCOUNTABILITY

Management's purpose is to provide leadership, oversight, clarity, coherence, and control so that all company operations work interactively and synergistically together to add and create value for the company's key stakeholders. The essential role of managers is to bring together ideas, people, competencies, and resources and shape them into a unified creative force that will achieve the company's anchorpoint objectives.

Management's primary responsibility, as a team under CEO leadership, is to establish the company's core business strategies and relevant performance capabilities, and to build and hold the company's marketplace and operations momentum to a level that will ensure lasting company strength.

ULTIMATE AIM

● Lasting company strength

THREE DIMENSIONAL MANAGEMENT

■ Strategic positioning   ■ Performance-capability positioning
● Momentum building

MANAGERIAL FOCUS

◆ Anchorpoint objectives   ◆ Accountability
◆ Momentum drivers   ◆ Momentum indicators
◆ Infrastructure

APPROACH TO OPERATIONS

■ Company-wide unity of cause   ■ Involvement-oriented operations
■ Meaningful performance appraisal   ■ Performance-based compensation

MANAGERIAL ACCOUNTABILITY

■ Astute core strategy   ■ Market-position strength
■ Organizational vitality   ■ Productivity gain
■ Financial performance   ■ Protection of resources and assets
■ Value: for customers, employees,
  and shareholders.

● The two principles and ◆ five paths of Three Dimensional Management

Figure 2-4: Perspective on Management Accountability

Each strategy area needs frequent review to keep it aligned with external and internal changes, and a flexible hand to permit the exploitation of unexpected market opportunities. Defining specific, meaningful, and clearly articulated strategies can be time consuming for management, but once established and proven, they do not normally change rapidly.

It is the CEO alone, with advice and consent from the board of directors, who is accountable for approving, setting in place, and maintaining effective strategic positioning for the company. Nevertheless, all policy managers play key roles in developing strategy. When they have conflicting views, the CEO has to make final decisions and resolve different viewpoints in a way that each policy manager can support while remaining enthusiastic about the company's direction. The CEO must also make certain that assumptions about market-place potential are realistic and that the company has or can obtain the necessary competencies, capabilities, and resources to implement the strategy. Simultaneously, the CEO must ensure that the appropriate indicators of company momentum are in place and that they are routinely reviewed and acted upon. Policy managers, individually accountable for the performance of particular capability areas such as sales, manufacturing, product development, administration, and others, are accountable for that aspect of strategy which is unique to their area. As management team members, they are also accountable for the compatibility of their strategy with the company's overall needs.

THE DYNAMICS OF MARKET-POSITION STRENGTH

Market-position strength is the ultimate objective that, when achieved at a high enough level, makes possible long-term, consistent growth in the company's financial performance. Without adequate market strength, a company will struggle to stay alive. Market strength comes from the synergistic integration of strategic positioning, performance-capability positioning, and momentum building combined with the imaginative use of company infrastructure. Perhaps most of all, however, it comes from organizational vitality—committed people working creatively and energetically in the company's best interests.

Market-position strength is not simply a matter of concern for the company's sales people. Everyone in the organization has to contribute to it.

ORGANIZATIONAL VITALITY: THE ENGINE FOR COMPANY PERFORMANCE

Organizational vitality is the intellectual power and energy of the company's people. A high level of vitality applied on the company's behalf is essential to meet the company's ambitions and goals over the long term. Lasting company strength depends on the self-renewal and momentum obtained from this vitality.

The degree of organizational vitality is evident in people's individual attitudes, their behavior, and the initiatives they take on the company's behalf. How the company's people interact, what they say and what they do, the extent of their interest in the daily activities, their thoughts on how to improve things, their actions for self-improvement, and their job satisfaction are all indicators. Managers have to be able to read the many different aspects of human behavior, be sensitive to the forces at work, and develop approaches that will foster and nurture the company's organizational vitality.

The ultimate test of management superiority is the ability to consistently and simultaneously produce growing value for the company's customers, employees, and shareholders. This result is the true bottom line for management. Long-term, sufficient value growth can take place only if all employees, managers and nonmanagers, are pulling together for a company-wide unity of cause. The ability to raise and maintain organizational vitality is a manager's most important competency and a fundamental area of individual accountability.

PRODUCTIVITY GAIN

Making regular and important improvements in company productivity is essential for profit growth, both in the external environment of aggressive competition and in a climate that is relatively stable. When competition is aggressive, the need is normally more urgent, but even in a stable environment productivity gain is necessary to improve profitability and to stay ahead of inflation. Because revenue generation is where the largest cost is, this is where improving productivity has the most impact. In the other areas of the company, productivity gain is important for reasons that go beyond cost considerations. Improving cycle time in product development, for example, can be a major factor in market leadership, so it can contribute substantially to market position strength. Productivity gains in administration, cencon, and management all help keep the company's overall cost structure down and contribute to value produced for employees and shareholders.

To keep the company lean, competitive, and profitable, policy executives have to act continuously to achieve productivity gains. The company needs to set specific goals for productivity gain throughout the organization and to evaluate managerial performance on the basis of the results obtained.

FINANCIAL PERFORMANCE

The CEO and all other policy managers are directly accountable for consistent growth in the company's revenue margin, operating profit, net income, cash flow, and overall balance-sheet strength. Managers influence financial results by strengthening operational areas that actually determine financial results: core strategy, organizational vitality, market-position strength, and productivity gain. The company's financial performance ultimately determines whether a CEO remains in his or her job, and because the CEO depends on other policy managers, their jobs too are at risk if financial performance is not satisfactory.

Ensuring sufficient cash flow is a particularly important aspect of financial performance. Assuming that a company's receivables, inventory, and payables are well managed, cash flow is primarily influenced by growth in revenue. If a company's operating cash flow or cash reserves are not sufficient to support growth in the working capital needed to support revenue growth, then cash has to be obtained from other sources. Otherwise growth in revenue has to be curtailed. Top management's primary financial consideration is keeping revenue growth in line with cash availability.

For a publicly traded company, share price growth is also an important facet of management's financial performance. Share price is set in the open market where it is based on the collective opinions of investors and analysts about the company's future financial performance; their mood and feelings about the direction of the financial marketplace in general also plays a role. More directly, share price growth is related to the level, growth, and consistency of the company's net income and cash flow, and by how well management communicates the company's story to the financial community. Although the vagaries and emotions of the investment community affect a company's share price in the short term, eventually share price becomes aligned with the company's past financial performance and the estimates for its future success.

Whether justly or not, the financial community uses consistency in growth of quarterly net income as a key yardstick to assess the performance of public companies. The only way to predictably achieve this consistency in earnings growth is to reach a high level of market position and operations momentum. Although nothing can assure consistent quarterly earnings growth, momentum building is the most likely route.

The board of directors share accountability for share price growth with the CEO to the extent that they set policies in the areas of dividends, cash flow (depreciation, amortization, goodwill, etc.), use of free cash, and equity and debt structure.

PROTECTING RESOURCES AND ASSETS

A company's resources and assets include all the tangibles and intangibles that it utilizes or employs to conduct its affairs. These resources and assets provide the basis for the organization's operational infrastructure. They range from non-balance-sheet areas such as the company's reputation, people, trade secrets, proprietary information, and market position, to all the assets included on its balance sheet. Every manager, whether policy or operating, is individually accountable for protecting the resources and assets situated within his or her area of responsibility.

VALUE TO CUSTOMERS, EMPLOYEES, AND SHAREHOLDERS

The primary measure of management superiority is the company's capability to consistently and concurrently produce growing value for its customers, employees, and shareholders. This result is management's bottom line, and it is achieved by meeting important goals in each of the anchorpoint objectives year after year. The momentum indicators described in chapter 3 provide a means for routinely and continually measuring company performance in these important value areas.

MEASURING MANAGERIAL PERFORMANCE

Evaluating the performance of individual managers is an essential process for every company if it is to secure genuine, comprehensive accountability. Managerial performance has been measured primarily by the company's financial reports, and while financial reports and market share information are important, they focus on the past, are limited in scope, and are slow in arriving. Far more realistic are indicators of likely future performance, qualitative and quantitative, that are promptly and readily available.

Nothing can foretell the future with accuracy, of course, but monitoring appropriate momentum indicators that reflect dynamic change can provide some insight about future company performance. Momentum measures also can supply a reality test for near-term (six to eighteen months) performance forecasts by managers. Perhaps most importantly, they empower management with early warning signals that can help avoid unpleasant surprises. Taken together, the company's financial reports and momentum indicators can provide the directors, the CEO, and all other policy managers with a reasonable perspective on how well the management team is performing in strengthening and growing the business.

Evaluating each of the three areas of managerial performance—company performance, performance of the manager's capability area or business unit, and the manager's personal effectiveness—requires a separate evaluation approach. Company performance is directly measurable, and the performance of the specific province under the aegis of an individual manager can be measured by tracking goal achievements. Personal effectiveness, which relates to the individual's wisdom, abilities, and behavior, is the least tangible dimension and is therefore open to differences of opinion. Figure 2-3, which outlines the elements that constitute the managerial job, offers a basis for objectivity in evaluating individual effectiveness.

People feel good about their past accomplishments and justifiably take pride in them. Relaxing a bit when things are going well is normal. If this easing up goes too far, however, "reality myopia" can set in. Curing this affliction is part of the performance appraisal process. The central purpose of performance appraisal is to help the person being evaluated find ways to personally grow in capability in order to contribute more to the company's future prosperity and to her or his personal future success.

BOARD OF DIRECTORS ACCOUNTABILITY

In defining effective corporate governance, the National Association of Corporate Directors (NACD) has noted that a board of directors

> ensures that long-term strategic objectives and plans are established, and that the proper management and management structure are in place to achieve those objectives, while at the same time making sure that the structure functions to maintain the corporation's integrity, reputation, and accountability to its relevant constituencies.[5]

The board of directors is not a part of company management; its primary role is providing oversight of and guidance to management and challenging management's strategies to help make them more effective. The board is accountable to shareholders for company financial results and to employees for the fairness and balance of the company's policies and value sharing.

The chief financial officer (CFO), while reporting to the CEO, should be separately accountable to the board for the integrity and completeness of the company's financial information and for compliance with accounting and legal requirements. The human resources executive also should be separately accountable to the board for company legal compliance in the areas of employment, payroll, and benefits. The board must have confidence in how these executives perform in their areas of specialty. In addition, the board must periodically assess significant risks of liability and possible litigation from unhappy (or exploitive) shareholders or employees. Determining liability risks for environmental issues should also be a routine part of management activity and regularly reported on to the board.

As part of their oversight accountability, directors must encourage both reality and creativity in management's thinking. To do this, they have to be constantly aware of where the company stands in its marketplace and whether sufficient company momentum is being generated to address the changes taking place in that marketplace. Understanding the company's performance dynamics in terms of its marketplace situation is a vital aspect of corporate governance. This awareness is missing today in the boardrooms of most companies. Directors should also be familiar with the leading indicators of future company performance and use them as a matter of routine.

How well is management anticipating those company needs essential to sustain growth in financial performance? Poor company financial performance is almost always traceable to management's lack of early understanding and action on change forces that affect the company's future performance. Management has to design the company's information system to provide momentum indicator information that they can use and also routinely provide to the directors.

Another principal responsibility of the board is to define clearly, in conjunction with the CEO, the performance result expected from the CEO, and to set demanding, specific performance goals that are mutually agreed upon. Once these are established, the board must evaluate the CEO's performance on the basis of these goals. (See Appendix B for an example of a CEO position description that can provide a basis for performance review and the structure for conducting it.) A key part of the CEO's job is managerial development. To fully carry out the CEO performance evaluation process, the directors therefore must have an intimate understanding of the strengths and weaknesses of the policy managers who report to the CEO. The CEO's evaluation of the performance of these policy managers should be made available to the board.

While the board must avoid interfering with the CEO's authority and management actions, it must at the same time observe and assess the effectiveness of management's decisions and actions, and note the impact of these on the effectiveness of the organization as a whole. The NACD calls this NIFO, an acronym for "nose in, fingers out." Each board member should be free to talk with any person in management at any time without prior approval of the CEO.

CEO succession is arguably the most important matter that will face a board of directors. Being absolutely right in selecting a successor is essential and requires the active involvement of every director. Board members need to know first hand about potential internal candidates, which means they should ensure that managers who report to the CEO are often present at board meetings and social venues so that the directors can become acquainted with each of them. When the directors go outside for a new CEO, the board as a whole must be confident in the new person. To ensure this confidence, all board members should meet with the final candidates. This will also help the candidates become aware of the makeup of the board and of its performance expectations for the CEO and his or her managerial team.

To avert awkwardness and potential conflict of interest, the board's oversight should permit no more than two members of management as directors of a nine-person board. The role of chairman of the board is also best assigned to an independent outside director who can maintain a supportive but arm's-length relationship with the CEO. When the CEO is also chairman, board oversight of management is considerably more difficult. A nonemployee chairman or lead director should help set the agenda for board meetings and arrange for executive sessions to be attended only by the outside directors. For the board to function effectively, explicit charters should be established for the board chairman's job as well as those of the board committees: executive, audit, compensation, nominating, finance, or others.

Each member of the board needs to be conscientiously involved with all issues of company governance. The old reference to "sitting" on a board has to be revised to "acting." Board members need to spend much more time than has been traditional on important company matters in a board environment in which members are expected to be knowledgeable, engaged, and important contributors. Given the necessity for greater commitment, they should also be better compensated than in the past. A significant part of their compensation should be in company stock that they are required to hold for at least one year after their board service is completed. They should also be expected to personally invest in the company's stock, over and above compensation. A significant ownership commitment helps keep each director's focus on lasting company strength. Board members should not be permitted to sell company stock except under special circumstances.

A committed, active, at-risk board must be both a significant resource for management and an important stimulant to company momentum.

THE CEO'S ACCOUNTABILITY

As noted by the Conference Board, the CEO's ultimate accountability to the company's stakeholders is for company growth, as demonstrated primarily by financial performance; character as demonstrated by the favorable reputation the company has earned; and perpetuation as visible from the company's capacity for self-renewal and sustained momentum. The seven accountability areas in Figure 2-4 provide the specific means to evaluate how well the CEO has met these ultimate conditions of accountability.

The position of CEO confers on its holder both exceptional benefit and a heavy burden. The benefit comes in the form of challenge, few restrictions, prestige, power, and money. The burden is from the ever-present isolation and spotlight, and the immense expectations and demands inherent in the job. Much is expected of the CEO, the most important executive in a company. All concerned expect the CEO will put and keep the company on a successful path of self-renewal and sustained momentum. This takes an unusually wise, competent, and durable leader with a deep sense of personal accountability to the company's various constituencies.

In every company, the CEO plays four separate roles: leader, delegator, change agent, and business generalist. All four are conducted simultaneously. The kind of leadership needed in a business must be of the highest order if there is to be sustained company momentum. The CEO sits at the one vantage point in the enterprise that reflects the entire picture of the company's involvements, relationships, and accomplishments, as well as its problems and opportunities. As a leader, he or she has to be perceptive and imaginative, anticipate needs, see opportunities, be willing to take a wide variety of risks, and creatively solve company-limiting problems. Above all, the CEO needs to communicate reality in a way that maintains enthusiasm in the company's people even at times when the company faces serious problems. And as often as necessary, the CEO must make, correctly and perhaps courageously, a small number of critical strategic decisions that determine the level of future success achieved by the company. There are also failures from which to recover in the course of shaping a company's future. The CEO's decision making is the most important long-term influence on the stability, profit, and growth the company achieves. The challenges to be faced, first in positioning the business, then in guiding its affairs in a momentum-building manner, are imposing.

As both leader and delegator of authority, the CEO is expected to shape policy management into a high-performance, cooperative team with a company-wide perspective that works creatively as a group. This includes setting company values and policies that foster organizational vitality, instill high standards for ethical and legal behavior, and protect company interests. As leader, the CEO is the company's chief architect of the company's strategy for management and the one who selects the people who will form the management team. As the delegator of authority, the CEO is responsible for defining the specific responsibility and accountability of each policy manager and for evaluating his or her job performance. The policy managers are responsible for developing specific business strategy, establishing diverse operational capabilities, and seeing that the company actually achieves operational and market-position momentum. The CEO's leadership effectiveness is determined in part by his or her behavior (constructive and destructive) and setting in place an explicit strategy for company management. Leadership ability, decision-making wisdom, judgment in selecting and involving people, personal learning, and breadth of competency are important personal success factors.

Much has been said about empowerment or similar terms that describe the delegation of authority by managers. The purpose of these terms is to emphasize the importance of initiative, decision making, and action by people involved in the organization's everyday activities. Delegating sufficient authority coupled with maintaining clear boundaries is essential if an involvement-oriented, flatter organization structure is to work well. No matter what terms are used to describe delegation, it should be clear that power remains with the company's managers; revised organization structure or use of "soft" terms cannot change that. Business is not a democracy, nor can it be in most situations. The critical consideration for all managers is to avoid abusing their power and to use it in a manner that makes the work of others more interesting, challenging, and easier to accomplish. Successful delegating means emphasizing accountability while specifying the authority and boundaries for decision making and action. As there will be different "right" approaches for different situations and at different times, the nature of how to use power and delegate authority effectively is a primary issue for every manager to consider and resolve.

The CEO needs to be particularly adept in the role of change agent. Insightful understanding of why and how the organization works as it does, good and bad, is vital for making the kinds of decisions in strategy, people, and structure that can produce high company momentum. Constructive change stems from an in-depth understanding of where change is needed. Establishing a means of measuring company momentum in market position and operations opens a path to that understanding. An explicit program for momentum building then becomes the route to actually making the desired change.

As a generalist, the CEO has to understand clearly what is expected of each of the company's specialist areas that are involved in revenue generation, value creation, cencon, administration, and management. What are the external change trends in the specialty areas, and what are other companies doing in these areas? How do these activities relate to the unique needs of the CEO's company? Without focusing narrowly on the work of the specialties, which is the province of the specialist managers, the CEO's task is to perceptively evaluate the result being achieved in each specialty area and to shape the organization so it can deliver the desired overall company results. The CEO also has to understand the impact of the company's cencon system and the informal communications network on the efficacy of company overall operations.

Often the least-considered role in the CEO's position is that of being a "real person," one whom others at any level in the company can respect and trust, and who will listen to and respect all employees as important contributors to the company's performance. Even in the context of the superior/subordinate authority relationship, a good CEO generates a sense of partnership based on fairness and sensitivity about working relationships. This is not easy to accomplish for either party, yet it is the only possible basis for open, direct communication. The CEO should encourage this kind of fluid company culture.

Because the CEO has virtually absolute authority, others in the company are cautious about what they say in his or her presence. Ever-present stroking by others can enlarge the CEO's ego to unrealistic proportions. Filtered, selective, and sometimes deliberately distorted communication can isolate the CEO and limit his or her view of reality. To be effective, the CEO has to find ways to break through the veil of distortion to see reality as it is, not as he or she would like it to be, or as it is painted by others. Each CEO has to find the path to reality in whatever manner works best. A CEO also needs an innate sense of his or her own personal accountability to all the company's stakeholders. Lack of a broad enough sense of accountability and lack of awareness of the veil of distortion are the principal reasons why otherwise capable people fail at the job.

Boruch B. Frusztajer has made this trenchant comment about underperforming companies:

> There must be undercapitalized companies in almost every industry, but I have never seen one. What I have seen are organizations that have tackled projects inappropriate for their size and beyond their abilities, though not the ambitions, of their management teams. I have also seen company Presidents using the seemingly sophisticated concept of undercapitalization to cover up their inability to run a profitable operation.[6]

The CEO is also accountable for the actions of others that could cause the company serious harm. Examples of abdication of accountability are not uncommon, and in extreme cases they can lead to serious and perhaps fatal company problems. This usually occurs when the CEO delegates responsibility but does not retain a diligent sense of accountability for the results. An example of an extreme case is Kendall Square Research Corp. in Massachusetts. A *Boston Globe* article on December 2, 1993, by Josh Hyatt of the *Globe* staff, reported:

KENDALL SQUARE CLEANS HOUSE
Cofounder demoted, others replaced as firm's accounting crisis detailed.

> Kendall Square...yesterday replaced several top executives and said that its loss for 1992 was much bigger than previously reported...that sales for the first nine months this year would be $14 million less than previously reported....A company spokesman described a company whose accounting acumen fell far short of its technical sophistication. He said that the fiscal problems resulted from "contracts that were unclear and vague. Sales people made changes and added provisions and conditions that either were not appropriate or made accounting treatment complex and murky." He added: "We didn't have internally the kind of sophisticated organization to write, monitor or review these contracts."

The caveat that avoiding accountability is dangerous to the CEO's well-being applies to every other corporate officer as well. They too are accountable for their actions or lack of same, as well as for those who work within their oversight.

POLICY MANAGER ACCOUNTABILITY

The top managers who report to the CEO are accountable to him or her for their contributions to company performance. In essence, these managers have the same ultimate accountability as that of the CEO, because they are the ones on whom the CEO depends to actually guide the company's operations. The results these managers achieve in their particular capability areas, their contributions as members of the policy management team, and their personal effectiveness are the normal areas for individual performance evaluation.

Each policy manager has to perform the same four roles as the CEO, but within a more specific and narrower scope of accountability. The responsibilities, accountability, and performance requirements of the CEO's job must be translated into the job definitions of the other policy managers; collectively it is up to them to produce the overall company performance that the CEO is personally held accountable for by the board of directors.

In general, policy managers must successfully establish an open relationship with the CEO so that constructive dialogue can take place between them. Pleasing a CEO is hardly a minor consideration, and managing this relationship in a way that is in the company's best interests while not scuttling one's future personal opportunities requires good judgment and integrity. Keeping the CEO's thinking within a realistic context while being responsive to important challenges is a routine part of the relationship.

Unlike the CEO, the policy manager requires skill at peer relationships. In most smaller companies, three to seven people make up the policy management team. While their individual jobs require different specialty areas of accountability, they are nevertheless accountable as team members for the overall performance of the company. They have to work cooperatively together and should be able to openly discuss company strengths, weaknesses, and business opportunities without the fear that a peer will undercut them or talk behind their back. If policy managers' variable pay is based largely on overall company performance, peer group cooperation and openness are more likely. Such a shared climate also promotes a greater degree of realism in their discourse, which generally affords more astute decisions and actions for the company as a whole.

NOTES

1. Peter F. Drucker, *Managing for Results*. New York: Harper & Row, 1964, p. 5.

2. Peter F. Drucker, *The Practice of Management*. New York: Harper & Row, 1954, p. 47.

3. John W. Gardner, *On Leadership*. New York: The Free Press, 1990, p. 2.

4. John P. Kotter, *The Leadership Factor*. New York: The Free Press, 1988, p. 29.

5. National Association for Corporate Directors, Washington, DC.

6. Personal correspondence, Boruch B. Frusztajer, president and CEO, BBF Corporation, Waltham, Mass.

CHAPTER 3

Momentum Indicators

The Instrument Panel

MEASURING PERFORMANCE

Over the past decade, dissatisfaction with existing practices for management reporting and the accounting methods used for measuring company performance has been growing. The three most important problems are the inadequacies of cost accounting; the only marginal usefulness of traditional financial reports for decision-making in internal operations; and the overall paucity of vital nonfinancial information. Addressing these problems means constructing realistic new performance indicators, establishing teams to evaluate qualitative measures, and redesigning internal financial reports. The payoff to the company for improving performance measurement and reporting can be huge when critical problems are illuminated and successful action is taken to eliminate their root causes.[1]

Successful managers have always followed the axiom, "What is visible gets attention, and what gets attention gets done." An essential part of momentum building is therefore establishing a select group of key business performance indicators that are specifically designed to monitor both market-position and performance-capability momentum. This chapter presents a group of indicators, shown in Figure 3-1, that can highlight and clarify the trends in a company's performance and allow managers to anticipate and alleviate problems before they become rooted.

MARKET POSITION STRENGTH

- Net new order growth
- Revenue margin growth
- ★ Competency advantages
- ★ Customer focus index
- ★ Product quality index

FINANCIAL PERFORMANCE

- Operating profit growth
- Operating cash flow growth
- Return on net assets
- Working capital turnover
- D&A expense/REM ratio

ORGANIZATIONAL VITALITY

- ★ Unity of cause index
- ★ Innovation level index
- ★ Three C's efficacy index

STAKEHOLDER VALUE PRODUCED

- ●★ Customer value produced
- ●★ Employee value produced
- ●★ Shareholder value produced

PRODUCTIVITY GAIN

- Payroll/revenue ratio
- Cost-to-sell ratio
- ★ Productivity rating matrix

★ indicates a qualitative indicator

● indicates a quantitative indicator

Figure 3-1: Momentum Indicators

Momentum indicators are performance measures that provide ongoing guidance on progress toward company strengthening. Four of TDM's five anchorpoint objectives—market position strength, organizational vitality, productivity gain, and financial performance—are key areas in which quantitative and qualitative measures should be focused. The fifth anchorpoint, astute core strategy, is not directly measurable, but its validity is confirmed by the performance results in the other four areas and in the value produced for key stakeholders. The specific parameters noted under each of the five areas are the momentum indicators for the overall company. For internal levels below that, appropriate indicators need to be defined separately; however, the areas of organizational vitality and productivity gain should be considered for every level.

PROVIDING ACCURATE FINANCIAL INFORMATION

Financial accounting based on generally accepted accounting principles (GAAP) is in routine use by virtually all businesses. GAAP procedures have evolved over many years to satisfy the needs of auditors and boards of directors, for shareholder reporting, and for compliance with Internal Revenue Service and Securities and Exchange Commission laws and regulations. As the legal and regulatory requirement, GAAP obviously must be the essential foundation for every company's accounting processes. However, standard GAAP financial reports are not very useful for decision making in internal operations. This is not surprising, as they are not structured to aid decision making but to report after the fact (often many weeks after) on the overall financial performance and condition of the company.*

The word *expense* has a specific meaning under GAAP; expense is a period cost for income statement reporting. This definition is the one used in this book. The word *cost* is used here in a broad, general sense. It can refer to expense or the amount of money, time, or effort used in a particular undertaking or activity. The word *expenditure* is also a general term often used to describe a specific cash use that is not an expense, such as a capital asset purchase.

At the center of all accounting systems is the general ledger (GL) database. Every financial transaction by a company is recorded in an appropriate GL account or in a subsidiary journal account. There are no basic constraints in GAAP requirements to prevent accumulating data within the accounting database that would be useful for internal reports. Including such supplemental data can simplify the preparation of reports that are specifically designed for internal use only. In most computer-based accounting, the transactions are (or should be) entered into the accounting database in near-real time. Prepared in this way, reports for internal operations use can be available almost immediately. To provide new internal information, it may be necessary to redesign some of the account structure within the GL or subsidiary journals. This can normally be done without in any way affecting the requirements for GAAP compliance, and without significant changes in the relevant accounting system, software, or equipment.

All financial accounting is numerical, which conveys an impression of exactness. While most of such accounting is in large part exact, GAAP, in order to have universal applicability, permits subjective and policy decisions that can significantly alter reporting results. These "soft" areas include inventory, receivables, depreciation, amortization, expense capitalization, repairs and maintenance, intracompany allocations, and future expense reserves. GAAP requires consistency in applying accounting methodology unless there is disclosure of a change, but even with consistency there remains the possibility of arbitrarily shaping, intentionally or otherwise, reported results. Anyone who uses these financial reports should become aware of situations that could distort reported trends or operating results.

---

* GAAP in the United States is the accounting profession acronym for *generally accepted accounting principles*. Explicit definitions on accounting treatment for all transactions, report formats, and policy matters have been established by the Financial Accounting Standards Board. Both the SEC and the IRS employ GAAP standards in setting their own extensive rules and regulations.

COST ACCOUNTING

Accurate product cost accounting is a matter of vital importance to every business. Yet the only requirement for product cost accounting under GAAP is to value, in the aggregate, the goods sold during the accounting period and the goods held in inventory on the closing date. This means valuing direct materials, direct labor, and applicable overhead, a process that is relatively easy, as only a company-wide, single total for each is required. But GAAP does not adequately address the issues involved in cost allocation to individual products or to product lines that share services, processes, or resources with other products.

Over time, various methods for cost allocation to specific products have evolved that are in common use today, but because of the policy-set cost allocation assumptions in use, they often provide incorrect information. These distortions in costs assigned to individual products can lead to incorrect pricing or to cost-reduction efforts that are useless or improperly focused. Such distortions are usually silent problems, but they can have a significant negative impact on operating profit. Inadequate cost information is a particular problem in "flexible" or "lean" manufacturing, in which various products use the same manufacturing facilities. In these cases, the profitability of some products can hide the losses in others. "Product mix" is often used as an explanation for an otherwise unexplained change in revenue margin. Establishing better product cost accounting can help find the root causes of the "mix" issues.

Every company has to decide explicitly on how it will perform product cost accounting for internal management use. Setting this policy is an important decision that warrants the careful attention of top management. From the perspectives of both managers and operational people, accurate and timely cost information for every product is not just desirable but absolutely essential. As a matter of routine, product cost information is used to make individual product pricing/volume decisions, set priorities for cost-reduction programs, and guide product and process development. Establishing accurate cost-accounting methodology that satisfies both GAAP and all the company's internal uses is a necessity for every company that seeks higher momentum.

A relatively new method for product cost accounting, called activity-based accounting (ABC), is potentially much more accurate than traditional methods in situations where multiple products share labor, materials, supplies, or internal services. ABC allocates cost based on resources consumed by each product in every activity from raw material receipt to delivery to the customer. Specific activity drivers (the reasons the activity exists) are defined for each activity, and the total cost of each activity can then be allocated to individual products, based on the extent to which each product drives the activity.[2]

The ABC approach is also useful for determining the cost of operations other than those in manufacturing, as it can be applied to any kind of activity in any area of the company.

An ABC approach was put into use by the Roseville Networks Division of Hewlett-Packard when operating people there did not believe the numbers the accounting department produced. The company revised its accounting system to measure the factors that truly drive costs. In describing the result, company people said:

> The cost-driver or activity-based system is more accurate, more timely, and ultimately more useful to its "customers," the manufacturing, R&D, and marketing people....In fact, Roseville has been held up as a model for other Hewlett-Packard organizations, and the computer manufacturing division, which is a level above us, has mandated that all its manufacturing organizations use a cost-driver accounting system based on ours.[3]

MAKING MORE ACCURATE PLANS AND FORECASTS

Nearly all companies prepare annual profit (budget) plans that are based on backlog and new-order forecasts. From these forecasts, they estimate revenues, production schedules, sales and manufacturing costs, and capital expenditures. Estimating expenses in non-revenue-generation areas (including product development, administration, management, variable pay, debt service, and taxes) is also part of this process. The basic purpose of profit planning is to target a specific profit goal by aligning expenses with expected revenue margin, and to preauthorize some of the expenditures. Typically, profit plans are revised as often as significant changes occur in forecast assumptions. These financial forecasting, budgeting, reporting, and analysis efforts take up an immense amount of management time in every company, and far too much in most. Streamlining this process is a potentially fruitful area for productivity gain. Some companies regard profit plans as the minimum-realistic expectation for actual conditions. Others consider them optimistic projections that normally require innovation to be fulfilled. Under TDM, a company can adopt either a minimum-realistic approach or an optimistic one. The important factor is for everyone to know the basic premise. When plans embody significant "stretch" goals, the preferred approach to profit planning is one that is realistic for normal budgeting of recurring operations. The incremental profit improvements from momentum-building projects are then separately shown so that their progress can be tracked more easily.

Profit plans depend on forecasts, and forecasts depend on assumptions that are based both on past experience and judgment about future circumstances. This subjective side of the budget process has considerable potential for normal human error, particularly in the areas of forecasting new orders and estimating the time to complete product- and process-development projects. Even the most competent, conscientious person is unable to foresee with high certainty the timing of future orders, or the problems that might arise in operations or development work. To some extent, order backlogs can buffer revenue generation from the uncertainty of new-order timing, but with ever-shortening cycle times, this backlog buffering becomes less effective. Order backlogs of much less than sixty days are now becoming commonplace.

Refining forecasting methodology is an important step toward eliminating some of the uncertainty, but even with the most sophisticated techniques, forecasting will remain a process open to error. The most useful way to minimize the impact of uncertainty is to frequently review and update forecasts. Although this takes time, the shorter period between reviews means relatively less time is required for analysis, and the magnitude of error is normally reduced. For new orders, this update should take place weekly. The need for sales people to review and update their own new-order forecasts every week can also motivate them to stay in closer touch with their customers' plans.

When variable pay is linked to profit performance, some sophisticated gamesmanship can go on within the budgeting process, which leads to both over- and understating expected results in different areas at different times. Care in the design of annual cash bonus plans can reduce the incentive for this gamesmanship. One useful technique is to adopt multiple-year performance averaging as the basis for calculating bonus payment.

THE VALUE FLOW IN A PRODUCT COMPANY

As noted earlier, the core purpose of all business activity is to produce economic value. Figure 3-2 shows a graphic representation of the value flow in a stand-alone product company.

The value flow begins in the marketplace. Every company's market-position strength and performance capability define its potential to obtain customer orders and thereby to produce revenue. When the two costs of revenue generation—selling and manufacturing—are deducted from revenue, the remainder is *revenue margin*, the primary source of profit from company operations. Revenue margin pays for the two sources of value creation, company development and product development. The objective of these activities is to produce growth in company momentum by increasing market-position strength and improving performance capability. When these development efforts are successful, they contribute directly to the company's capacity to obtain more orders and thereby to long-term company strength.

Investment for improving performance capability should take place throughout the company, in product development, administration, management, cencon, and revenue generation. The basic test for deciding where and how to invest for improved performance capability is assessing the direct or indirect long-term impact of the investment on obtaining customer orders. If

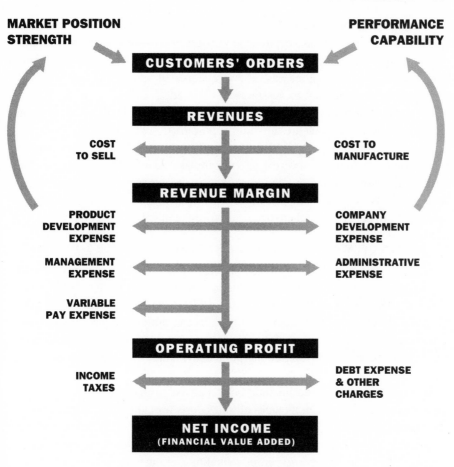

MARKET POSITION
STRENGTH

PERFORMANCE
CAPABILITY

CUSTOMERS' ORDERS

REVENUES

COST
TO SELL

COST TO
MANUFACTURE

REVENUE MARGIN

PRODUCT
DEVELOPMENT
EXPENSE

COMPANY
DEVELOPMENT
EXPENSE

MANAGEMENT
EXPENSE

ADMINISTRATIVE
EXPENSE

VARIABLE
PAY EXPENSE

OPERATING PROFIT

INCOME
TAXES

DEBT EXPENSE
& OTHER
CHARGES

NET INCOME
(FINANCIAL VALUE ADDED)

Figure 3-2: Financial Value Flow

this investment succeeds, the company's improved cost structure and/or capabilities will help keep it more competitive in the marketplace.

Revenue margin also pays for administrative, management, and variable-pay expenses. Variable pay refers to all pay that is not salary, wages, or sales commissions. This includes bonuses and profit- and gain-sharing payments. What remains after all the non-revenue-generating operating expenses are deducted from revenue margin is the company's operating profit, from which debt expense, other nonoperating charges, and income taxes are subtracted to arrive at net income. The only ongoing sources of long-term growth in operating profit are growth in revenue margin and gains in company-wide productivity.

A company's financial assets are easily stated in numerical terms and are therefore included on its financial balance sheet. These assets include the company's physical infrastructure, which is composed of tangible assets such as working capital, property, plant, and equipment, as well as some intangible assets, such as goodwill and capitalized costs. The company's human resources and operations infrastructure includes its financial assets as well as customers, employees, company processes, and intellectual property that are not easily valued quantitatively and therefore are not included on the company's balance sheet. As Drucker has pointed out, accounting deals with measurable things, not necessarily those that are the most important.

If significant company growth is to take place, normally all the cash provided from operations must be invested in company assets, including working capital. Often, the cash required to support growth is greater than that generated from operations. When there is rapid company growth, bank loans or some other form of long-term debt or capital are necessary to supplement internal cash flow.

REVENUE MARGIN: THE SOURCE OF OPERATING PROFIT

A quantitative indicator of market-position strength is a necessary measure for every company. Unfortunately, no single financial parameter in the present lexicon of business or accounting can readily provide this vital information. There is, however, one concept that I have found particularly useful over many years: revenue margin.

As previously noted, revenue margin (REM) is that dollar amount which remains from net sales revenue after all the period expenses of revenue generation have been deducted. These include both the cost to manufacture (goods sold) and the cost to sell, which includes all sales costs normally in the sales, general, and administrative (SG&A) expense line on a GAAP income statement. These are: field selling expenses (payroll, commissions, prospecting, salesperson expenses); customer services expenses including field maintenance and customer support expenses; marketing expenses, including product management, sales promotion and advertising; and distribution and delivery expenses.

> *REM is the profit obtained from the company's revenue-generation system. This metric is a financial measure of market-position strength; therefore, change in REM is the primary quantitative indicator of market-position momentum.*

REM is the aggregate total revenue margin for a company calculated for each accounting period. Two subcategories are also important here. Product revenue margin (PREM) is the aggregate revenue margin produced by a specific product or product line; variable product revenue margin (VAREM) is the incremental revenue margin produced by changes in unit volume of a particular product or product line. Both PREM and VAREM are useful for analyzing or forecasting the impact of product mix and unit volume on company REM; they are also primary references for making pricing decisions.

Gross margin, as an indicator of company performance, should be retired in most companies. It is an archaic carryover from the past, when cost of goods sold was the most important variable in revenue generation, a situation that no longer holds. Grouping sales expense with general and administrative expense in internal reports is also misleading, as sales and administrative expenses arise from totally different business activities and should be monitored separately. To avoid unnecessary disclosure, however, using the traditional SG&A grouping may be desirable for external reports.

REM is normally the only source of operating profit for every product company. It is what pays for all the non-revenue-generating activities in value creation, administration, and management, and what delivers the company's operating profit, net income, and operating cash flow. When REM increases or decreases, the change has a direct impact on operating profit, net income, and cash flow.

DESIGNING AN OPERATING FINANCIAL STATEMENT

Currently, internal company financial reports take many different forms, ranging from detailed information on expense incurred in each capability center to complete GAAP financial statements. The internal report most important to all managers is the internal income statement. It is an easy step, using the value-flow model depicted in Figure 3-2, to develop a useful internal financial report that can serve as the source of data for analyzing and graphing momentum. I call the one proposed here an operations financial statement (OFS), as it is more comprehensive than a conventional income statement. The format for the OFS is shown in Figure 3-3. (See Appendix B for an example of an OFS for the hypothetical company Multi-Med, complete with monthly, quarterly, and annual performance and plan data.)

The purpose of the OFS is to provide, quickly and clearly, actual and planned performance data that will directly influence operating decisions and actions. The company's profit plan should be organized to be in alignment with the OFS format so that plan forecast data are easily entered into the OFS. While monthly reporting is shown, the format could readily be adapted to reporting biweekly or weekly. With the advent of on-line analytical processing, weekly reporting will no doubt become the preferred approach. The OFS shows the actual performance to date, monthly and quarterly, as well as the plan for the remainder of the year. Combining actual and plan data provides a rolling forecast for subsequent periods and for the year. Because users of the report are also the sources for the forecasting, they can put together appropriate forecast changes for inclusion in the next issue when they review the most recent report.

Gross margin has not been included because revenue margin provides more meaningful information on the current profit result of the revenue-generation system. Revenue margin as a percentage of net revenue is provided simply for

OPERATIONS FINANCIAL STATEMENT	MONTH			QTR ENDING				YEAR PLAN	% up from Last Yr
	Mo 1 4 wks	Mo 2 4 wks	Mo 3 5 wks	Actual MAR	------ Plan ------ JUN	SEP	DEC		
# NET NEW ORDERS (NNO)									
NET REVENUES (NR)									
Std Cost to Manufacture									
Manufacturing Cost Variance									
Cost to Sell*									
Sales Commission									
Write Offs: AR & Inventory									
Cost of Revenues Total									
# REVENUE MARGIN (REM)									
% of NR									
Manufacturing Development Expense									
Product Development Expense									
Company Development Expense									
Admin & Mgmt									
Variable Pay Expense									
Dev & Admin (D&A) Exp Total									
# D&A EXPENSE % OF REM									
# OPERATING PROFIT (OP)									
% of NR									
Debt Expense									
Goodwill Amortization									
Other (Income) Expense									
Policy-based Exp (PBE) Total									
INCOME PRE-TAX (IPT)									
Income taxes									
NET INCOME									
% of NR									
Non-Cash Expense									
Capital Asset Expeditures									
# OPERATING CASH FLOW (OCF)									
FREE OPNG CASH FLOW (FCF)									
# Sales Cost % of Revenue (SCR)									
# Payroll % of Revenue (PPR)									
# Return on Net Assests (RONA)									
# Working Capital Turnover (WCT)									
Net Receivables > 60 days									
Inventory < 3 Turns									

# Denotes that the line item is a momentum indicator.
*includes all sales costs except sales commissions.

Figure 3-3: Format for Operations Financial Statement

information. Although it is not a momentum indicator, this information is useful for context in understanding the dynamics of revenue-margin changes. To highlight cost problems, cost of manufacture is separated into two line items to show the period variance from standard costs. A supplemental analysis report on variance is necessary to help identify root causes of the variance.

Cost to sell is an intrinsic cost of revenue generation and is considered at the same level as the cost of goods sold. Sales commission, a component of cost to sell, is a separate line item because it is usually large and varies directly with revenues. If advertising is a major cost, this too should be a separate line item. Separating these variable sales costs clarifies trends in the semifixed sales costs and makes them more visible.

Writeoffs in inventory and receivables are also shown separately to avoid distorting trends in the other revenue cost line items. Normally monthly reserves are accrued for writeoffs to prevent infrequent large charges from negatively affecting any single month or quarter. The accruals are periodically reconciled to actual.

A new expense category, development and administration (D&A), has been established that differs from the grouping in a GAAP income statement. The OFS shows these basic expenses in an unallocated "pure" form to keep perspective on their magnitude and to monitor trends.

Development expenses are assigned to three categories: manufacturing, product, and company. Manufacturing and product are the same categories as those now commonly in use. Company development is a new line item that includes noncapitalized expenses for human and infrastructure development throughout the company. Administration and management line items include the company-basic recurring expenses that are fixed or semifixed, such as rent, insurance, administrative salaries, management salaries, and other items contained in a traditional G&A grouping. Variable pay expense is that which is paid, in total, for the entire company. It includes bonuses, profit- and gain-sharing, and 401K direct or matching company contributions; it does not include sales commissions or similar compensation arrangements that are in lieu of salary.

A second new expense category, policy-based expense (PBE), covers expenses that are not directly incurred in operations. The PBE group includes debt, goodwill amortization, allocations by a parent company, contingency reserves, and all other nonoperating expenses. Although it is not a momentum indicator, the trend in the PBE/REM ratio should also be monitored.

Net income in the OFS is the same as in a GAAP income statement. The OFS must agree with the company's GAAP statement as a confirmation of correlation between internal and external reports.

The line items below net income contain calculations from data that do not normally appear in an income statement. Data for these are separately determined and entered as information on the OFS. Capital asset expenditures and the two cash flows provide an important perspective on cash generation and use in company operations. Operating cash flow (OCF) is calculated for the period by adding noncash expense to net income and subtracting the capital asset expenditures. Free operating cash flow (FCF) is calculated by adjusting operating cash flow for the period changes in working capital. FCF is the *net* cash generated by operations that is available for future use. When FCF is declining or negative, management may need to consider additional debt or equity financing, or a reduced rate of revenue growth. It is worthwhile to keep in mind that in accrual accounting, cash flow is not equivalent to funds put into the bank; there are time delays, sometimes long ones, between cash flow and spendable cash. Forecasting cash receipts, and therefore spendable cash, should be a routine task in the controller's office.

Two productivity-gain momentum indicators, sales cost percentage of revenue (cost-to-sell ratio) and payroll percentage of revenue (payroll/revenue ratio), are included. Following these two are return on net assets (RONA) and working capital turnover (WCT). The last two line items, net receivables over sixty days and inventory less than three turns, both in dollars, are included to highlight high-risk situations in working capital. Although they are not momentum indicators, these ratios are important to monitor because values above normal for either is an early-warning indicator of possible future write-out expense and a signal to take early corrective actions. Each company sets its own relevant number of days and turns in these last two categories.

While it is not shown on the OFS, *order backlog* is also an important part of revenue and cost forecasting, and detail on trends should be separately provided.

Although it is concentrated, the OFS is easy to follow because all the vital information is on one page, which makes it particularly useful. Its line items are grouped on the OFS in a way that provides the greatest insight with minimum analysis time.

The period OFS should be available very soon after the closing of each report period; one working day should be the aim. This will probably require important changes in the company's accounting office processes.

GRAPHING MOMENTUM INDICATORS

Momentum information is normally presented best in graphic form, which makes change easier to see. The OFS has been designed for computer graphing of individual line items; the aim is to convey well-communicated, timely, easily understood information that shows performance history, trends, and goals. Including a goal reference (baseline) will show the performance gap that needs to be closed. Moving averages and ratios also are often useful. Maintaining consistency in methodology is important, as change is the momentum indicator, not the actual data.

Graphs that indicate momentum trends typically show the parameter being measured on the vertical axis, and corresponding time on the horizontal axis. Figure 3-4 shows examples of three simple, well-designed momentum trend graphs, which appeared in the October 1996 issue of *Economic Times*, a monthly publication of the Conference Board.

USING QUANTITATIVE MOMENTUM INDICATORS

What follows describes the quantitative momentum indicators for the categories of market-position strength, organizational vitality, productivity gain, and financial performance that are shown in Figure 3-1.

The two indicators for market-position strength, *net new-order growth* and *REM growth*, are universally important to all companies. Market share growth is sometimes considered as an indicator of market-position strength, although it is not particularly useful as a momentum indicator; in a fast-growing (or changing) market area, a company could show reasonable growth in new orders, or REM, or in both together, while its market share declines. This condition in itself is neither good nor bad. Share information has to be interpreted in the context of the situation and each company's specific marketplace objectives. In most niche markets, market-size data is not

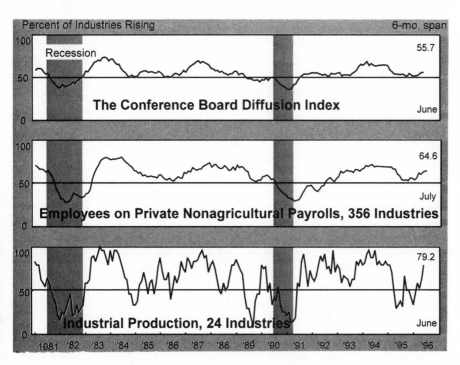

Figure 3-4: Indexes of Economic Momentum

gathered objectively, accurately, or rapidly, so that useful statistical information may not be readily available or reliable. Generally, if new-order growth rate equals or exceeds the growth rate of the overall market niche, and if REM is holding or rising, then spending time and money trying to measure market share for a niche is usually unimportant. Watching competitors is more productive.

New Orders Growth

New orders precede revenues, and their growth rate is a leading indicator for future revenue levels and for changes in the company's market share. A weekly line graph showing both net new orders and a rolling moving average (one to three months) is one means of showing order growth trends. Some companies monitor "book-to-bill" ratio or order backlog instead of net new-order growth. As these are indirect measures, however, they lack clarity and need more interpretation.

A growing rate of new orders is an indicator that the company is satisfying market needs in a competitively effective way. But it could also mean that the company is "buying" orders through low pricing, so new-order growth needs to be considered in context with the REM level provided by the orders, and by the company's sales growth strategy. New orders can also be used to predict future REM levels when accurate cost-accounting information is available for individual products.

As a precaution, it is important to be aware that certain situations will distort new order trends. Sometimes, orders are booked that are not firmly scheduled for shipment. These should not be included in momentum reports until they are firm. In periods of product shortages, for example, a customer sometimes hedges by placing the same order with two or more suppliers with the intention of canceling part of each. Another customer might place a larger order than needed so as to gain delivery priority, also with the intention of cutting the order back later. If caution is taken with high-risk orders so they are not recorded into backlog until they are confirmed to be real, distortion in new-order trends can be avoided.

REM Growth

REM is the most useful, broad-gauge, quantitative indicator of market-position strength. It combines in a single number the impact of four variables: revenue level, product pricing, product cost, and sales cost, all of which must be in harmony to provide sustained REM growth. The only way to confirm growing market-position strength is to track the long-term growth trend in REM. REM is also a leading indicator for trends in operating profit, net income, and cash flow. Without REM growth that is significantly larger than the inflation rate and large enough to support necessary development programs, a company ultimately faces net income decline. A useful means of showing REM trends is a weekly line graph that shows current revenue margin and the rolling moving average (one to three months).

By itself, revenue is not an indicator of market strength, although it is obviously useful in analyzing operational performance. Revenue is an important measure of a company's short-term ability to convert its finished goods inventory, order backlog, and new orders into revenue margin. When revenue is down, regardless of whether the cause is too few new orders, too little backlog, scheduling or manufacturing problems, or inadequate inventory, then revenue margin and operating profit are also normally down.

Payroll/Revenue Ratio

Payroll as a percentage of revenue is a broad-based, company-wide measure of organizational productivity that is much more sensitive than the sales-per-employee measure in common use. If total payroll costs (direct payments plus taxes and benefits) are not declining relative to revenue generated, then overall company productivity is likely to be static or declining.

To supplement the overall company payroll/revenue ratio, similar indicators should be in place for each of four areas: revenue generation, value creation, administration, and management. Separate monitoring of these areas identifies where productivity problems may be developing. These supplemental indicators provide a perspective important for both the CEO and the board of directors. Graphing the supplemental indicators is not necessary, however, as they are not rapidly changing except when significant payroll policy changes are made.

The indicator for payroll cost of management should provide guidance for setting management salary and variable pay. Here, two ratios—one for management base salary as a percentage of operating profit, one for management variable pay as a percentage of operating profit—are useful. Generally, the cost of management should not exceed a preset goal and should gradually decline as a percentage of operating profit as the company grows. Only when this occurs is management becoming more productive.

Cost-to-Sell Ratio

Cost to sell as a percentage of revenue is an important measure of productivity in selling activities. A downward trend in this ratio should be evident except during periods when selling capability is being expanded or the company is engaged in an unusual and expensive promotion program. The ratio should improve as revenue increases and when there are gains in selling productivity. A useful presentation here is a graph that shows actual and moving average data. To supplement this graph, a breakdown of sales cost by product line should be supplied, using an ABC approach if significant differences in resources are used for each product line.

Operating Profit Growth

Operating profit (OP) is the indicator that combines REM performance with the expenses incurred in the company's development and administration (D&A) areas. Sometimes called earnings before interest and taxes (EBIT), operating profit is the profit realized from current operations. OP is the key indicator for overall management efficacy in achieving short- and long-term financial results.

Operating Cash Flow Growth

Operating cash flow is the gross cash generated by operations. It is called gross because it does not yet reflect working capital adjustments. Consequently, it is a "purer" measure of cash generated by operations than free operating cash flow, and as such it is a better momentum indicator. Free operating cash flow includes changes in working capital that mask changes in cash flow from operations. As noted earlier, however, free operating cash flow is an important indicator of a company's capacity to internally finance growth in revenues, and from that perspective it should be carefully monitored.

Return on Net Assets

Internally, return on net assets (RONA) is the most useful long-term return measure as compared to return on equity or investment, as RONA is directly under operating management control and a more stable point of reference. Decisions and conditions that affect a company's equity or debt have no direct effect on RONA, whereas they do affect the other return measures. Return on sales (ROS) is often considered as a return measure, as it encompasses both the "top and bottom" lines. While on the surface this might seem useful, ROS can foster the wrong emphasis in revenue-generation strategy. The variable of importance in revenue generation is revenue profit (REM dollar) growth, not return on sales per se.

Calculations of return for external reports usually use net income as the numerator. For internal use, however, the best approach is to use *operating profit*. This provides a direct measure of profitability from operations that is unaffected by nonoperating expense and taxes.

Working Capital Turnover

A company's working capital, although not shown directly on a balance sheet, is the sum of its cash, receivables, and inventory less short-term payables. In most companies cash balances are kept relatively low, so that receivables, inventory, and short-term payables are the primary determinants of working capital. For product companies, inventory and receivables are likely to be the largest net asset on the balance sheet. For these companies, a primary measure of asset utilization is working capital turnover (WCT). WCT is calculated by dividing annualized revenue by working capital. The larger the ratio, the more efficiently working capital is being employed.

D&A Expense/REM Ratio

D&A expense encompasses all value creation and company-central administrative, management, and variable-pay expenses. These are core expenses incurred to keep the company in business and to sustain and grow its capabilities, competencies, and infrastructure. Many of these expenses are discretionary, and some are semifixed.

The D&A expense/REM ratio is the percentage of REM that D&A expense represents. This ratio monitors overall discretionary and semifixed expenses relative to the profit available to pay for them. Management should aspire to a permanently declining ratio, obtained from productivity gains and increased REM. A rising ratio is a serious concern except when new development undertakings cause a temporary rise. It is important to monitor REM contribution from new undertakings to keep track of value creation relative to project cost.

ECONOMIC PROFIT

Economic profit (EP), sometimes called economic value added, is a financial measure once used primarily in macroeconomics and currently occasionally used to evaluate management performance. EP is not an effective momentum indicator but it is a useful analytical tool.

As a measure of effectiveness in the use of a company's financial assets, EP indicates what the net profit of a company would be if the company had to pay its shareholders a market-based return on equity capital. EP of less than zero would indicate that the company's net income is not sufficient to cover the cost of its equity capital. If the company is not earning a return comparable to normal market rates, the question arises if the capital is not better off in some other investment.

EP is calculated by subtracting the "cost" of capital from net income. The cost of capital is calculated by multiplying balance-sheet owner equity by a defined market rate of return. If past operating losses have reduced equity below invested capital, then invested capital should be used in place of equity in the calculation. The market rate of return can be easily approximated by adding a risk-related premium to the thirty-year treasury bond rate. This premium is judiciously established by assessing the company's financial strength, the quality of its earnings, and the conditions in the capital markets.

Some large companies have adopted EP as a primary measure of their financial performance, and some use it in their executive variable-pay plans. In 1993, it was reported that some companies, including CSX, Briggs and Stratton, Coca Cola, and AT&T have adopted EP in their management processes and credit it with effectively aligning management decisions and actions with shareholder interests.[4]

EP is not useful as a performance measure in companies where the emphasis is on growth. Such objectives as market-position strength and organizational vitality are far more important than a purely financial asset-allocation measure. EP can be useful, however, as a measure of a company's progress toward earning sufficient profit, and for making basic decisions on the restructuring or possible sale of a company. It can also be a useful benchmark in setting long-term goals for return on net assets.

USING QUALITATIVE MOMENTUM INDICATORS

While quantitative indicators are relatively easy to present numerically, the qualitative indicators, important as evidence of momentum trends, require alternative ways of measuring and communicating momentum. The most useful approach is to establish a process based on making judgments of progress in meeting strengthening goals in each indicator area.

This approach works best when the company assigns teams to the specific areas to be monitored. Team members then decide what best reflects the nature and quality of the company's strengths. Each team can provide a periodic report card in which they grade the company's overall performance. On a scale of 0 to 10, a grade of 10 would represent the ideal condition; a zero would indicate a crisis in need of urgent attention. A momentum index could be based on a composite of all the grades issued by team members. Once determined, the index can be graphically plotted relative to time.

Grading for each area can be done by each team member by answering the question: What is our current level of strength, and are we now strengthening at a sufficient rate? In addition to the team members' personal opinions, periodic, objective surveys of employees, customers, shareholders, and suppliers should be conducted to indicate the relative satisfaction of these constituencies with the company's performance. These survey results should be factored into the grading judgments. Providing, for all company employees, a safe and direct communication route to a responsible team member is another means of bringing problems to the surface. The value of well-designed surveys and confidential feedback from conscientious people is that these signal how well things are really going and can help bring reality into the judgments of those doing the grading and setting priorities for action.

After each grading session, team members can consider priorities and budgets for actions in the areas that need strengthening. The frequency of each review session should be set by the nature and extent of the needs.The company's ultimate benefit from establishing qualitative momentum indicators is the fact that its team members are engaged in analyzing these matters on a regular basis, determining what improvements are taking place, and concerning themselves about where more action is needed. The process itself and the heightened awareness of the trends it produces should ensure constructive, timely improvements.

MARKET-POSITION STRENGTH

A company's market-position strength is directly determined by its own particular competencies, products, customer satisfaction, marketplace presence, and, of primary importance, its reputation in the marketplace. The quantitative indicators of net new-order growth and REM provide an overall measure of the company's performance in the marketplace. The three qualitative indicators, competency advantages, customer focus index, and product quality index, reflect the underlying strength of the company's operations to achieve its desired financial performance.

Competency Advantages

In the long term, the level and nature of a company's future customer orders are determined by its overall company competency relative to market opportunities, and the competency of its competitors. Competency advantages are the specific, identifiable company attributes that underpin product or service leadership in the marketplace. To be an advantage, an attribute has to be superior to a similar attribute of competitors and has to provide definitive customer benefits. Some attributes that can provide competency advantage are proprietary technology or designs in products or production processes, more efficient operational processes, key people, unique customer services and support, well-executed activities in all company operations, and company values that nourish satisfied employees and contented customers. Usually a competency attribute has no meaningful gradations; it is either an advantage or it is not.

Combining two or more competency advantages to achieve much stronger performance capability can sometimes provide dramatic results, as the success of Wal-Mart Stores attests. Wal-Mart grew from a small beginning in Arkansas into a multibillion-dollar enterprise, outdistancing all its more entrenched competitors by a combination of competency advantages. These advantages included basic values like honesty, fairness, and respect for employees and customers, in combination with an astute market strategy, sophisticated purchasing and distribution processes that kept costs and inventories low and stores fully stocked, and low selling prices that derived from low operating costs.

In a competitive marketplace, competency advantages are usually temporary. This is why it is so vital to sustain a continuous effort at strengthening current company competencies while adding new ones. Managers must carefully define specific company competency advantages and then monitor their utility in the market, which is the only means of determining their impact on company momentum. Using customer surveys and evaluating competitors' performance are important ways to confirm where and why advantages exist. No index can usefully portray momentum changes in market position that occur because of changes in competency advantages. Only periodically analyzing the company's competency advantages and establishing realistic programs to strengthen them will supply the required momentum. Indirectly, competency advantages can be related to trends in revenue margin and pricing firmness.

Customer Focus Index

Customer focus means totally *satisfying* company-selected customers while *learning* from them about their needs and the ways the company can better satisfy them. Acting on this information is, in part, how market-position strength is built. Customer focus also means looking carefully at potential customers, particularly those now in the camps of competitors. Customer focus, to the point that it is and remains a marketplace advantage, is essential for continuous growth and a fundamental requirement for achieving lasting company strength.

What factors contribute to customer satisfaction? Product performance, quality, value, range of product choice, services, and delivery lead time are all significant. This means ensuring first-rate sales and support services, providing customer contact and coordination with the company that is easy and pleasant, and solving customer problems with speed and goodwill. The ultimate consideration is to find out what it takes to make the customer a loyal, repeat buyer and act on it.

One way to assess customer satisfaction is to use formal and informal customer surveys, but the most important way is to analyze what happens at the company's interface with its customers. The points to be scrutinized include people behavior and competency, lost orders, lost customers, order processing and delivery time, order fulfillment errors, product returns, customer complaints, growth in existing customer sales, response time to customer inquiries, and how the public responds to the company's advertising and sales literature. All these areas should be benchmarked against competitors as well as superior-performing companies in other industries.

Monitoring the second aspect of customer focus, learning from customers, is more elusive than measuring customer satisfaction. Probably no genuine way exists other than for policy managers, together with company operating people, to spend time with customers in everyday interactive situations. Observing how the company's people acquire useful information is essential. Equally important is how this information is passed along to the appropriate people in the company so it can be pooled with other information and idea sources. Once information has been received and pooled, someone has to evaluate it in the context of company strategy and goals, and then decide on actions, if any. This process of acquiring, passing along, and using information from customers is as much an informal as a formal process. Much of it depends on the care and concern each person takes to initiate communications and to follow up on the necessary details. Top management needs to know how all these things work and to formalize as much of the process as possible. Even so, only a sense of personal accountability by the people involved ensure that the informal aspects of the process are effective.

Perhaps the only way to monitor both aspects of customer focus is to establish an index using the report card method. Based on these judgments, a composite index can be established that indicates the degree to which customer satisfaction and learning from customers are being attained.

Product Quality Index

A minimum requirement in the marketplace is product quality that is fully competitive; a higher level may or may not be advantageous. The importance of product quality cannot be overstressed, for there will be few repeat sales to customers who are dissatisfied to the point of anger if a product doesn't work as they expect it to, or who find it works initially and then fails prematurely.

Obtaining quantitative data on product quality includes monitoring product out-of-box acceptance rates, product failure modes and rates, defect categories and rates in manufacture, rework percentages, and cost-of-quality problems. Qualitative measures should include assessing workmanship consistency and actual versus market-expected quality. The most useful indicator for tracking quality improvements is an overall quality index that combines quantitative measures and qualitative judgments.

ORGANIZATIONAL VITALITY

I have noted that the engine which powers company performance and therefore company growth is organizational vitality—the combination of intellectual power and human energy. Measuring organizational vitality is perhaps the most important need in every company, because without this information, problems will go undetected until they become serious enough to cause major difficulty. Change in organizational vitality is the most important leading indicator of long-term company performance.

The key elements that contribute to organizational vitality are accountability; innovation; the three C's of communication, cooperation, and coordination; and rate of learning, both individual and organizational. Without a sufficient level of these elements, a company will fall behind in market-position strength. It will be constantly playing catch-up and never achieve a leadership role in the marketplace. Rate of learning is at the core of organizational vitality; staying at the cutting edge of change depends on maintaining a state of insight about opportunities and the ability to capitalize on them.

The quantitative evaluation methods most commonly used include surveying employee attitudes, the number and nature of employee suggestions for improvement, employee turnover, and absenteeism and lateness studies. These are useful, but they do not provide much understanding of people contributions to company momentum. For example, one new idea that provides a product design breakthrough can spark greater impetus to company momentum than almost any difficulty its contributor might cause by being grumpy or perpetually late for work. Most creative people work according to their own rhythms.

The starting point for measurement here is to establish an index for each of the three proposed areas—unity-of-cause involvement, innovation level, and three C's efficacy. Key people who are able to make insightful observations about the company's situation in the indicator areas are the main source of information. Others include meaningful contributions made in one-to-one sessions during informal, constructive performance appraisals. As with market-position strength, using a team approach for grading each of the three indicator areas is the most effective approach. Each policy manager, operating manager, and team participant is expected to evaluate and make judgments on the extent to which each of these areas is actually a momentum-driving force. Again, rate and direction of change are the most important considerations.*

Unity of Cause Index

This index is a measure of individual and team accountability. The extent to which positive attitudes have taken hold within a unity of cause is best determined through one-on-one talks and in observing behavior in day-to-day activities. Attitudes are shown through initiative, persistence, responses to change, organizational esprit, time-use awareness, and the care and concern demonstrated in work performance.

Innovation Level Index

Innovation is the output from individual learning, competency, creativity, risk taking, and initiative. Its ingredients are the frequency and importance of useful ideas, imaginative strategy, creative actions, and problem solving. Assessing whether people who are in key positions are sufficiently innovative is an essential part of determining momentum level and trends in organizational vitality.

The key considerations in analyzing a company's innovation level are those activities and behaviors of managers that encourage or inhibit innovation by others.

---

* As defined by Peter F. Drucker in *The Effective Executive* (New York: Harper & Row, 1966), *efficacy* combines the terms *effectiveness* and *efficiency*. Effectiveness means doing the right things, and efficiency means doing things right; efficacy means doing both the right things and doing them right.

While management controls that encourage conformity are important in some areas, they also restrict the kind of innovation that may be necessary to build momentum. Balancing the tension between innovation and conformity is essential. Carefully considering whether existing policies and controls are being applied in the right places and in the right way is a vital part of momentum analysis.

Three C's Efficacy Index

Communication, cooperation, and coordination determine the rate at which organizational learning takes place, and therefore they significantly affect organizational vitality. Nothing slows down momentum building more than limitations and blockages in these three areas. Open, meaningful communication, oral and written, is the primary means by which information flows, and the conduit through which it is converted into useful knowledge and action. Communicating effectively depends on cooperation and coordination throughout the company.

The company-internal channels of communication—downward, lateral, and upward—all need to be kept open and unencumbered by fear or indifference. For numerous and sometimes subtle reasons, most organizations contain impediments in all three. Impediments also flourish in the outside channels that link the company's people with customers and with suppliers. Identifying those obstructions and eliminating them are key steps toward building organizational vitality.

PRODUCTIVITY GAIN

The rate at which productivity gains take place has important effects on a company's competitiveness and capability to produce stakeholder value. The only operational actions that will increase long-term company profit are growth in REM and productivity gains. In every company, productivity is directly related to organizational vitality and to the efficacy of operational processes in use.

Productivity throughout a company determines its overall cost structure and rate of accomplishment. In aggressively competitive markets, it is often difficult to increase prices, and declining market prices are a fact of life for many companies. Facing such difficult market environments means routinely making substantial company-wide gains in productivity and enlarging the company's customer base if it is to counter competitive pressure and concurrently produce growth in stakeholder value.

Most successful companies spend 15 to 40 percent of REM on product- and customer-development activities. They do this to maintain and strengthen their market position and to stimulate growth in their performance capabilities. Other contributions to productivity gain and growth are explicit efforts to strengthen customer focus, improve and add products, enhance competencies, simplify processes, and encourage continuous improvement in how things are done. Assessing quality, cost, cycle time, throughput unit volume, inventory levels, and related matters in manufacturing are all important in analyzing productivity.

PRODUCTIVITY RATING MATRIX

Because productivity is important in every part of a company, establishing a productivity rating matrix provides a realistic way of qualitatively analyzing momentum trends. This overview of productivity in a company's eight principal capability areas supplies a surprisingly clear perspective on how well the company is performing and illuminates the areas that need improvement. Fig-

PRODUCTIVITY RATING MATRIX CAPABILITY AREA	OVERALL PERFORMANCE	OPERATING PROCESSES	TECHNICAL PROCESSES	COST TO PERFORM	TIME TO PERFORM
SELLING					
CUSTOMER SERVICES					
PRODUCT MANAGEMENT					
MANUFACTURING					
PRODUCT/PROCESS DEVELOPMENT					
COMPANY DEVELOPMENT					
ADMINISTRATION					
MANAGEMENT					

A 0-10 rating is assigned based on actual performance relative to the needs of the company, or to an established benchmark.

10=Excellent   4=Marginally Acceptable   0=Crisis

Figure 3-5: Productivity Rating Matrix

ure 3-5 shows the format for this matrix and how it reflects productivity gains in the company.

The matrix rates the company's capability areas on productivity in each of five categories: overall performance, operating processes, technical processes, cost to perform, and time to perform. A benchmark for each of these categories needs to be set, based on external marketplace standards when possible. Rating, on a 0-to-10 scale, is done by those people, managers and nonmanagers, who are in a position to clearly understand and communicate the company's operations. Zero indicates a crisis situation; 10 means there is little room for improvement. The overall grades indicate the areas that require specific undertakings to raise productivity; future grading charts what progress has been made.

MEASURING VALUE FOR CUSTOMERS, EMPLOYEES, AND SHAREHOLDERS

The indicators of value growth for stakeholders are the ultimate bottom-line measures that demonstrate management performance over time. Management's job is to produce important, simultaneous growth in each stakeholder-value area year after year to ensure lasting company strength.

Customer Value Produced

A useful qualitative indicator of value growth for customers is the company's *reputation* with its customers, as this is a quality built on company performance that maintains customer respect, trust, and loyalty; it is also the foundation for opening new customer relations and retaining existing ones. Measuring reputation has to be based on information that comes directly from customers. Obtaining genuinely objective facts depends on research and surveys conducted by outside organizations.

The most useful quantitative indicator for growth in value provided to customers is *revenue margin*. Customers buy on value as they perceive it; the long-term growth in revenue margin made possible by firm prices is a direct measure of the extent to which customers indicate their satisfaction with the company. Analyzing revenue margin trends for each major customer and in aggregate for smaller customers can indicate value for customers. When revenue margin trends decline, the long-term value provided to customers is almost always also declining.

Employee Value Produced

The qualitative indicator that best measures growth in value for employees is one that monitors *company culture*. Cultural change that helps employees deepen their accountability to the company and strengthens their participation in its unity of cause indicates that management is succeeding in its efforts to make the company more attractive, psychologically and financially, to its employees.

A useful quantitative indicator for growth in financial value for employees is *profit-sharing pool size*. If company growth in operating profit provides a corresponding increase in each employee's share of a company-wide profit-sharing pool, this is a direct measure of growth in value for the employee.

Shareholder Value Produced

A useful qualitative indicator for value growth to shareholders is *company stature in the marketplace*. In the minds of shareholders and analysts, company stature is a direct measure of the esteem these constituencies have for the company. Using research and surveys conducted by outside organizations is an objective way of obtaining overall judgments about company stature. The company's stock price-to-earnings ratio is another indicator of stature, as it is determined by outsiders based on their judgment of the potential for future company growth in financial performance; it is an integrated indicator of their attitudes on management competency and on overall company effectiveness toward building lasting strength.

A helpful quantitative indicator for shareholder value growth is *total return* to shareholders, the sum of share price growth and cash distributions to shareholders.

Simply noting the range and depth of the momentum indicators described here conveys TDM's coverage of typical company activity. The following chapters show how to harness this activity to generate lasting company strength.

NOTES

1. Robert G. Eccles, "The Performance Measurement Manifesto," *Harvard Business Review*, January-February, 1991; Robert S. Kaplan, "Yesterday's Accounting Undermines Production," *Harvard Business Review*, July-August, 1984.

2. Peter Flentov and Eric Shuman, "Activity-based Costing: The Case for a New Costing Paradigm," *CFO Magazine*, March-April 1991; Robin Cooper and Robert S. Kaplan, "Measure Costs Right: Make the Right Decisions," *Harvard Business Review*, September-October 1988.

3. Debbie Berlant, Reese Browning, and George Foster, "How Hewlett-Packard Gets Numbers It Can Trust," *Harvard Business Review*, January-February 1990.

4. "The Real Key to Creating Wealth," *Fortune*, September 20, 1993.

## CHAPTER 4

Momentum Drivers

The Catalysts for Growth

Momentum in business refers to *rate of accomplishment*. This chapter focuses on understanding the importance of the contributions that strengthen a company's market position and performance capability and finding ways to intensify those contributions.

Eight momentum drivers, shown in Figure 4-1, individually and collectively enhance achievements in the company's anchorpoint objectives. The basic three, unity of cause, accountability, and learning are the *core drivers*. They strengthen the other five, organizational vitality, risk taking, creativity, quality, and control, which are called *key drivers*. Organizational vitality, the foremost key driver, is considered in chapter 5.

UNITY OF CAUSE

For a company to benefit fully from the talents of every employee, each has to see his or her role as a contributor to an important company need. A company-wide unity of cause aimed at company strengthening can be that common purpose, for it links the entire organization's basic need to a benefit for the employee: if career and financial opportunity are to develop for the employee, the company first has to grow in strength with its customers and in its performance capability.

To function in an authentic way, the cause has to be clearly and briefly stated so that everyone is able to identify with it and be guided by it. All have to genuinely believe in the cause and understand that it transcends individual and group interests. They must know how they personally can contribute to it. Individually, each must believe that the most important insurance for continued employment and opportunity for personal advancement is spirited momentum-building by everyone in the company.

Some people may feel that momentum is just a euphemism to compel them to work harder and to put in more time on the job. They must come to see that momentum building is primarily working smarter. They must also accept the reality that the marketplace sets the required rate at which company strengthening must take place. These may not be easy concepts for some people, including some managers, to identify with, even when they understand them intellectually.

Gaining employee support for a unity of cause may also be hindered because of deep-rooted but unspoken cynicism toward causes in general, especially if earlier attempts at unity have failed to take hold. People do not want to feel manipulated by management. Even when they support the unity of cause, it takes constant reinforcement and lots of management attention to actually get people to work creatively and effectively together within it. One important ingredient for rallying support for the cause is to establish a company-wide profit-sharing program that includes disclosure to employees of information about company financial performance. The profit sharing can be based on a defined percentage of operating profit above a specific threshold, the proceeds of which are put into a pool that is paid out to every employee,

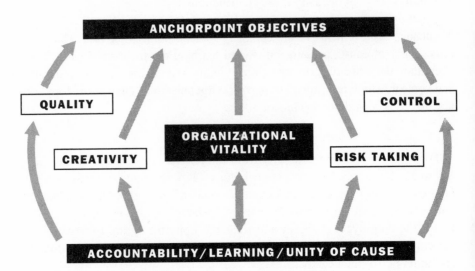

Figure 4-1: The Momentum Drivers

preferably once every three months. This tangible reward for both conscientiousness and personal attention to company interests is an important component for generating enthusiasm for the cause over the long term. This kind of company-wide gain sharing puts a specific burden on management, however. It means that managers have to make certain that the necessary results are achieved so the payouts occur and are also of a meaningful size. If they are not, enthusiasm will quickly turn into complacency and perhaps even anger toward management, in which case the employees will blame management for the lack of profit growth in the company.

Whatever the unity of cause, it should be formalized and made part of a company's mission statement; it then must be incorporated into the company's performance appraisal process for all employees, managers and nonmanagers. If the unity of cause is a sincere and functional part of the company's mission, then every manager will be able to refer to it frequently when setting priorities for actions.

ACCOUNTABILITY

Functions, responsibilities, and *tasks* (both explicit and implicit) are words that describe what people do to perform their jobs. Accountability describes the achievement expected from job performance. Momentum building depends on individual accountability accompanied by the necessary authority to act. For most everyday activities in a company, getting the right things done, in the right way, at the right time, and for the right cost is a complex process. When accountability and authority are unclear, things take too long to do and are often done wrong or late. A manager checking closely on what is happening is not what drives important accomplishment; what does is a competent and accountable person getting done what needs to get done.

Distinguishing between responsibility and accountability is essential. When a job is defined in terms of accountability instead of tasks, the job holder is expected to find out what needs to be done and then get it done in a way that produces the necessary results. When the situation changes, it is up to the individual to adapt and find the new appropriate action that will accomplish the job. If accountability is clearly understood and management provides a supportive environment, most of the time people can decide on their own what is important without the need for supervision. Accountability nourishes the initiative to become aware of needs, to take appropriate actions, and to confirm that the results are satisfactory. It also enhances the dignity of the company's people.

Building an organization in which the daily work is carried out in a manner that needs minimum supervision by policy managers depends on a clear understanding of job accountability. This means that each person has a serious interest in his or her job and a willingness to be accountable for results. Real accountability exists only when people want to be accountable. Partly this means being aware that if they don't do something it will not get done, and that it is up to them to get it done on time and in the right way. When this condition exists, most people will usually do whatever it takes to get the job done.

Nothing is more important for company performance than a high degree of accountability in each person for his or her own job performance. Directly supervising others can change their behavior, but not their thinking or their attitudes. Intellectual activity cannot be supervised or managed. Becoming accountable is the only way to bring one's full intellectual and creative power to bear on the company's behalf.

For people to be accountable, to take an interest in their jobs, and to make an intellectual contribution to them, the following conditions must obtain: specific expectations for performance; clearly defined boundaries for the use of their authority; a minimum of cultural, process, or structural inhibitors; necessary help and guidance; frequent constructive feedback on job performance; and relatively limited supervision. The shift to accountability-based relationships does not mean abdication of managerial responsibility, just engaging in a different kind of involvement, one based on trust, patience, and tolerance for mistakes.

An attitude that appropriate change is vital for growth in company performance is an essential and powerful driving force. To build that force, all the company's people have to believe their ideas and contributions are important. They need to believe that customers must be satisfied, that quality must prevail, and that time lost wastes both money and opportunity. Most importantly, they have to personally identify with the company and know their initiatives to improve things will make a difference, and that they will share in the fruits of company achievements.

Some people are naturally inclined toward being accountable. Many others just want to be told what to do and then perform their job without having to feel accountable. Such attitudes can be difficult to change. "What's in it for me?" "It's not my problem!" These and a variety of other such parrying positions have to be moved into the background before those who adhere to them will venture into the less comfortable role of being accountable not just for the performance of tasks but for a result.

Fostering Accountability from Others

The willingness to accept meaningful accountability becomes more limited at levels below the CEO. Most people tend to look upward rather than inward for their direction. They devote their talents and time to carrying out their job responsibilities in the way they think will best satisfy their boss, even when this is not the most productive way for the company. People do not want to make mistakes, and because they often lack clarity about priorities or have inadequate information, it is common for them to rein in their abilities and do the job in the safest way. If a manager wants to obtain real accountability, he or she has to be sensitive to this normal behavior; while respecting an upper manager's views and seeking his or her counsel is part of a subordinate relationship, the subordinate also has to be free to act independently, without fear of reprisal, according to the needs of each situation.

Unfortunately, some managers will not accept being challenged by their subordinates and insist that their way is best, whether or not the subordinate agrees. And some subordinates believe their personal interests are not synonymous with the company's interest, which might also be true under some managers. When managerial ego interferes or top managers function by punishing subordinates, it is not possible to obtain real accountability.

Often problems that deter accountability are weak relationships between managers and between managers and nonmanagers, and upper managers who delegate responsibility without imparting sufficient authority and support for the subordinates to do their jobs without higher-level intervention. A manager may rationalize this situation on the grounds that it minimizes mistakes, or that the manager is more experienced and can help subordinates get a better result, or that past attempts at generating accountability have failed. But more commonly, the manager simply has never really considered doing things in a way that encourages accountability from others.

To foster involvement and accountability, a company must let it be known that everyone's thoughts, ideas, and suggestions, although they will not necessarily accepted, will be seriously considered. Encouragement and support should take precedence over control, blame, and punishment. People need the room to experiment with ways of doing things better, and the more they feel like partners in an enterprise, as opposed to simply subordinates, the more likely it is they will feel accountable to that enterprise. Perhaps most importantly, people need a sense that they are well regarded, trusted, and respected by upper management. Upper-level managers must see to it that feedback about job performance is timely, informal, frequent, and helpful. The company's pay policies must also be perceived as fair and reasonable.

Most people, most of the time, behave responsibly in a low-supervision environment if they know clearly what is expected from their performance. Clarifying performance expectations starts with revising job descriptions to more concisely and broadly define responsibility, while being specific about authority, relationships, communications, and accountability. The company's people must have relatively broad latitude for decision making and actions. When upper management establishes guidelines for the kind of decisions that are to be reviewed, in advance or after the fact, and when easy and frequent vertical communication takes place, upper management can have more confidence in the decisions and actions of others. For this to work well, however, upper-level managers must have the discipline to avoid personal intrusion in the normal activities of others, even when invited to do so.

A relationship between a manager and his or her subordinates based on involvement and accountability is the only really productive one for achieving superior long-term performance. Involvement means that each person is an important contributor of ideas and to operating decision-making. Accountability means people are committed to their jobs and by their own initiative will usually find ways to produce the right result for the company. To become accountable, people need to be sufficiently self-confident and competent and feel they have sufficient managerial support. They also need to believe that consistently accountable behavior over time earns rewards, and that if they fail to perform as their job requires, this "no result" situation will carry penalties. Nearly everyone has the potential for a reasonable level of accountability, which is usually evident by how we behave in our personal lives.

Aubrey C. Daniels makes the point that getting top performance and gaining a world-beating organization in the process is possible, but that it takes a lot more than common-sense management or the latest fad management practice. Most managers, he observes, fail to understand that people are not merely a component in the business machine, but are the engine of it. Daniels has evolved what he calls Performance Management as the means for bringing out the best in people. He describes the qualities of human nature and then applies this understanding of human nature to using positive reinforcement as a way of encouraging desired behavior. His approach uses two vital questions: Why do people do what they do? What would cause them to adopt more positive, productive on-the-job behaviors? [1]

One important step toward building a more accountable company is to focus on refining a sophisticated, helpful central information and control system (cencon) that makes available both financial and nonfinancial information, with the purpose of helping those doing the work to do a better job. If the system simply puts more ammunition in management's hand to apply downward pressure, the result will be not more but less accountability, and a lot more time spent in meetings. To be fully effective, a good cencon system needs to obtain and process relevant information and then disseminate it in a useful, timely, and condensed way. The timeliness of communicating information to those who must act directly on it is absolutely essential; these people have to regard the information system as a tool for doing their own particular job.

Perhaps the most obvious facet of accountability is that to some extent, every manager is a role model. By nature, managing is not a time-structured job; situational needs have to determine when a job gets done. A manager who works by the clock rather than by the needs of his or her job is sure to be copied by many others.

LEARNING AND RENEWAL

Learning is the most fundamental momentum driver. Everything else emanates from it. Individual learning is driven by a need to know, curiosity, and a desire for self-improvement. Both personal and organizational learning—that is, people learning from each other and thereby stimulating new organizational knowledge—are vital for momentum building. The only way a company can hope to achieve and retain competency advantages that will provide long-term, market-position strength is to engage in continuous learning. It is the dynamic force that keeps both people and companies at the cutting edge of important achievements. The organizational culture of every business plays a key role in setting the kinds of attitudes that encourage or discourage learning.

Sometimes the need to learn is urgent, as with the arrival of new technology that makes what currently exists obsolete. The advent of the transistor and related devices in the 1950s and of integrated circuits in the 1960s rendered nearly all earlier vacuum-tube technology obsolete and opened the door to countless new or improved products. These technologies also made many people obsolete. Those who develop products, services, and processes have to be able to quickly gain competence in newer technologies if they are to remain productive. Even if a business is based on technology that is relatively slow to evolve, changing needs constantly exert pressure for greater or different competencies. Growth in knowledge and competency is equally important in management, sales, manufacturing, and administration.

The need to upgrade performance, quality, and value in products and customer services, which began in the 1970s, has accelerated and continues today to stimulate the need for rapid learning. People throughout every business must be constant learners if they and their company are to keep pace with change in the operating environment. The internal and external dynamics of change are always present—people leaving the company; products, processes, and people aging; new needs arising; customers wanting new things; and competitors making new offerings. These changing situations all contribute, sometimes rapidly, to making a company's competency and capability obsolete.

The growth of knowledge comes from purposeful learning activity that involves listening, reading, observing, experimenting, analyzing, and synthesizing and relating bits of information. Learning is further stimulated by putting new knowledge into a useful context and by a purpose for doing so. The purpose may be to learn more just to gain new insight, or it may be to get something tangible done. One important stimulus comes from reviewing results of important undertakings to learn why things came out as they did. Aristotle's observation that an unexamined life is not worth living has a management parallel: an unexamined result is a lost opportunity to learn. Time set aside for introspection is likely to be highly worthwhile when the purpose is to learn, not to blame.

Learning is also an important aspect of renewal, those measures taken to adapt and revitalize a company's collective competencies and capabilities that provide its operational and marketplace strength. In people, renewal means regenerating enthusiasm and pursuing new personal competency. In a business enterprise, knowledge growth has to take place in whatever specific areas, individual and company wide, provide the competency advantages for the company that ultimately lead to market-position strengthening. Building momentum depends on the rate at which new useful knowledge is absorbed and put to use in the company.

Observing the nature of organizations and their people, John W. Gardner has said:

> When organizations and societies are young, they are flexible, fluid, not yet paralyzed by rigid specialization and willing to try anything once. As the organization or society ages, vitality diminishes, flexibility gives way to rigidity, creativity fades and there is a loss of capacity to meet challenges from unexpected directions.

Gardner also has observed that as people become more competent to function in their environment, they become less adaptive to making changes. He believes that this is a maturing process that is not only inevitable but desirable in its early stages. If the maturing process is not to bog down, he notes, the organization's people have to be encouraged to continuously "think young." Gardner's concept of thinking young means curiosity, openmindedness, experimentation, and accepting the inevitability of failure along with success.[2]

Over time, most successful businesses tend to lose their openmindedness, adaptiveness, and enthusiasm for new challenges. The earlier in a company's life that management becomes aware that it is at high risk of losing its future competitiveness because of the effect of its earlier successes, the easier it is to decide that continuous renewal and growth in company strengths is a vital area for everyday management concern. Renewal requires transforming established and comfortable situations into new forms of strength that will provide advantages to the company under changing market conditions. The process is sharpened when the company's people actually put new knowledge to use, and when new people join the company.

Managers can help those who work for them to "stay young in thought" by providing an open environment for changing the nature of activities and by offering different kinds of challenges—for example, in the form of changes in job assignments to introduce them to the need to learn. Companies sometimes unwittingly encourage obsolescence in people by keeping them in a job they are good at when the importance of the job is declining because of technology or marketplace changes. Boruch B. Frusztajer points to an example in the semiconductor field:

> Consider a young engineer who worked on diodes. Since his employer has an investment in the man's knowledge of diodes, a more recent graduate is put to work on transistors. After a few years, the diode specialist is obsolete. However, if the diode man was given a chance to move to transistors, he would be even more effective than the new graduate and the process of obsolescence could be reduced. The same, of course, applies to other areas of changing technology and other departments of most enterprises.[3]

At its root, company renewal is an *organizational learning* process. Essentially, organizational learning is a process that combines the knowledge of individuals—tacit, intuitive, and explicit—into new explicit group knowledge that will foster better understanding and new approaches for organizational undertakings. Understanding the concept of organizational learning is relatively easy; achieving it in the real world is not. Peter M. Senge's view, expressed in his book about how organizational learning comes about, emphasizes the need to break out of traditional mindsets and be open to new ideas and knowledge.[4] Chris Argyris looks carefully at the many obstacles to learning that exist in organizations and offers considerable insight on how to overcome them. He points out that in many companies, intelligent policy managers are the slowest learners, not because they can't learn, but because they are out of touch or overconfident.[5]

Referring to his book, Warren Bennis has said: "If I were to put everything in *An Invested Life* into one phrase, it would be this: that the key to competitive advantage in the '90s and beyond will be the capacity of top leadership to create a learning environment, an adaptive, agile, athletic, social architecture capable of generating intellectual capital. Now that's very abstract, but the key to it is intellectual capital."[6]

Although technology is an obvious area for continuous renewal and learning, others are equally vital, and perhaps the primary one is management. Managers at every level have to be leaders in continuous learning, first by practicing it themselves and then by encouraging others to do the same. Once sensitivity to learning is heightened, the very atmosphere it creates almost inevitably produces growth in organizational vitality with attendant greater accomplishment. A curious, open mind that challenges past assumptions and is not blinded by ego or defensiveness can lead to many new ideas and opportunities.

If it is regarded as an essential everyday effort, renewal through learning need never be instigated by panic from a traumatic experience. Company trauma usually occurs when market strength is lost with the consequence of poor financial performance. Individual trauma usually occurs when a person has been passed over for promotion, or terminated from a job. Unfortunately, too many of us need such a crisis to propel us into renewal, but we then deny ourselves its gratifications. If learning is only a chore, it will lack the dimensions of pleasure and play.

An essential foundation for innovation that depends on individual and organizational learning is a CEO's awareness of how important learning is as a continuous process in his or her company. Learning and renewal can keep the reshaping of a company ongoing so it can best exploit its marketplace opportunities at a pace consistent with the rate of change of its internal and external situations. It is unfortunate indeed that the top executives of General Motors, IBM, Sears, and many other companies that fell on hard times did not foster renewal and learning early enough. The pain they experienced, and in particular the pain of those whose jobs were eliminated by radical downsizing, would have been much less severe or avoided altogether.

RISK-TAKING

People in business take risks of varying size every day. Usually they do it because they have to, not because they want to. Most people would prefer to be safe in what they do. But nothing of significance happens in a business if its people hide from risk. Momentum building entails constant risk taking by managers and nonmanagers alike. When carefully calculated risks are a part of decisions and actions, progress comes in bigger steps. Counting on a safe and sure path may be necessary for many things, but knowing when and how to take risks is equally important. Setting sights high for new product performance, organizational change, new strategies, new people and teams, and new technology all involve risks. Acquiring another company is a very risky undertaking; failing to achieve the hoped-for result is far more common than success.

The mistakes that go with risk taking are part of the price of progress. Because businesses cannot avoid taking risks, managers are charged with the crucial judgment of which risks to take, when to take them, and how to minimize the possibility of failure. Often the biggest risk of all is being too cautious or conservative, or doing nothing. The gain or loss of company momentum occurs with every problem or opportunity, whether action is taken or not.

In an intriguing perspective on risk, Andrew Grove, CEO of Intel Corporation, describes a new market, personal conferencing, that Intel plans to enter:

> Twice before we sat by and played the components supplier as a systems business grew haphazardly. These things aren't an Erector set that jumps together on its own. Somebody has to package our technologies and sell them. This time we're going to

go out and help create the market, build the systems as well as the components, and compete in the marketplace. We'll either succeed or fail in a big way. We're willing to take the risk.[7]

New markets and products are where most companies take their major risks. If a company harbors important growth ambitions, there is no alternative to significant risk-taking.

Most risk-taking is not of the singular, dramatic kind like what Grove mentions, or like the acquisition of a company. Many risks are taken every day in routine activities, such as delegating authority. Hundreds of related little decisions usually are made for each big decision, and while managers need to be involved in big decisions, their involvement in those smaller decisions is frequently unproductive. They need to exercise tolerance and patience when others with good intentions make wrong decisions. What is important is not that a mistake was made, but whether or not it was recognized and promptly corrected. The company culture has to be tolerant of mistakes, but intolerant of behavior that avoids acknowledging and correcting them.

Taking risks with people is a routine part of every managerial job. If the wrong person is in a job, the cost will be high in lost opportunity, time, and money. Putting new people into a job is risky, for the variables involved in successful job performances are often difficult to evaluate in advance. Only time on the job can test a person's behavior, interpersonal relationships, integrity, intellect, and growth in competency.

Many smaller companies without the capacity to pay top salaries are compelled to place relatively inexperienced but high-potential people in key jobs. These people require lots of support and help but not the kind of close supervision that includes an upper manager making most of the decisions. When a person is given some space within which to build confidence, the payoff can be large, because less-experienced people are more motivated to learn and work harder, a dynamic that can sometimes lead to important creative achievement.

Taking worthwhile risks is a fundamental part of being a momentum-building manager, and so is anticipating the pitfalls in risk taking that can cause trouble. Unexpected problems will almost always arise; Murphy's law has not been repealed. What matters is being prepared for the unexpected and reacting quickly and judiciously to it.

CREATIVITY

Nothing happens until someone does something. The "core unit" of achievement is an individual doing one thing at a time so each completed task contributes in part toward a greater purpose. The principal determinants of achievement are knowledge, competency, and creativity combined with the motivation to succeed. Creativity is the wild card in the equation, and without an ample measure of it results are likely to be ordinary.

Creative innovation is the most powerful force in business operations, far more powerful than money or an entrenched market position. It is creative innovation that enables a company to adapt to and lead change in its marketplace. Ensuring an adequate supply of creative ideas is of vital importance to momentum building. Because there is no direct way a manager can do this, the only route is to foster a high level of organizational vitality and to staff key areas with people who have a creative bent. Cooking from recipes requires skill, but generating important new ideas requires creativity.

Karl Albrecht has noted that a creative corporation should be able to:

- sense or anticipate changes in its operating environment and conceptualize them accurately
- evaluate its own success in terms of how well its processes fit the demands of the operating environment
- transform its internal processes on a relatively continuous basis to become what it needs to be to survive and thrive in the environment [8]

Creativity is not limited to the realms of the technical or the artistic. As Albrecht notes, management too needs to be creative in its analysis, decisions, and actions.

Drucker has defined innovation as change that creates a new dimension of performance. This definition implies that a change has to provide useful improvement to qualify as an innovation. Webster's New World Dictionary defines *creativity* as "creating or able to create; having or showing imagination or intellectual inventiveness." These definitions imply that:

- creativity precedes and drives innovation and is the intellectual source for improvement
- creativity involves both new ideas and the adaptation of existing knowledge to new situations
- the potential for creativity resides in all of us

Exploring the qualities of creativity, Robert Fritz has said:

> The creative process is both predictable and unpredictable. It is both composition and improvisation. There is a balance of the intuitive and the rational. There is an ever-increasing process of learning. Each creator has his or her own personal rhythms. [9]

Deep interest (Fritz calls it "love") in a subject, curiosity to learn more about it, and an intense desire for a new perspective all apparently need to be present before creativity can spring forth. Emotion, not just logic, seems to play an important role in the process. Creative people think and work in nonlinear patterns; sometimes the patterns seem almost random. But there is usually an inner goal toward which all the effort is ultimately directed. Patience is a necessary part of the creative process.

An innovative idea is one that is regarded as important in the context of its application. We can distinguish between adaptive innovation, in which the source for the idea comes from existing knowledge, and creative innovation, which describes a new idea. One way of looking at the distinction is that adaptive innovation can be planned or programmed based on existing competency and incremental change, whereas creative innovation depends on a fresh idea that provides a leap ahead in insight and opportunity.

Problem solving depends heavily on creativity. Applying normal competence to problems usually leads to an acceptable result, but the horizon for gaining a breakthrough broadens immensely when both adaptive and creative innovation are present.

The mental process that produces "leap-forward" ideas is still a relatively obscure matter. We know that high intellectual capability is a factor, along with enough knowledge to understand situational interactions and possibilities. People with a high sense of accountability are also likely to be creative, because they have a deeper interest than others in the result of their pursuits. A deep interest that leads to a person's immersion in the pursuit of a result can produce at different times both brilliant ideas and blindness to the big picture. Interaction with others often stimulates ideas and broadens one's perspective while keeping it in the zone of reality. Sometimes it helps to look at a solution as a "black box" with an input and an output. Defining what the box has to do can lead to different ideas on how the box should function.

We understand more about what shuts down the process of creativity. At the head of the list are all the factors that demotivate a person and the kinds of situations that discourage a deep interest in one's job. People who work at a job primarily for the pay are less likely to be creative. In an organization, a work environment that encourages accountability and job interest is essential if creativity is to be nourished. Creative innovation cannot be predicted or programmed, but management can work conscientiously to provide the environment that encourages it.

Selecting people with a demonstrated capability for developing important ideas is the manager's most important way of obtaining creativity when it is an essential job need. Certain people seem to have more creative potential than others, and seeing to it that they are in key roles is an important managerial responsibility.

QUALITY

The Re-vision Era that began in the West in the 1970s was launched by the belated realization that the Asians were establishing tough new standards for world-class value and quality in products. Since these standards were set, those companies that either were disadvantaged or saw an opportunity to gain competitive advantage through higher quality have imposed a quality imperative as a top priority. The word *quality* now permeates every part of the business world.

Business and industry's most visible broad-based response to the competitively intensifying marketplace was TQM (total quality management), a movement that took root in the U.S. automotive, consumer electronics, and copier industries, whose products were clearly lower in quality and performance and higher in manufacturing cost than those of the new Asian competitors. The TQM initiatives were adopted primarily by larger companies; most successful smaller companies had been more sensitive all along to the quality and value aspects of their products. Nevertheless, they too were forced to look further and deeper into the role of quality in sustaining competitive effectiveness.

Employing the principles of W. Edward Deming, Joseph M.Juran, and Philip B. Crosby, many companies launched quality improvement initiatives to correct product design and manufacturing weaknesses and to improve productivity. The programs that made the most progress emphasized product redesigns that incorporated high intrinsic quality, reliability, and user value. Manufacturing processes and practices were also redesigned to shorten throughput time, reduce inventory, minimize variances, and reduce costs. Independent quality control within production was often eliminated, and responsibility for product quality was assigned to production people. Best-of-class benchmarking was widely applied as a reference to measure quality and productivity improvement. A company culture evolved that valued quality, with lots of employee training and participation in problem analysis and solution. Manager-manager and manager-worker relations were steered toward improved communication and cooperation.

Motorola, after feeling the pain of Japanese competition and exiting the consumer television market, decided that its future consumer markets would be in wireless products such as cellular phones and pagers, and that a world-class quality level was necessary if they were to succeed. The company installed a program called Six Sigma, with a defect rate goal of 3.4 per million, to which was added the achievement of a 90 percent defect rate reduction every two years and a 90 percent reduction in cycle time every five years in such areas as customer order processing and developing new products. To help integrate quality into Motorola's culture, management defined common terminology and measurements for quality. Bonuses were tied to measurable improvements. Robert Galvin, then CEO, estimated that over the five-year period starting in 1986, the savings Motorola achieved from Six Sigma totaled $2.2 billion.

Deming has pointed out through his "fourteen points for management" that the constant pursuit of quality brings many benefits, including the cost advantages that accrue when problems have been pinpointed and corrected at the source. Crosby makes the point: "Quality is free. It is not a gift, but it is free. What costs money are all the unquality things—all the actions that involve not doing jobs right the first time." In this poignant way, Crosby calls attention to the importance of quality and the hidden cost of quality inadequacy. He notes too that quality takes time and resources but will pay for the investment. Juran provides specific methodology for creating a company's plan of action on quality for any industry. He specifies criteria for selecting projects to improve quality and picking a team to carry them out.[10]

Using the term *total quality* to describe a broad-gauge management approach implies that quality is the only vital ingredient for successful management. This is a misleading and probably a dangerous oversimplification, as many other attributes are essential for business success. The full complement of momentum drivers, along with the anchorpoint objectives, provides a working perspective of these considerations. Another narrow view is to regard quality as a "miracle path," and thereby sometimes to overlook the real root cause and effect, good and bad, of actual performance.

Quality is an attribute that refers to a degree of excellence. It is a word that can apply to almost everything and therefore needs a context if it is to convey real meaning. For example, quality can usually be defined clearly and objectively in assessing products, many processes, services, and workmanship, but it is imprecise and not useful in describing strategy, performance capability, decision making, creative activities, and people and their relationships. How do we define and evaluate the quality of a person? Management's interest in people, for example, lies not in ill-defined quality, but in more objective areas, such as accountability, motivation, competency, suitability for a particular job, and achievements.

None of this is intended to minimize the need for a quality imperative in appropriate areas or at appropriate times. Quality in company operations has always been important and will continue to be of critical importance in the future. Continuous improvement in quality is essential in virtually all businesses. In the Momentum Era, exceptionally high-quality standards for a company's products, processes, and services are vital simply to be competitive. High quality in these areas is now taken for granted by customers, who do not necessarily expect to pay more for it but nonetheless insist on it, and thereby set the standards for what constitutes quality acceptability.

Achieving world-class quality, particularly if the objective is quality leadership as a marketplace advantage, can be very costly both in time and money. Done early and correctly, however, the pursuit of quality can often deliver a high return on this investment by gaining a more secure market position. By being forced to act on quality and getting a late start, General Motors reportedly spent more than $40 billion on a "restructuring mission" over five years through 1986, and tens of billions more since then, without gaining full quality parity in products with leading Japanese producers or with some of its American and German competitors. Even after GM's Cadillac Division received the coveted Baldridge Award, Cadillac was rated last, below all other cars in its class, on the 1994 car reliability list published by *Consumer Reports*. Unlike Ford and Chrysler, GM seemed not to take quality seriously enough in the early 1980s to make it a top management priority. By 1994, the company was still paying a high price for this mistake.

As a momentum driver, quality refers to products, processes, services, and workmanship. It encompasses consistency, reliability, and durability, as well as compliance with specifications. A company's momentum-building efforts should include using the strategies and techniques for quality improvement developed for use in TQM and ISO 9000 (an international standard for quality assurance in design/development, production, installation, and servicing in product companies). There should be no tolerance for mediocre quality. Unless product and service quality equal or exceed the expectations of both customer and competitor, a company will have a serious problem in the marketplace.

Management must decide whether market-position advantage is best reached by leadership in product quality, or in combination with market-acceptable quality, leadership in such areas as product performance, services, productivity, price, or market presence. This is a fundamental and explicit strategic decision. The challenge is to develop multiple points of leadership, where possible.

CONTROL

Control means to exercise authority, to regulate, to verify, to measure, or to set boundaries. That improvement (strengthening) occurs by innovation is almost universally acknowledged; there is less awareness that improvement also depends on control. Juran has observed that company survival and growth require that managers continually "break through" into new, higher levels of performance and hold those gains once achieved. This does not mean an undue emphasis on control, but it does means exercising enough of the right controls to achieve and maintain necessary performance levels.[11]

A bureaucracy is control- and rules-driven, but a progressive business has to be driven by opportunity and performance. Like pharmaceutical prescriptions, a certain optimum dosage is necessary, but too much control can be troublesome in any business that seeks innovation and growth. Controls must be aligned with a company's core business processes in a way that will keep company-wide attention on market-position strength and performance capability.

All managers' jobs require that they protect their company's assets and resources by exercising authority-based control over polices, processes, programs, people, and money. Without adequate controls, a business cannot operate; controls provide the structural foundation on which a company's normal operations take place. Internal controls are based on clearly stated policies and processes that provide for the accuracy and trustworthiness of all information used internally or externally, for compliance with applicable laws and regulations, and for safeguarding company assets and resources. Operational controls are based on explicit policies and processes that provide for effectiveness and operating consistency throughout the company. While these control policies, a code of conduct, and related processes form the basis for control, they are not enough to ensure that controls are working; this requires a personal sense of accountability and high ethical standards for all people involved in company operations.

Controls have become more sophisticated with the advent of the computer. Today, the mechanisms of management control permeate every corner of every business. In manufacturing, extensive controls in all processes are part of production, procurement, inventory, and product movement. Quality control is a central need, and company policies govern product and service quality, customer services, and other areas that affect the company's reputation, its position in the marketplace, or its costs. Management and administrative control processes abound in information distribution and profit (budget) and other business plans, as well as in employment policies and practices.

Control-oriented policies and processes are employed with varying degrees of usefulness and pain for both the company and its people. Although many control mechanisms seem important, hidden cost is associated with each. This cost is not only in money, but in the time consumed by nonproductive activity and in the frustration caused by the red tape associated with them. Too much control, too little, or the wrong kind can all undermine operational productivity. When businesses tend toward too much control, there are work delays, and innovation is stifled. The cost of these losses can be much higher than the cost of the mistakes that might occur without the controls. Most companies exercise far more control than is necessary. Managers need to routinely confirm the usefulness of existing controls with the aim of eliminating or simplifying them.

In the past, most organizations established formal controls to satisfy specific needs, without regard to the reduced motivation and loss of momentum they might cause. Often, the dictum seems to have been, the more control the better. Preventing mistakes was considered crucial. Today, controls must be designed to support company momentum building; the focus must shift from avoiding mistakes to company strengthening. The issue for managers is to decide where and what kind of controls should exist to satisfy the company's business needs while simultaneously encouraging momentum building and recognizing the necessary balance where tight explicit controls remain important.

There is always tension between control and innovation. If controls are too burdensome, they become a roadblock to innovation—in particular, to creative innovation. If they are too loose, they may encourage poor performance. Developing useful but not excessive controls requires considerable sensitivity and insight. A common error in many companies is to leave the matter of control in the hands of the administrative and financial people. When the prevailing point of view in deciding where and how controls are to be established is set by people who are not directly involved in the work activity, the business processes are likely to be made unduly cumbersome. Administrative interests, of course, have to be taken into account, but the tension between innovation and control has to be balanced on the side of encouraging momentum-building.

Control mechanisms must be "friendly" to the company's operating people. The purpose is to establish a workplace environment that is based on individual freedom to act. The most fruitful approach is to carefully design a well-defined operating process and to judiciously select the people who will work well within it. Then control is based in accountability, appropriate training, the right tools, and pertinent metrics. When an operating process includes rigid controls, the people involved should clearly understand why this kind of control is present. If they do not, the prescribed control mechanism is likely to be largely ignored.

If the people who initiate controls are sensitive to the perspective of the people who are affected by them, ways can usually be found to ease the pain they cause, real and perceived, and at the same time get the right job done. Most people accept most controls, if not with pleasure, with tolerance and understanding. If they perceive them, from their vantage point, to be unnecessary, unfair, or unreasonable, however, tension around them will rise, which can be a principal cause of discontent, complacency, and lack of job interest, and can even precipitate a worker's leaving the company.

Under Three Dimensional Management, a manager minimizes direct supervisory control of other people. Too much supervision dampens organizational vitality, accountability, and creativity, which slows down progress in all undertakings. Instead of micromanaging, managers must act in a spirit of supportive involvement. The seed of higher momentum is an impulse or idea that can lead to improvement in something. Whether that seed dies or blossoms will depend on how it is nurtured. Excessive managerial control is hardly an environment that encourages developing ideas or shepherding them from concept to actuality. Momentum building calls for generating improvements through innovation in both breakthrough activities and control methods. For guiding activities that depend on creativity, the best approach lies in exercising the least control, relying instead on boundary guidelines and individual accountability.

DEVELOPING THE MOMENTUM PLAN

A momentum plan (MP) is the action document which emerges from the company's sessions that define market and operations strategy. It replaces the traditional strategy implementation plan and is distinct from a profit or budget plan. The MP is the vehicle that unites priorities, projects, and budgets for accomplishing desired change in existing market position and performance capability. Its purpose is to define, in a single roadmap, the undertakings that will collectively move the company toward its strategic-positioning objectives. The MP establishes the what, why, where, who, and when for company-wide momentum-building. The "how" aspect of momentum building should evolve naturally, during the process of putting the plan to work.

Usually everything that is desirable cannot be simultaneously pursued, and attempting to do too much risks failure of the entire effort. Identifying the vital few most worthwhile initiatives and concentrating resources on them will usually provide the most cost-effective result in the shortest time. Additional people or outside help may also be needed if what must happen cannot otherwise get done within the necessary time frame.

The CEO should be the overseer for the creation of the momentum plan, but people at every level in the company should participate in preparing it so it does not become simply a top-down management mandate. If it is to be realistic and lead to desired results, the MP needs to be both a top-down and a bottom-up undertaking. Setting its direction requires the knowledge of all the company's key people, managers and nonmanagers. Insight and guidance should come from many sources, including customers, suppliers, and people who actually perform the company's daily work activities. The plan should embody considerable flexibility to attract creative innovation as it develops and is carried out.

Most of the specific work to be done under the MP will normally be of a one-time, nonrecurring nature. The most practical way of proceeding is probably to establish teams to carry out the major projects, perhaps including people with unique competency from outside the company. Resolving the ever-present conflict of getting today's work done while simultaneously working on strengthening projects will need continuing management attention and considerable ingenuity.

Typically, expense authorizations for company-strengthening actions are buried in operations budget plans, which obscures their visibility and their practical value. The finances allocated to momentum-building undertakings should be distinguished from operations expenses and defined separately within the momentum plan so that how and where money is being used for company strengthening is always both apparent and flexible.

Many companies use financially based return-on-investment (ROI) analysis as a way to look at cost-benefit for improvement projects. Although quite useful in some instances, ROI analysis requires making assumptions based on forecasts, and many worthwhile projects can die early as a result of incorrect assumptions. To avoid a cycle of disappointment and progressively less-ambitious new projects, it is essential to carefully study the qualitative as well as the quantitative assumptions, so that managers can stay aware of the hazards, inaccuracies, and biases inherent in forecasting. The right direction is not always in the numbers.

A MODEL MOMENTUM PLAN OUTLINE

The following outline for structuring an MP has seven parts, one for each of the anchorpoint objectives, one for momentum drivers, and one to define terminology.

1. Core strategy
2. Market position strength
3. Organizational vitality
4. Productivity gain
5. Financial performance
6. Momentum drivers
7. Terminology definitions

The nature of the action involved is the best guide, so no particular format is required within each part. As a first step, momentum indicators should be securely in place within the company's cencon system.

Part 1, Core Strategy

This part summarizes the company's mission, ambition, and values, and the strategy for operations and market positioning that has been decided on in the strategic thinking sessions. Company organizational structure and strategy for management should be clearly set forth.

Parts 2 through 5

These parts specify the particular goals and describe related projects for improvement in the other four anchorpoint objectives, including the projects to be undertaken to achieve the goals. Here is where team charters and membership, individual accountability, and budgets should be defined. Continuous improvement programs in each capability center should also be outlined and sanctioned. The new standards set for the company's financial performance should indicate the specific goals for each line item in the company's internal income statement and balance sheet.

Part 6, Momentum Drivers

This part describes the specific goals and the related actions they require for improvement in the core and key momentum drivers and for the three C's—communication, coordination, and cooperation—for the company as a whole, and for each capability area.

Part 7, Terminology Definitions

This section should define any terms, jargon, or acronyms used within the company that might otherwise be unknown or misunderstood. The purpose is to establish a uniform standard of meanings throughout the company. Included here would be any definitions and conditions for specific momentum indicators in use by the company.

THE THREE C'S: COMMUNICATION, COORDINATION, AND COOPERATION

Nearly everything that gets done in a business happens because people communicate, coordinate, and cooperate with each other. The three C's are the means by which people inform and are informed about specific situations and act together to get things done. When allowed to flow freely, they are also the catalysts for generating enthusiasm for and interest in company activities and for building useful knowledge from raw information. Talking through ideas and issues with others is the most expeditious way to sharpen one's own thinking and focus on the areas important to operational results.

Meetings are a common and useful vehicle for communicating and coordinating; whether they work well depends on the skill of the meeting leader to engage the participants toward a specific purpose. A vague purpose and overtalking minor issues are common faults that deter people from attending or contributing to meetings, so advance planning is vital. Listening to and talking with others, whether in meetings or one-to-one, is the common way of obtaining, in context, useful information. Reports, letters, and memos are also helpful but usually less so than face-to-face interactions because the context and interactive exchange are missing.

Cooperation is a critical part of learning, preparing, taking actions, and following up, yet securing it is often more difficult than accomplishing meaningful communication and coordination. To cooperate, each person involved must want to be helpful to the others. Cooperating takes time, which some people may be reluctant to spare simply to help another person. Slow response to memos and not returning phone calls usually signal a lack of interest in cooperating. Cooperation occurs freely only when the parties involved have a common interest in the outcome.

THE THREE C'S AS MOMENTUM CATALYSTS

The three C's are critical to enhancing company momentum. They are the catalysts for shaping the organization into a unified force for momentum building. The only way to encourage meaningful information interchanges and provide the opportunity for serendipitous information flow are opening all communication channels—formal and informal, upward, downward, and horizontal—and keeping them open. Doing this demands constant managerial attention because so many natural impediments stand in the way of full and open communications. For example, people who need specific information may not know it exists and therefore do not ask for it. Those who have important information may not be aware of its importance to others. Some people believe in the adage that information is power and therefore share what they have only when it serves their best interests. Often people deliberately do not communicate for a great variety of personal reasons that are usually not obvious.

Two elements that stimulate open communications are taking an involvement-oriented approach to management and organization structure, and establishing a culturally accepted unity of cause. The only way to ensure the free flow of the three C's is to adopt a horizontal organization structure based on communication paths as opposed to managerial authority. Such a structure can keep open the communication moving between people on the front lines and also between these people and managers. Without an easy flow of information and interchange, the intellectual power of the company will be stifled. All operational processes and controls should be designed to encourage and support the three C's.

Managers have no easy way of controlling what information is received or given or how it is put to work within the company. Sharing information voluntarily is essential. Only when the company's culture and organizational structure work to overcome the difficulties typical of information-control problems based in issues of power, security, and other personal matters can the channels of information flow be made fully productive. Open communication, which encompasses sufficient coordination and cooperation, will take place only when people believe they will be helped, not harmed, in the process.

THE IMPORTANCE OF MOMENTUM DRIVERS

Company momentum occurs when managers are creatively performing their primary responsibility toward achieving anchorpoint objectives while focusing on the individual momentum drivers as an integral part of their efforts. Figure 4-2 shows this relationship. The level of company momentum achieved depends on the extent to which specific goals under the anchorpoint objectives are being met. An important contributing factor to goal achievement is the effectiveness of communication, coordination, and cooperation throughout the company.

It is impossible to rank the importance of individual momentum drivers. Any one or more of them may be paramount at any given time, depending on company circumstance. Over time, the emphasis changes with changing situations within the company and in its marketplace. The task is to continually exert the proper emphasis on each at all times, and one of management's ongoing responsibilities is to set this priority.

As managers work to strengthen momentum drivers, it is helpful to keep in mind the law of diminishing returns: when there is enough of something, more of it has relatively little value. Examples of the validity of this principle abound; perhaps the most obvious regards food consumption. When hunger has been satisfied, more food on the plate is of little interest, and if consumed, it may cause heartburn. This law is apparent in the ever-present challenge of knowing how much is enough for certain of the drivers, including risk-taking, quality, and control. There is also the danger that marginal or barely adequate is taken as good enough. As applied in TDM, the point of diminishing returns is reached when further gain will be small relative to the cost or time involved to achieve the added incremental gain. In other drivers, the law specifically does not apply. When levels are increased in the realms of unity of cause, accountability, learning, organizational vitality, and creativity, benefit to the company does not diminish, but is enhanced, sometimes exponentially.

The momentum drivers and the three C's are at work to some degree in every business. Understanding their current significance and then finding ways to make their contribution more important is a major requirement for momentum building. Each should represent values in the company culture that are be-

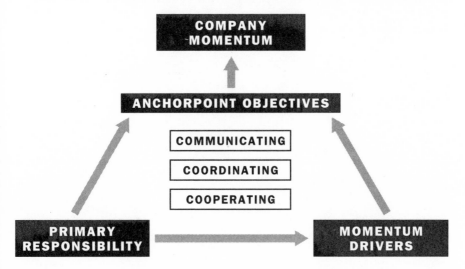

Figure 4-2: Building Company Momentum

ing constantly reinforced by everyone. Raising everyone's consciousness level on the importance of the momentum drivers is a key task for all managers that will probably never be fully accomplished, given the vagaries of human nature and range of attitudes of individuals. Continuously keeping the momentum drivers and the three C's in everyone's mind's eye, however, is an essential counterbalance to the ever-present forces that encourage complacency.

NOTES

1. Aubrey C. Daniels, *Bringing Out the Best in People*. New York: McGraw-Hill, 1994.

2. John W. Gardner, *Self-Renewal*. New York: Harper & Row, 1963, p. 3.

3. Personal correspondence, Boruch B. Frusztajer, president and CEO, BBF Corporation, Waltham, Mass.

4. Peter M. Senge, *The Fifth Discipline*. New York: Doubleday, 1990.

5. Chris Argyris, "Teaching Smart People How to Learn," *Harvard Business Review*, May-June 1991.

6. Warren Bennis, in an interview with A.J. Vogl about his book, *An Invested Life: Reflections on Leadership and Change* (Boston: Addison Wesley), *Across the Board*, September 1993.

7. Jeffrey Young, "Computers That Look You Over," *Forbes*, December 6, 1993.

8. Karl Albrecht with Steven Albrecht, *The Creative Corporation*. Chicago: Dow Jones Irwin, 1987, p. 30.

9. Robert Fritz, *Creating*. New York: Fawcett, 1991, p. 5.

10. W. Edwards Deming, *Out of the Crisis*. Cambridge, Mass.: MIT Press, 1982; Philip B. Crosby, *Quality Is Free*. Mentor, 1979; Joseph M. Juran, *Juran on Leadership for Quality*. Quality Press, 1989.

11. Joseph M. Juran, *Managerial Breakthrough*. New York: McGraw-Hill, 1964.

## CHAPTER 5

Organizational Vitality

The Engine for Performance

VITALITY

A company without its people is a lifeless mass of material things that has no capacity for thinking or acting. It is people, working individually and in groups, who provide organizational vitality, the intellectual power and human energy that produce company accomplishment. This vitality arises from human contributions to company operations and provides the potency for momentum building.

An organization's intellectual power is its capacity to develop ideas, strategies, decisions, and actions that will provide performance results of value to the company. It depends on individual and group knowledge, competency, creativity, and judgment. A company's human energy is based on individual motivation that leads to initiative, action, and achievement. High-vitality organizations are characterized by a flow of insightful ideas and decisions, performance-focused action, and persistence in getting the right things done within a time frame set by conditions and opportunities in the companies' marketplace.

In most companies, the actual organizational vitality level is well below the potential available. Finding ways to tap into the unused potential can make a significant difference in company performance. This unrealized potential, although not easily measurable, is costly because it keeps the company's rate of achievement lower than it should be and induces the employment of more people than are really required. As managers seek superior results, they must routinely attend to organizational vitality, which means finding ways to assess, monitor, and stimulate it. Motivated, focused, imaginative people working co-operatively with appropriate tools and processes are a hallmark of superior management and the best assurance a company can have that it will prosper.

FINDING THE RIGHT PEOPLE

Nothing is more important for building organizational vitality than having the right people with the right attitudes in every job. Finding the right person takes insightful judgment and patience if the demands of the job are to mesh with the individual's intellect, capability, motivation, demeanor, ambition, and potential.

Who *are* the right people? Ideally, they are people who are productive, imaginative, and organizationally synergistic. They do their jobs exceptionally well and beyond that contribute measurably to the strength of the organization as a whole. But ideal people are rare, so the manager's task is to get the best fit possible between company needs and an individual's apparent qualifications. Some people enjoy challenge and problem solving, some enjoy a high-energy, demanding environment, and some just want to get by. If the job calls for teamwork, a person who is impatient with others might be a problem. Job-specific competency may not be necessary if the company is willing to train. Job competency does not necessarily mean education level or years of experience in a particular job; many people who work in a job for a long time do not grow in competency, or can become rigid and narrow-minded in their thinking. Intellectual level is always an important consideration. A job should be interesting, and the more complex it is, the higher the level of intellect needed; on the other hand, the attitude of a person who is intellectually overqualified for a position can deteriorate into disruptive arrogance or boredom if the job is not sufficiently challenging.

Perhaps the most critical factor in identifying the right person is to become aware of the level of the candidate's internal need to perform well. People with a clear sense of their own accountability can usually master a new job situation in a short time. If a constructive attitude toward self- accountability is combined with sufficient intellect, interest, and curiosity in learning new things and the *why* of things, the person will invariably grow in capability at a rapid rate. An individual who is her or his own toughest taskmaster and is a learner will be of special value to any company. People like this are usually hard to find, but in filling key positions they are worth the search.

Most managers, if they are candid, will admit to a success rate of under 70 percent for their decisions in matching people and jobs. Hiring mistakes usually are caused as much by situational pressures as they are by managerial judg-ment; these factors include time pressure, budget limitations, inadequate job definitions, limited background checking, and a normal desire to get on with essential business tasks. Hiring decisions invariably involve compromise, and compromise always risks failure, but the chances of success are far greater if managers plan on how to integrate a newly hired person into company opera-tions and give him or her the necessary support. Often the failure can be sim-ply the result of an inadequate post-hiring process, in which the person hasn't received sufficient help or support to reach a satisfactory level of job profi-ciency. When a potentially capable person is put into a job and expected to perform it without much help or support, there is a high risk of failure. Tossing people into deep water as a method of teaching them how to swim sometimes works, but more often it does not.

The most desirable approach, of course, is to promote or transfer a person from within the company, but when that is not possible it is essential to avoid shortcuts and take particular care in both the hiring and post-hiring processes. Badly considered actions regarding people are among the most costly mis-takes a company can make, for they take a heavy toll in lost money and time and reduced morale. People who have been put into jobs in which they do not fit and thereby will likely fail suffer special frustration and disappointment, and it is even more devastating for them when situations do not work out be-cause a manager failed to anticipate and act on the involvement needed to sup-port their success.

Managers cannot afford to compromise much as they seek to build compa-ny competencies by carefully selecting and developing the company's people. Encouraging people to learn and develop their abilities is essential, and be-cause circumstances frequently change, it is vital to keep track of current job performance. Moving people around from time to time to provide continuing interest and challenge is a good way to stimulate learning and enthusiasm.

Management's acumen in selecting people generally sets the upper limit for a business's operational results. The actual level of company accomplishment is set by the extent to which management succeeds in building organizational vitality.

ORGANIZATIONAL DEVELOPMENT: THE BEDROCK FOR VITALITY

Sustaining growth in organizational vitality depends on the steady ground-work of organizational development: judiciously selecting, involving, and nourishing growth in the capability of people, and establishing a constructive, energizing company culture. Ongoing projects toward organizational strength-ening are essential to sustain and raise a company's momentum level. While it is universally acknowledged as important, organizational development is often lower in priority than other "more pressing" needs. Of course, these needs are more pressing usually because of inadequate organizational development in the past. When this negative feedback loop exists, beleaguered managers need to play catch-up to break it.

Few decisions have more impact on organizational vitality than those concerned with selecting, involving, developing, promoting, transferring, and demoting the company's people or terminating their employment. Handling these situations carefully as well as clearly and concisely defining the personal attributes necessary for each job are key tasks, particularly in light of how mistakes reduce momentum.

MOTIVATING PEOPLE

Much has been written about how managers can motivate others; a great deal of it misses the mark. Of course, a manager can alter behavior through close supervision, but this cannot genuinely motivate. Motivation comes from within a person. The production miracle in the United States during World War II took place because most people were eager to help out in the war effort. The way motivation is stimulated is by igniting the inner flame of desire to do something.

Inner motivation, a desire to perform well, and competency are the principal contributors to superior job performance. A person must truly want to do something before it will be conscientiously undertaken. This want, or lack of it, comes from a complex combination of forces, only some of which are related to the job. Most competent people want to perform well, and they will if the work-based demotivating factors present in the company culture are at a low level. Demotivators can be anything, real or perceived, that reduce an individual's motivation and thereby diminish job performance. As a foundation for motivation, all employees need to believe that top management cares about them as individuals, will treat them equitably and fairly, and will support their efforts. If this perception exists, the potential for motivation is high. Other important factors that influence motivation are interest in the work, respect for the company and its management, affinity with the company culture, co-worker pressure, desire to advance, fear of failure, and the possibility of gain or loss in prestige, power, or money. How people are paid and their sense of job security and advancement opportunity are also central issues. People have to feel good about most of these factors if motivation is to be high.

Ironically, if a person has the desire to perform well but management's standards for quality in work performance are not clear, the work done might be mediocre or unsatisfactory. This in turn can engender criticism that will then reduce future motivation. Setting a high standard for quality in work performance can be a significant stimulus to motivation, since work done well draws compliments.

Pep talks, threat sessions, or money can sometimes temporarily alter a person's attitudes and seemingly motivate them more highly. Yet if a worker perceives a job primarily as a source of income and lacks a reasonable measure of interest in it, job performance is likely to be well below his or her potential. Trying to change underlying attitudes, which can be time consuming and often risks failure, is the only way managers can influence long-term motivation. If someone's negative attitudes are deeply rooted, managerial action may not be able to change them.

Other matters that can have a major effect on a person's motivation level at work can range from health and family problems to drugs and alcohol. Although it is not a manager's business to probe into such non-work-related problems, managers are responsible for eliciting satisfactory job performance and constructive behavior at work. There is usually no easy answer when a manager is faced with a motivational problem that is externally derived, yet when job performance is less than satisfactory, a solution must be found.

THE COMPANY'S SOCIAL
AND OPERATIONAL ENVIRONMENTS

Along with the legacy of company traditions, every company has two environments, social and operational, that help shape the attitudes and behavior of its people. Each environment influences the other, and the two merge with company traditions into what is generally referred to as the company culture.

The operational environment should be stimulating, comfortable, and safe, not inhibiting or demoralizing. Employees should look forward to going to work each day because they derive psychological as well as monetary benefits. They should enjoy their work as well as their social experiences. The company's social environment is formed by the way people interact with each other. Whether people are generally friendly, helpful, and caring, or indifferent or troublesome makes a big difference in how all people feel about the company. If people enjoy both their work and social involvements, there is a much greater likelihood of high company esprit, with its attendant constructive attitudes toward working and cooperating with others.

Although managers can seldom be involved in everyday interactions between employees, they can still play an important role in fostering a constructive social environment. Most important is first to recognize the existence, importance, and nature of the company's social environment and try to understand its impact on company operations. To the greatest degree possible, a company should be an enjoyable place where one can do serious work. If managers have a realistic perception of the social environment, they can usually find ways to influence it constructively. This is a dangerous area to meddle in, however, as situations can be made worse as well as better.

ENRICHING THE COMPANY CULTURE

Undergirded by healthy organizational development, an energizing company culture is the foundation for high organizational vitality. Shaping its design is one of the most important responsibilities of the CEO, who, consciously or not, sets the company's core values and policies that define the framework for a company's culture. Unless the CEO recognizes the role played by culture in the company's momentum level and insists that other managers recognize its importance as well, there is little likelihood that the company as a whole will achieve its highest potential for organizational vitality. This is a key area for CEO leadership.

A company culture is founded on the beliefs held in common by most of its people. It is based partly on how individual employees perceive the operational and social environments; partly on traditional customs about "the way things are done here"; partly on company performance history; and partly on employees' perceptions of the effectiveness of management.

The many factors shown in Figure 5-1 influence the nature of a company's culture. These diverse factors shape attitudes toward the company and powerfully affect motivational level on the job. An amorphous but nonetheless real presence, the company culture sets the level of group esprit and the tone and nature of interpersonal relations within the company; it is a significant contributor to, or detractor from, individual motivation. Depending on its nature, the

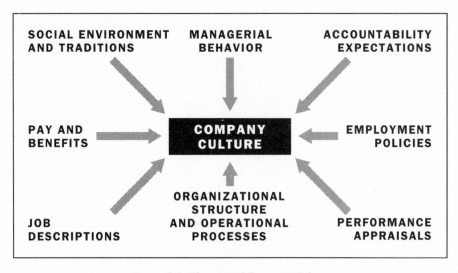

Figure 5-1: Elements of Company Culture

culture fosters attitudes that encourage the climate to be either activity oriented or performance focused.

An activity-oriented culture is characterized by its complacency: people
avoid controversy and tend to do things by the clock. Breaks, lunch hours, and
quitting time are key events, and trying to get something done is often regarded as good enough. Schedules frequently slip, over-budget expenses are ratio-
nalized, and accountability for nonperformance is vague. A veneer of calm
and good intentions prevails.

Hard issues, such as lost customers, lost orders, quality problems, delays in
product development, and premature product releases are often glossed over
without serious introspection or prompt corrective action. Cultural mores and
peer pressure are stronger influences on attitudes and behavior than what the
company needs. A air of cynicism is generally present just below the surface.
Usually, a few people are hard workers who take pride in their effort and work
ethic; most others are conscientious but only within narrow bounds.

In a performance-focused culture, most people are enthusiastic about their
jobs and take sufficient pride in the company and its achievements to recom-
mend it to their friends as a place to work. High performance standards and
clear individual accountability prevail. The needs of the company are a top
priority, second only to personal emergencies. Performance problems are routinely examined, with a constructive approach to corrective action. People
trust and respect management and feel secure about making suggestions for
improvement. They want the company to succeed because they know this will
help their careers. Company communications are reasonably open and honest,
upward, downward, and horizontally. When schedules are at risk of slipping,
people respond with extra effort to get things back on track. Constructive
changes are readily implemented.

A performance-focused culture allows room for relationships to be tested,
and frank dialogue is an accepted part of getting things done. Divisiveness, arbitrary confrontation, and personal attacks, no matter how subtle, are not toler-
ated. People focus steadily on getting things done right, on time, and at reasonable cost. Initiative and innovation are encouraged. People find their work
enjoyable and challenging and will normally do what needs to be done with a
minimum of direction. When problems arise, they respond quickly. They
might also seek out better ways to do things.

Companies with fewer than fifty employees normally maintain little formality and are able to make decisions in a relatively uncomplicated fashion,
conditions that tend to produce a healthy performance-focused culture. As a
company grows, its culture usually becomes more complex. People at the operating level become more isolated from policy managers and acquire self-
protective attitudes and behavior that they feel they need to be safe. They tend

to do what they are told and let managers worry about problems and improvements. The company's people begin to form highly distinct cultures that distance management, professional, and associate groups from one another. Policy managers may become unable to properly perceive the culture within each group or the general company culture. Unless policy management takes countervailing actions, the culture(s) that influence professionals and associates will generally drift toward an activity orientation. If this drift goes too far, some of the company's more innovative and productive people will leave because the more stratified and less comfortable culture limits their opportunities. The mediocre performers will usually stay.

Most company cultures function somewhere between the two poles of activity oriented and performance focused. But whether a culture moves in the direction of reinforcing complacency or reinforcing initiative is largely up to company managers. Whom they employ, their behavior, whether their decision making is imperious or inclusive, and how they establish the operational environment all contribute. If the management approach is imperiousness, the trend will be toward complacency with a prevailing attitude of, "I'm going to do what the boss wants and do it her or his way. My main task is to find out what that is." If the management approach is involvement oriented, people will tend to take personal initiative with a prevailing attitude of, "I need to find out what's right for the situation and get it done well."

If a company's organizational vitality is to reach levels that produce high momentum, it is necessary to change a complacency-based, activity-oriented culture to one that is performance focused and initiative based. All the separate cultural elements (Figure 5-1) should be carefully reviewed so that helpful changes can be made as needed. A necessary precondition is respect for all employees, with demonstrated genuine concern, care, and support for their needs and problems. It is also essential that all the company's people understand the need for culture change and become aware that it is in their own best interests. This will have to be accomplished by actions, not just talk. The most important issue is to reach the point where there is a community feeling of common interest and shared involvement in the company's future. It may be necessary to remove people who are uncooperative or who otherwise exert a negative influence on the culture.

If positive cultural attitudes are to develop, people have to know what is expected of them, who in management they are accountable to, and who will review their performance and thereby control their advancement in pay and job responsibility. They also need to know what is expected of the other people they work with, both managers and peers. Perhaps most important of all, managers must understand the cultural forces at work and be sensitive to their personal role and influence as contributors to that culture.

The work environment should offer a sense of security so that each person feels safe about trying out new ideas, even if they result in failure. Of course, it is essential to promptly correct an action that turns out to have been mistaken, but making a mistake should be regarded as a routine cost of building momentum. To censure people in these instances invariably leads to their withdrawal into safe postures that stifle their initiative and capacity for creative achievement.

A culture that encourages concern and care about company performance and stimulates initiative and persistence in all undertakings is enormously rewarding to both the business and the people in it. In this way, it is a major contributor to organizational vitality.

PAY AND BENEFITS

To a large degree, the employment marketplace sets the nature of a company's pay and benefits policy. Under normal circumstances, each company establishes its own policy based on what is necessary to attract and retain employees, what is common practice in its industry or geographic area, and management's perceptions about appropriate pay and benefits. From the perspective of organizational vitality, the principal issue is the attitude of the employees. Do they consider the company's policy and practices to be fair and reasonable, or do they feel the company is taking advantage of them? All of us are sensitive to whether or not we are being underpaid or fairly paid relative to our peers and to our own abilities, and whether a company's compensation practices are in line with those of similar companies. The same applies to benefits such as insurance, employer contributions to 401K plans, profit sharing, and equity ownership. A company has to be clear about all these matters.

Although a company's pay and benefits policies and plans are important to every employee, unless they are perceived to be unfair or noncompetitive, they are not normally the major factor in influencing the attitudes that affect motivation; other constituents of the company's culture are a greater influence. When people can see firsthand that they are benefiting financially from the company's growth and prosperity, their frame of mind will be constructive and supportive toward helping the company. But if a company's pay and benefits practices are considered to be stingy or out of line, they will be significant demotivators.

STYLES OF MANAGEMENT
AND THE PERILS OF MANAGERIAL BEHAVIOR

The two basic styles of managerial behavior, imperiousness and involvement, express different points of view. When a manager proceeds with only a minimum of involvement by others, his or her style is perceived to be imperious. People are regarded as work units, necessary to get things done but also a source of continuing problems. Authority reigns, and there is little effort to understand what others think. Often an imperious manager is arrogant, listens too little, seeks compliance by intimidation, issues orders, makes arbitrary decisions, and is unwilling to explain the why of things.

An involvement-oriented manager, in contrast, engages others in the decision-making process by routinely seeking out their views and ideas. People are regarded as important contributors and as individuals with unique capabilities and knowledge that can improve decisions and actions. A management style that fosters involvement in decision making does not mean decision making by consensus; it means bringing the greatest degree of insight to bear on each decision. The accountable manager must still provide leadership and ensure that the decisions made are sound ones.

Every manager uses both these behavioral patterns to some degree, but one usually predominates. Some people regard imperiousness as the proper persona for a manager, as it reflects the image of the dynamic, take-charge tough guy. In the context of company turnaround situations, imperiousness may be the only approach that works. Bringing the company quickly onto a successful new track often requires a strong, autocratic management style. Once redirection takes hold, however, a long-term, momentum-based strategy for management is necessary to avoid a repeat of history in the future. Even in a relatively less troubled situation, a predominantly imperious style can often succeed if a manager is exceptionally competent in his or her field of specialization. Rarely, however, can it work well in the long run to build organizational vitality; regardless of a manager's competence, imperiousness becomes a serious liability as a company gets larger.

Most company "values statements" include some version of the assertion that management regards company people as contributors. When reality within the company reflects the "work unit" attitude, however, people easily see the hypocrisy and regard all policy management's statements with suspicion.

What managers do sets the tone and the level of enthusiasm in an organization, not simply what they say. People look to how managers behave for clues as to whether management has integrity, whether it treats people fairly and with respect, whether prejudice, bigotry, or harassment are condoned, whether open communication on problems and suggestions are met with retaliation, whether managers are competent in their jobs, and whether managers put company needs ahead of their own personal interests. If a manager takes himself or herself too seriously while not taking accountability seriously enough, it creates a formidable barrier to effective communications and good interpersonal relations, and it limits the company culture to one that is predominantly activity oriented.

Respecting working hours is also an important influence. If managers arrive later than others are expected to arrive, the negative role model quickly produces a casual attitude by others toward starting time. If a manager who is routinely late attempts to discipline others for the same fault, resentment is natural. Equally important, arriving late conveys a feeling of indifference to the value of time. Some managers regard arriving late as a privilege conferred by their status, or because they put in a longer work day than the others. This rationalization might justify their own behavior, but the negative impact on the company work environment remains.

If managers seem to value turf, control, pay, prestige, power, perks, and privilege more than they value commitment to company performance, the company culture will come to be based on self-interest first and company interest second. Organizational vitality will be held down, and management will be unable to expand it without changing its own attitudes, values, and behavior. Eliminating all special treatment for management is usually neither possible nor necessarily desirable, but it is desirable to maintain the highest possible degree of equality for all categories of employees. Management must demonstrate, by the daily behavior of its members, that the company interest comes first, to be followed (with some exceptions) by the interests of professionals and associates, and last, managerial self-interest. Attitudes that support a caste system of managerial privilege will seriously handicap the company. Few managers think through or even notice all the problems caused by managerial privilege and behavior. This is an area that will amply reward introspection and subsequent corrective actions.

ESTABLISHING
A FLEXIBLE ORGANIZATIONAL STRUCTURE

There is no "correct" organizational structure. A model that works today may cease to be effective in the future, and one that works well for one business may fail in another of similar character. Nonetheless, structure plays an important role in company operations, as it determines how work actually gets done and how decisions are made. An unsuitable structure or poorly designed operational processes slow down the company's work flow and distort the timing and quality of decision making. Under these circumstances, momentum is not easily developed.

In the best possible structure, decision making and action taking are easy to accomplish, operational processes are free of any structural barriers to rational work flow, and the people who conduct the work are able to engage in uncomplicated communication, coordination, and cooperation. The structure must also be flexible enough to accommodate valuable people who may be atypical. One approach for an involvement-oriented company is an I-beam organizational structure, discussed in chapter 7. It can be used by any company and can readily accommodate future change while it remains essentially permanent in structural form.

Job titles linked to organizational hierarchy are a particularly sensitive area. People like titles that sound important, because they convey prestige and implied or real authority. Some executives like to confer titles that have been deliberately inflated for reasons of employee morale or to impress outsiders. Loan officers in banks, for example, frequently have a title such as assistant vice-president even when they have relatively little authority. But inflated titles can also breed an unwarranted feeling of self-importance and arrogance. Further, once a title is conferred, changing to another that may be viewed as less important is usually difficult. To retain organizational flexibility, many successful managers try to create titles that are more generic and that describe job function rather than authority; some try to eliminate titles altogether.

ATTAINING ACCOUNTABILITY

A company that intends to build organizational vitality needs to achieve a high level of individual accountability from all its people. The level it attains will be closely related to what level of expectation upper management has conveyed. Obtaining accountability for performance is more complex than simply delegating authority. Other essential ingredients are an effective strategy for management, managerial leadership, and a performance-focused company culture.

Accountability requires that people take initiative in their work with the least possible reliance on upper management for direction and supervision. The guiding principle is that operational decision-making should be able to take advantage of the most complete and up-to-date explicit knowledge and to involve those people who have the most tacit and intuitive understanding of the specific situations. These people are not normally policy managers as they are not close enough to the activity; it is the people who have the best situational understanding and a high stake in the outcome of their decisions who will usually take meaningful action sooner and with greater commitment to get things done right.

In moving from responsibility-based delegation to performance-focused accountability, the first question to be asked is: Can the current job incumbents perform well in an accountability-based, low-supervision environment? Most people will need time to digest the change and fully understand and accept the new expectations for their job performance. Prematurely placing people into a situation that is beyond their capability is a common mistake here. Those who face significant change may need mentoring or other help to succeed in the transition. Some people probably will be unable to change enough to perform well in a high-accountability environment.

Attaining accountability is neither easy nor straightforward. People who have been accustomed to frequently confirming their work with their boss to seek direction and decision making will find it hard to accept the role of decision maker and action initiator, with all its attendant risks. To achieve authentic accountability, it is essential to have the right person in the job, in terms of both competency and attitude. He or she has to understand clearly what results are expected and to accept the challenge of delivering them. The manager has to stay out of the way unless there is trouble, yet stay close enough to provide frequent, constructive help and performance feedback. While it is normal for people to want to do a good job, the manager's task is to get them to achieve superior performance.

PREPARING RELEVANT JOB DESCRIPTIONS

Companies prepare job descriptions for most of their jobs, many of which are based on models in old reference books. While these descriptions specify responsibilities, most do not address accountability or authority except in a superficial way. Worse, these descriptions usually are so bland that they are of little value either to the person whose job is described or the manager who looks to them for guidance in performance appraisal.

The starting point in redefining a job scope that encourages higher vitality is to prepare a written job description that specifies accountability, communication, and decision-making and action authority. It should also delineate what support for and obligations to others the job requires, both within and outside the person's own performance area, as well as to customers, suppliers, or other outsiders. If specific tasks are defined only minimally, the brevity encourages the job holder to think more carefully about how best to get things done. The formality of putting aside existing responsibility-based job descriptions and preparing new ones centered on accountability helps focus a shift toward raising momentum. The job description's presentation of accountability should be sufficiently clear and succinct that it can be the basis for a common understanding in future job performance appraisals.

If a job description is to be relevant and dynamic, it must include the essential capabilities needed to perform a job. To prepare a description, some of the important questions to ask are: What specific contributions are expected of the person holding this job, and to what standard will he or she be held accountable for performance? What are the specific personal qualities, experience, and competency necessary for superior job performance? Is team membership, leadership, or managerial capability a part of the job? Do we need a star performer or team player? If someone is to be recruited for the job, some additional questions need to be answered. Should we pay more for someone with a strong background, or less for someone with potential but fewer credentials?

What kind of training should we provide?

While it is a burdensome task, taking the time to thoroughly define each job will be rewarded in several important ways. The new description increases the chance of getting a better fit between job and person, thereby improving the prospects for a successful outcome. The job holder, when in place, will have an enhanced understanding of what job performance is expected, and his or her action is thus more likely to be relatively more effective. Finally, with the existence of a commonly accepted point of reference for comparing actual to required performance, future performance evaluation will be fairer and far more useful.

APPRAISING PERFORMANCE

Every person in the organization, including the CEO, needs constructive, useful feedback on job performance and help in improving it. In many companies, however, the process in use calls for a formal approach conducted only once a year and requires only a "report to file" for future reference in salary reviews and promotion considerations. The basic problem with such a formal annual process is that feedback on performance does not take place at the time when it is most helpful. The highest benefit from feedback occurs immediately after an event that needs reviewing. The result of poor timing is the development of a perception gap on performance for both the reviewer and the reviewee. If no review at all takes place when poor performance is an issue, performance standards are even more easily disregarded in the future.

Commonly, formal performance appraisal sessions are not very helpful to either reviewer or reviewee, and they can often be troublesome when discussions center on subjective matters rather than objective ones. The person doing the reviewing is often uncomfortable in the process and concerned that the one being reviewed will be either unhappy with criticism or, after a favorable review, unhappy if he or she doesn't get a salary increase. The person whose performance is being reviewed is often defensive. The final report is typically bland without offering much insight or help in improving performance. Another frequent problem is that the review process fails to take into account the inadequacies and biases of the person who is performing the evaluation and the subsequent unfairness and inaccuracies that can result. To overcome this in part, it is desirable that more than one person be involved in the evaluation. This helps moderate biases, and the greater objectivity derived allows greater insight into the process.

A potentially useful review process has two phases. The first is informal: review and discussion take place frequently when current situations are fresh in mind. No written reports are involved. If the reviewer is oriented toward helping rather than criticizing, the process can be highly constructive. Any problems need to be candidly discussed, however. The second phase of this process is a perspective review that takes place every three to six months, during which the effectiveness of overall job performance is discussed. Both the reviewer and reviewee keep notes on what contributions are being made toward the company's anchorpoint goals, the extent to which momentum drivers are being strengthened, and the specific overall job results the reviewee has attained. The review should include useful guidance on areas for improvement. Salary should not be a part of the discussions; salary and other compensation and benefit matters should be taken up separately, outside of the framework of informal and perspective performance reviews. If an annual report-to-file is needed, it can be prepared from the notes taken in the perspective reviews. There is no need for an annual, formal review meeting.

When a person assumes a new job, frequent informal performance reviews are especially important during the first few months. This is the period when the job holder is most receptive to constructive help that will improve job performance, and it is also the time when a manager can most easily correct problems and build the right kind of rapport with the person.

When a manager is faced with correcting unsatisfactory performance, an approach called discipline without punishment is likely to be more productive than the traditional formal warning process in common use in most companies. The discipline-without-punishment process first requires two informal steps, positive contact with the job holder and then a coaching session. If the problem persists, three formal discipline steps follow: an oral reminder, a written reminder, and decision-making leave. If none of these steps adequately changes the situation, termination takes place. The time span for the entire process can be short if the problem is severe. The purpose of this approach is to treat the problem employee as a thinking adult capable of deciding on his or her own how to respond. As always with any situation of unsatisfactory performance, there is the potential of employee litigation after termination. This possibility should be considered at every step in the process.[1]

All managers should have their own clear ideas about the performance they expect from those under their oversight. Unfortunately, most managers do not adequately clarify their thoughts about these expectations and therefore cannot clearly and concisely communicate them. Without this clarity, misunderstandings are inevitable. With useful, accountability-based job descriptions, good rapport, and articulated specific goals to be accomplished, the more arbitrary aspects of performance and perspective reviews can be minimized.

One approach to goal setting and performance appraisal for key managers, used by Aerovox, Incorporated, links performance and the annual bonus. Every year in an open process, the company sets quantitative and qualitative objectives and goals. Beforehand, each person, including the CEO, sets his or her own goals. Then the full management team, including operating managers, meet in an open session to discuss them. On the basis of these discussions, changes are made. When goal setting has the benefit of group contributions, it is more likely to embody "stretch" rather than simply routine accomplishment. After six months and again at year's end, the entire management team reviews progress. At each review, each person reports to the group on his or her own performance against goals; the group also provides opinions on how well that person performed. A percentage depicting the group judgment on the extent to which goals were met is determined at year's end. This percentage is then multiplied by a predefined maximum bonus to determine the actual bonus to be paid. The people involved take this process seriously and work hard to meet their goals.

SETTING EMPLOYMENT POLICIES

A written company guide booklet, which is given to each employee, is a virtually universal practice in business today. It usually describes how the company operates, provides information on company policy and expected behavior, and specifies benefits and opportunities. One of the booklet's purposes is to provide a standardized approach throughout the company for handling routine people-related matters or issues that involve law and regulation compliance. The guide usually communicates rules that employees are expected to comply with and the company's code of conduct on matters involving ethics and other beliefs or values that are considered important. As there are complex legal implications in this pact between employer and employee, these policy statements require careful crafting. What is said needs to be comprehensive, clear, and precise, yet not unpleasantly onerous.

All employees are concerned about the company's policy on job security. The issue was highlighted in the early 1990s when IBM, long a role model as an employer that offered high job security through a no-layoff policy, began to hit hard times. When IBM's marketplace strength eroded and it started to post large financial losses, its no-layoff policy was abandoned and it began downsizing, eliminating more than a hundred thousand jobs by 1993 and more thereafter. Many other companies also downsized, before and after IBM, and millions of jobs were eliminated in the United States. The problems that caused this wholesale job elimination effectively brought most corporate paternalism to an end.

Another recent casualty has been the defined-benefit retirement plans. Regulatory requirement changes for funding these plans have caused billions of dollars of operating losses when companies were required by law to more fully fund their existing plans. It also became apparent that a retirement benefit defined many years before its need would in all likelihood be inadequate. Current and future retirees now look to fewer and fewer instances of defined-benefit pension plans to supplement Social Security. People are faced with establishing their own financial plans for retirement. An employee-savings plan, usually a 401K plan, named after the part of the Internal Revenue Service's code that allows such plans, is now the plan of choice for most companies and their employees.

A 401K allows tax-deferred saving but does not provide any certainty of a particular level of retirement income. Under such a plan, a company might make an annual contribution, but at present is not obligated to do so. When a company contributes, the amount is usually based on some percentage of profit, with a pro rata amount credited to each employee's account. Employees can also voluntarily contribute pretax dollars, up to a limit, to their account. To encourage saving, company matching of a part of the employees' personal contribution is now a common practice. The funds are usually professionally managed, often with the employee selecting the level of investment risk. Most employees routinely expect a 401K program as a job benefit.

Apparently the time has passed when companies could offer a firm commitment to employees for job security and pensions. What management can and should do, however, is to offer every employee the opportunity for self-development, to grow in knowledge and competency. A person's primary resource for job opportunity today is to keep her or his capabilities in step with the needs of a changing marketplace.

This is a new issue for many companies, because employee career development has not hitherto been of primary importance. In fact, such opportunities as job rotation, for example, which permit employees to broaden their skills, have generally been discouraged, as most managers want to keep their well-trained and fully competent people on the job they do best, even when the knowledge and competency involved are becoming obsolete. The situation is further complicated by the reality that people who are highly capable in a job are usually well paid and receive frequent increases in pay. This too discourages both managers and the employee from considering job rotation, which might involve lower pay, as a means of avoiding obsolescence. Yet obsolete capability carries a high risk of future job loss in a rapidly changing marketplace. The issue of individual career development has yet to be addressed in a way that fully satisfies the needs of the company and its people. But it is important to consider if a company hopes to sustain employee loyalty.

THE PARTNERS

In every business, four distinct groups of people are involved: directors, managers, nonmanagers, and shareholders. Each group makes a different contribution, and each contribution is essential to a company's long-term success.

An uncommitted outside stakeholder group—the company's base of customers—judges overall company performance by purchasing the company's products and services when they are perceived to be of sufficient value.

The board of directors has the following key tasks: to encourage and guide management; to consider the interests of all stakeholders; to evaluate management's performance; to initiate management change as needed; and to control and preserve the company's assets and resources. Management provides leadership, direction, and control for the company. Management must develop the company's social and operations systems to work together smoothly, synergistically, and profitably. Nonmanagers provide the specialized knowledge, competency, and ability to carry out the company's programs and activities.

The company's shareholders own the company, and it is they who ultimately control it. Shareholders are of two kinds: investors and opportunists. The investors are the long-term shareholders who understand that company interests must come first, while the opportunists have little interest in the company other than how they can make money through trading its stock. In the shareholder category, only the investor is a true partner, not the opportunist. Management decisions and actions must be concerned with long-term company strength, not with the short-term interests of opportunistic shareholders, even when their sale of stock might temporarily depress its price.

The four involved groups are partners in the sense that they are joined in an effort to satisfy customers, and by the avenue of company success toward that end, to succeed individually. The aim of the partners, individually and collectively, is to meet important company performance goals under each of the anchorpoint objectives and thereby to keep the company on a path of lasting strength. Unless these groups work together cooperatively under a unity of cause that exemplifies company strength-building, a company will underperform. To enhance organizational vitality and permit the greater company momentum that results from it, each partner must demonstrate a constructive attitude that puts company interest first. When this does not happen, everybody loses.

The CEO and the board of directors must attend carefully to how the interests of all the stakeholders are balanced. Customers want value and a dependable supplier; shareholders want share price growth; the board wants high-accomplishment management; managers want recognition, performance-based pay, and equity participation; and nonmanagers want to be respected, to be well paid, to have career opportunities, and to share in company profits. Nearly all employees want to grow in capability and have a secure future with attractive company benefits. Everyone wants to be proud of the company and his or her role in its success.

The board is the only partner that has the objectivity necessary to set policy on the balance of stakeholder interests. Balancing these interests is not easily done, for demands are always in a state of flux. If organizational vitality is to be sustained, it is essential that the policy set by the board be perceived as fair by all the company's employees, not just its managers. Unfortunately, few boards of directors ever address the matter of balancing stakeholder interests. This situation must change if a company is to succeed in the pursuit of lasting company strength.

Historically, three of the four partners have usually been working at cross-purposes, each seeking to gain a larger share of the company's income. The fourth, the board of directors, has often taken the position of being a friend of management, although this narrow view is now slowly expanding. Global competition has sent a shock wave through most companies and instilled growing awareness among the partners that company prosperity depends on harmony—the kind of spirit that will foster vitality in the company and be translated into a strong market position. Unless the partners achieve a workable, harmonious relationship based on trust, respect, and fairness, the company will encounter many unnecessary and debilitating problems on the path to growth.

Both managers and nonmanagers tend to overrate their own contributions to the company and to downplay the importance of the other. Discontent has been routine among nonmanagers, ranging from griping to real animus, usually about the fairness of compensation and benefits. Excessive compensation to management fuels this discontent, which is further fired when management and the board openly state that shareholder interests come first. These two visible situations continually reinforce the nonmanager employees' view that they are the forgotten partner. Their sense of underappreciation often leads to lethargy and complacency. Given the fact that both managers and nonmanager employees provide the capability that keeps customers satisfied and builds company momentum, it is crucial that fairness be addressed satisfactorily, both in terms of management's attitude toward nonmanagers and in sharing profit growth. Without the perception of fairness on the part of all employees, no real partnership harmony can be attained.

The company's board of directors and management are the partners who must provide the leadership that will arrive at partnership harmony. The directors must expand their roles to include being accountable for this partnership management. This means they will explicitly decide how much and when profit will be shared between the partners, and that they will set the guidelines for the company's employment policies.

NOTES

1. Dick Grote, *Discipline Without Punishment,* New York: AMACOM, 1995.

CHAPTER 6

Market-Position Strength

The Foremost Company Need

THE COMPANY'S CUSTOMERS

A chieving sustained long-term growth in a company's financial performance can take place only through consistent growth in profitable revenue. The only route to assure sufficient and growing revenue margin is building strength in the marketplace.

For decades, Drucker has emphasized that "the customer is the business." Customers are the ultimate decision-makers, and it is they who solely determine whether the company's reputation, products, services, and overall value provided are sufficient to warrant their business. Results in the marketplace set the boundaries for a company's overall success; market-position strength is the foremost need of every company and a key indicator of its performance.

Revenue is derived from orders obtained, one by one, from customers. Their orders flow only when they have confidence that their needs will be effectively, efficiently, and fairly taken care of. Even when a supplier has gained the confidence of a customer, the supplier may have been granted only a ticket to participate in order negotiations, not an assurance of obtaining the desired order(s). In arriving at acceptable terms, the relative strengths of the parties involved determine the outcome. Once the negotiations take place, a supplier with a high degree of market-position strength obtains considerably greater revenue margin.

The process by which orders are obtained is growing in complexity as customers become more and more demanding. Once the job of obtaining orders was confined to the province of a company's sales people. They remain the front line in the process, but if customers are going to be satisfied to the point of preferring to do business with a particular supplier, people in quality, engineering, manufacturing, management, and other areas must contribute. This kind of concerted effort is the only way to raise the probability that the right orders will flow when and as they are needed. Many companies concentrate on known customers. They, of course, are the first priority, for today that is "where the money is." But potential customers are also fertile ground, and finding latent market opportunity is often the route to creating a new market niche. Those with the foresight to do this are often handsomely rewarded.

While the fundamental importance of customers and orders deserves emphasis, there is also a caveat: all orders are not created equal. It is essential to ask, What customers should we seek orders from? Some customers are far more important to a business than others. It is critical to know the desirable customers and concentrate attention on them, while identifying and avoiding the undesirable ones. Sometimes the most desirable customers are the most demanding, as they push the supplier to new and higher levels of performance. Who are the undesirable customers? The most significant group is composed of those who do not fit into a company's core market strategy; serving them depletes resources, time, and effort from the company's mainstream direction. Of course, customers who are troublesome payers and those who are not trustworthy are always undesirable.

PURSUING MARKETPLACE ADVANTAGE

To have a marketplace advantage, a company has to provide customer-valued benefits that are sufficiently important and differentiated that they provide a preferred position for obtaining orders. Often the term *competitive advantage* is used interchangeably with *marketplace advantage*, but the word *competitive* implies that the purpose is to gain an edge on competitors. This is an important part of the consideration, but the more fundamental aim is to offer the value mix of product and service that best benefits the customer. Concentrating on customer needs, not the competition, is the most rewarding priority. Of course, knowing competitors' strategy, capability, and behavior is essential to achieving meaningful differentiation. So focusing on customers is the first priority, but knowing how to outperform competitors is also important if a company is to hold on to its desirable customers.

Many companies now offer a wide range of product or service features to customers in an effort to increase market-position strength. What constitutes real value to the customers, however, is leadership in offering the important few benefits that are critical to the customers' needs. To identify these, certain key questions should be addressed. Do the company's existing advantages offer sufficient value to the customers? Why, precisely, will they prefer to buy from us? Are our existing advantages getting stronger or weaker in the eyes of the customer? How do our competitors provide value to customers? How do we compare?

Making a company attractive enough to customers to stand out from its competitors while keeping company productivity high and costs low are the time-proven actions for gaining and keeping marketplace advantage. Of course, these same goals are being pursued by the competitor companies. The winner will be the company that has the most important ideas, makes the most perceptive strategic decisions, and has the highest momentum in getting the decisions acted on. If a company loses or does not gain sufficient marketplace advantage, then price becomes its only significant competitive lever. If such a company is not the lowest-cost producer, this situation usually leads to less desirable orders and marginal profitability. With value-based differentiation, price is less important.

Frequent changes in the marketplace complicate the task of establishing and maintaining sufficient differentiation in products and services. Competitors push forward, customers change their requirements, technologies mature and new ones arrive, all of which present both problems and opportunities. Top management must be keenly aware of how market change forces affect the company's own market position if they are to know how to effectively allocate resources. One vital aspect of this is to understand what is happening in the marketplace of the company's customers' customers and that of the ultimate end users of their products.

INTENSIFYING CUSTOMER FOCUS

Customer focus means two things: making certain that customers are satisfied to the point that they will be repeat buyers as needs arise, and continuously learning from customers about how the company can better serve them. The goal of customer focus is to secure customer loyalty. A letter to its stockholders, dated November 23, 1993, from the chairman of the Bank of Boston conveys the growing consciousness about this issue.

> At the end of October, we announced a strategic realignment of management responsibilities designed to focus on the needs of our customers by eliminating our group structure and essentially flattening the organization. We believe that this will serve to reduce unnecessary costs as well as layers of decision-making and will create a culture that rewards employee initiative and customer-focused teamwork. Our new organization puts more authority directly into the hands of line business managers and places a greater premium on decision-making speed and organizational cooperation. We maintain that excellence in financial services increasingly will be measured in

terms of customer satisfaction, and that the future will be driven by those who focus on the needs of their customers and engage employees directly and continuously in the process of customer satisfaction.

The overall guideline in working with customers is for the company's people to go above and beyond what customers expect, paying special attention to the company's most important customers. Customer focus, however, does not mean saying "yes" to every customer request. Customers sometimes can be unreasonable in their demands, and in these cases a supplier must often take a firm stand. If firmness is combined with an obvious desire to be cooperative and helpful, the relationship may very well be strengthened; customers usually know when they are pressing beyond the margin and generally respect a supplier who knows when and how to draw the line.

Irwin Gross has pointed out an important customer/supplier dynamic: "Customer satisfaction is one thing, giving the customer the upper hand is another," he notes. He describes a situation in which a supplier deals directly with large and powerful customers in what he calls a "win-lose" (zero sum) game involving the price and conditions under which a transaction will take place.

> Customers will conceal their satisfaction with the product and the supplier to keep their prices down. They do not reveal to their suppliers how satisfied they are or how valuable the supplier or the product is to them. They believe that such knowledge in their supplier's hands is likely to cause them to press for higher prices or other rewards from the relationship.

Gross points to examples in which companies that have a marginally profitable product are told by their sales forces that their product would "go down the tubes" if its price were increased. When customers are told the product is to be withdrawn, however, the customers often respond, "Well, raise your prices!" That is the only time a customer will tell a supplier to raise prices. Gross's message is that customers buy on need and value, not just satisfaction.[1]

A fundamental aspect of customer focus is for the supplier's people to get to know the customer's people, both decision makers and support staff, thereby building relationships that are welcoming and based on mutual trust. Customers need to know who in the supplier company, in addition to sales people, cares about them; for some customers this could require the attention of the CEO or a policy-level manager. The policy that transcends all others is to establish a relationship with the customer that is based on trust. Establishing trust requires honesty in presenting the company's position and in appraising whether the company's products will provide the performance the customer needs.

What customers say they want is often different from what they need. When customers and suppliers trust one another, insider information is often shared, and the privilege of learning more intimate details about the customer's situation can frequently lead to more creative solutions that put the supplier in a preferred position. A trust-based, privileged position opens the door leading to customer loyalty.

RETAINING CUSTOMERS

The basis for retaining customers is to provide value-based customer benefits. But more is required: keeping customers loyal also means eliminating potential problems before they arise. Every step, from sales calls to order delivery, must be part of a seamless process that is free of errors. Get it right the first time! An order must be confirmed quickly, and the product must be shipped on schedule and so that it is unlikely to be damaged or lost in shipping. When the product arrives, it should function as specified. This means 100 percent out-of-box acceptance. Being right 99 percent of the time is not good enough any more. Once a product is received, customers may need support so they can utilize it in the way they require. This support has to be prompt, accurate, and genuinely helpful. Sales and customer service people should routinely respond with speed and courtesy, which means they should be carefully selected and trained for effectiveness in solving customers' problems.

One path some companies are taking toward building customer loyalty and a more secure relationship is to establish a partnership arrangement with key customers. If this kind of arrangement is to succeed, the company must function at the highest level in all elements of customer retention; it must also share information on quality and new-product development in a way that allows the customers to anticipate in their own programs the supplier company's future capabilities. Reaching this level of mutual trust and confidence takes considerable time and an accumulation of many good experiences by both parties.

TRANSFORMING COMPETENCIES
INTO MARKET POSITION

A company attracts customers because of its *reputation, products, customer services, and marketplace presence.* Underlying these elements and at the foundation of its market-position strength are the company's *unique competencies.* The company's capability to perform in the marketplace depends on these core competencies. I have coined the word *strengthpoints* to describe these five elements of market position. Figure 6-1 shows their relationship. Meaningful marketplace advantages accrue when a company's market-position strengthpoints provide benefits to customers that they value higher than those of the company's competitors. Marketplace advantage can be analyzed by comparing a company's strengthpoints with those of its competitors.

A company's competencies deliver marketplace advantages only when they solve customer needs and fend off competitors, current and potential. The more successful a company can be in accomplishing these two ends, the more potential it has for profitable, secure growth. It needs to gain insight by carefully listening to customers, seeking their guidance, and observing their behavior. This working knowledge merges with the company's own ideas for strengthening its market position and must then be translated into its unique marketplace strengthpoints.

SUSTAINING UNIQUE COMPETENCIES

The scope of a company's competencies embraces both the company and its people. The competency of people exists only within themselves; company competency combines people and institutionalized competencies—those based on documentation, processes, and other resources that exist independent of any individual. Competency is derived from the creativity, ability, and energy of people; and competency requirements for a company are constantly changing as internal and external situations change.

Competencies in people, technologies, and processes are the tap roots by which a company sustains market-position strength. Unless the company has a group of unique competencies that together give it an edge over its competitors, marketplace advantages will be hard to achieve and sustain. Every customer always wants to know: "What are you going to do for me today?" What the company did yesterday is history and does not necessarily respond to today's needs, so people and organizational competencies have to be regularly

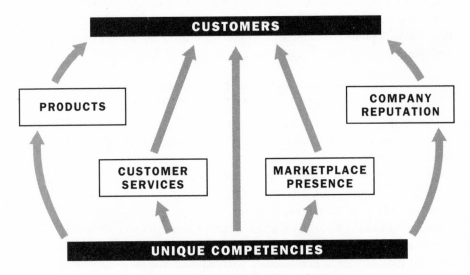

Figure 6-1: Market Position Strengthpoints

renewed, developed, supplemented, and kept at a high level. The requirement is to keep competency levels high enough so that the company can retain its marketplace advantages and keep barriers in place against competitors.

Over time, company competencies that are superior to those of its competitors are usually the only sources of marketplace advantage that a company can retain for a significant period. When a company's market-position strength is changing, whether for better or for worse, the root cause can normally be traced to competency factors. Top management needs to understand competency issues; they should be nurturing strong competencies and working on improving the weak ones. This activity lies at the heart of momentum building for market-position strength.

When new products are introduced into the marketplace, they must provide the kind of customer benefits that competitors cannot easily match. This means a company should limit its concentration on specific new product lines to areas where the company has distinct competency advantages. These advantages may be in people, technologies, processes, designs, cost, manufacturing, sales, distribution, or elsewhere, but they need to be real, not just perceived. When the right competencies are not present, it is vital they be developed or acquired in advance; otherwise a marketplace failure may be in the wings.

One critical competency for sustaining a strong marketplace position is a short cycle time in product development, from concept to customer delivery. What "short" means can vary considerably from situation to situation. When a product is based on designs and technology that are readily available to competitors, short can mean a matter of months to remain strong in the marketplace. When product development is complex—for example, when important technological development is involved—short can mean years. The aim is to be a market leader when the product line is introduced. To become a leader, a company must base the time frame for completing a product's development on realistic assumptions about future market conditions, which includes the time to achieve the capacity to manufacture. Then the project has to be organized and managed to meet that schedule. The most important parameters in the development projects are creativity and time.

It may seem appealing to reduce product development time by taking shortcuts. There is little to be gained, however, if a new product has "bugs" when it is delivered or is simply another also-ran. The only way a company can attain and perpetuate niche leadership is through superior competency in the entire process of product development.

Every company uses technology in some form. It is popular to glamorize high technology, but it is more useful to consider all technology as new, mature, or proprietary. New technology describes such areas such as biotechnology, computers and software, semiconductors, liquid crystals, and specialty materials; it often has a dramatic impact in the marketplace. Mature technology is that which is relatively stable, straightforward to apply, and widely available. Proprietary technology is based on either new or mature technology that has been adapted for a particular use and that is not readily available for others to use. Proprietary technology is usually considered a trade secret and may or may not be protected by patents or copyrights. It offers the only long-term source for a competency advantage from technology, and it is usually generated in-house.

New technology becomes mature over time and rarely lasts long as a competency advantage. Because technological advantages can be easily lost through the fast pace of change in the marketplace, there is a steady need for new competencies; what was superior competency yesterday can become commonplace today and obsolete tomorrow. As new technology matures and becomes diffused throughout an industry, maintaining marketplace momentum based on technology advantage becomes more difficult. The arena in which to establish competency advantage shifts to how creative a company can be in applying mature technology. One way to do this is to imaginatively combine multiple technologies that together generate better overall products or services.

Technology and processes are not the only areas that undergo constant change. The kinds of competencies needed by people also change over time. If employees are not continuously gaining necessary new competencies, they too are becoming obsolete. This can be a perplexing problem for top management, as the capable and important individual contributors of the past may no longer be as effective today or in the future. How management addresses this problem will have a powerful effect on the company's future performance.

Competency in people depends on their knowledge—explicit, tacit, and intuitive. Keeping sharp at all three levels requires curiosity, involvement, and study. Either overconfidence or declining job interest can lead to a slower rate of learning. A person's motivation to learn may also vary significantly at different times, often for reasons that have nothing to do with the job or the company work environment. Unfortunately, many people get left behind because they fail to perceive that they are not adapting to changing circumstances. Management can also unwittingly encourage competency obsolescence in their better people by failing to provide opportunities for them to gain different and broader competencies.

What standards can be used to assess competency? While it is relatively easy to recognize competency or its absence in a particular context, when effectiveness begins to wane, this is often difficult to perceive. Company growth adds greater complexity to many jobs, for example, and it is a primary cause of diminished effectiveness in people who do not simultaneously grow in personal competency. Managers must be vigilant and discreet in helping others understand the need to continuously develop their personal competency. As role models, policy managers should be engaged in pursuing self-development themselves if they want others to do the same. One reason why companies so often trip up in the marketplace after a period of rapid growth is that their competency has not kept pace with the more subtle or complex conditions of the new climate. This problem, never straightforward, has to be solved if the company is to continue to grow.

Managerial mindsets rooted in past successes must often change before advantageous answers can be found for new challenges. The CEO and other policy managers may find it difficult to alter their particular mindsets, especially if they are well entrenched and have lengthy experience. If obsolete mindsets remain unchanged, the only answer is to bring in new people. The many publicized cases of CEOs being replaced in the early 1990s, which usually took place only after deep-rooted problems became financially unbearable, exemplify the difficulty of introspection and a subsequent change of mindset. This malady is not confined to the CEO. For similar reasons, other policy-level and operating managers can fail to acquire the competencies critical to their job success in new situations.

Managers need exceptional competence, to the point of superiority, for they are the source of the decisions and actions that stimulate competency in all other areas. As the one who hires and involves all other policy managers, the CEO is accountable for the level of management competency in every company. The CEO's most important task is to establish a competency level in management that provides the company with unique advantages. Without an effective strategy for management coupled with superior performance in the managing process, a company usually becomes a follower in the marketplace; it is also be limited in organizational vitality. Competitors can usually find ways to gain access to most technology and process competencies, but attaining and sustaining exceptional competency in management, which is demonstrated by a high level of company momentum, is far more difficult.

THE COMPANY'S REPUTATION

A company's reputation for competence and reliability is at the core of its market-position strength. Customers have to believe their interests are of prime importance to their supplier and that the supplier will take care of their needs; otherwise, they will not do business with the company no matter how attractive its product or price might be. A company's reputation, as seen by its customers, is built step by step both by what it does and what it doesn't do. The catalysts that build confidence are integrity and responsiveness in transactions and relationships.

Customers see a supplier company as a continuum. In their eyes, the people they talk to in sales, customer service, engineering, quality, manufacturing, field service, or management and the quality and timeliness of the services and products they receive are the company. Their individual experiences collectively add up to form each customer's opinion about the company. In the end, the customer has to make a simple decision: Is this the kind of company I want to do business with? The collective opinions of many customers with many experiences determine the company's overall marketplace reputation. Making sure all customers have positive experiences with all the company's people and products all the time is the only way to turn reputation into a marketplace advantage. Even when a problem arises, if the company solves it in a prompt and appropriate way, its reputation can be strengthened.

If a company's reputation can be established to the point that it stands taller than its competitors in the eyes of the customer, then the customer will be loyal to its product even if the price is higher than its competitor's price. Gillette's reputation in razors and Merck's in pharmaceuticals have reached this lofty goal, and they are able to take advantage of it because they are perceived to be a more reliable source that their competitors.

Companies that are careless about their reputation will find their customers eager to move to a competitor at the first opportunity. A marginal or poor reputation with customers is one of the most serious problems a company can face and one of the most difficult to correct. A company becomes a known factor through the behavior of its people and its performance on orders, both of which are taken into account when future orders are considered. Image advertising is useful in some instances, but it usually cannot build reputation; only earning the esteem of customers has long-term significance.

THE COMPANY'S PRODUCTS

The centerpiece of a company's market position is its product position. What sets its upper level for market-position strength is the degree to which it succeeds in its efforts to make its products more desirable to customers, actual and potential, than those of its competitors. Customer benefits—what a potential customer looks at in making buying decisions—are created by a product's performance, quality, value, configuration, appearance, and availability, and all contribute to product position. Informed customers are not normally willing to pay for product features, including quality, that do not provide them with specific benefits. Accordingly, the primary route to gaining marketplace advantage from products is leadership in product innovation.

Offering a range of related products gives customers multiple options for satisfying their application needs. This can reduce their efforts to find alternate or new supply sources. Given a range, customers can often better optimize value or provide greater choice within their own marketplace. Different kinds of customers—end users, distributors, and original equipment manufacturers—

might require somewhat different variations of a basic product. Customers in different countries usually have special needs as well.

CUSTOMER SERVICES

Customer services encompasses all the many activities a company engages in to encourage customer business. They range from supplying sales and product application literature, offering trial periods and warranties, arranging contact with technical and management people, expediting orders, application problem-solving, and furnishing after-sale support, to product repair and preventive maintenance, customer training, and product upgrades or recalls. Determining what services are necessary and deciding on when and how to provide them are important top management issues.

Regardless of what services are provided, how a company interfaces with its customers is crucial. As consumers, most of us encounter situations every day that dissatisfy us. A product we buy fails to work as we expect it to, or it fails outright. Perhaps we were not cautioned about certain measures we should have taken, or we encountered a sales or service person who was unhelpful or snippy. Eliminating such obvious and simple aggravations is essential to establish a high level of customer satisfaction. In particular, company people in positions that involve customer contact must be able to tolerate stress and not become easily upset; they must genuinely want to be of help to customers, even when the customers are impatient or unreasonable. Providing backup support to these customer-service people is equally important. By the time customers need help, their patience is usually limited; they want fast, courteous, corrective action.

In the Momentum Era, every company must routinely provide superior services by helpful people who are sensitive to customer needs and are able to solve customer problems. Stimulated by insightful managers, all the company's people must seek ways to go beyond the norm and turn each service into a customer-valued benefit, and then in the aggregate of these services, achieve a marketplace advantage.

MARKETPLACE PRESENCE

A company's presence in the marketplace provides its basic communication link with a customer. Marketplace presence refers to the many ways in which a company stays in contact with customers, to the degree of its entrenchment with them, and to the breadth and depth of its marketplace penetration.

The most visible forms of marketplace presence are advertising and sales promotion. Field sales and service and inventory locations situated in areas that are convenient to customers is another high-profile aspect of presence. Others include visits by people from the company's central location(s) and phone conversations and correspondence that remind a customer of the supplier's presence and interest. If the customer knows a supplier is easy to contact for information and services, that awareness generates a sense of confidence and security about the company.

A supplier's degree of entrenchment with a customer depends in part on their personal relationships and the history of the company's performance in meeting the customer's needs. Establishing personal relationships offers a channel for insight that enables more effective performance. When a history of successful performance is established that has resulted in formal supplier and product approvals, it usually opens the door wider for new business opportunities. Product companies that wish to sell to quality-conscious customers find it is now a virtual necessity to qualify under ISO 9000, a quality standard for products, processes, and services that requires third-party certification.

Entrenchment also means the kinds of dependencies customers may have on their suppliers. The most obvious example is when a supplier is considered the sole source for a product or service. In the 1980s and earlier, IBM and DEC were often the only important computer hardware suppliers for many mainframe and midrange communications applications. There was very little product overlap between the two companies; the operating system software each employed was unique. Because applications software was developed mostly by independent companies and had to be compatible with the proprietary hardware and systems software, software migration to other hardware suppliers was neither easy nor economical. As a result, most IBM and DEC customers became totally dependent on these companies as sole-source suppliers.

Their entrenchment provided a major competitive barrier for each, and in large part this barrier was the reason IBM and DEC became such enormous businesses. Over time, however, many of their customers became exasperated with their lack of options. While these dependency-based, market-position strategies worked well for IBM and DEC for a long time, technology advances eventually provided new solutions for their entrapped customers. Neither of the suppliers embraced the new solutions early enough and neither chose to make obsolete their own installed base of equipment with newer open-system products that could use older software. Many of their previously captive customers were able to move to new suppliers, plunging both companies into a swamp of financial and operational problems. They found themselves out of step with the market in technical capability and endured many billions of dollars of red ink before they took adequate corrective actions.

Market presence also describes geographic coverage. Expanding a company's presence by opening sales and service offices in new regions is an important route to revenue growth, as well as a way to minimize monthly fluctuations in new order levels. Many companies find that expanding geographic presence is the fastest and easiest way to build profit growth. For some companies, this means going global.

INVESTING FOR REVENUE MARGIN GROWTH

The financial measure that best tracks changes in a company's market-position strength is REM growth rate. Growth in REM indicates a strengthening market position; declining REM signals market-position weakness and is a clear warning of serious problems.

The usual contributors to growth in REM are increased sales of existing products, the advent of improved and new products, optimized pricing, productivity gains, and more effective policies and programs for sales and product management. The fastest way in the short term to increase REM is to increase sales of existing products, always a high priority. Seeking productivity gains in the revenue-generation activities is also important, of course, and investing to acquire technology for future products can also be worthwhile, even when the exact requirements for future products may be uncertain.

Of the many issues affecting growth in REM, none is more important than product pricing. Every dollar, up or down, in price directly affects REM. Managers should be familiar with the price-volume elasticity in the company's market niches. When demand is relatively insensitive to price change, sometimes a higher price is the right route to higher REM. When sufficiently higher volume can be obtained by a reduction, sometimes a lower price is the right route. Analysis that uses PREM and VAREM can guide pricing structure and individual product strategy decisions. The relative importance of price is in itself a useful measure of market-position strength: being able to raise prices without losing volume or incurring customer anger is a key indicator of that strength. If possible, learning in advance what the probable reaction to a price change will be can avoid problems. Likely sources for gathering information on the relative importance of price (and other issues as well) include employees, customers, suppliers, and competitors, who can often be easily surveyed at trade shows, conferences, or in other informal settings.

As products and markets mature, REM from older products comes under pressure and usually declines as the result of price reductions and perhaps declining sales, brought on by the normal forces of marketplace competition. Alert managers find ways to extend product life cycles; one path for this is to develop new markets. As certain products mature, a healthy company anticipates the impact this will have on profit and focuses on bringing out improved or new ones early enough to supplement or replace the aging ones.

To remain competitive, every company has to make regular gains in productivity throughout the organization. Because of the magnitude of manufacturing and sales costs, productivity gains that lower these are of key importance. If productivity gains are routine, REM can rise when prices remain constant and hold firmer when prices decline. In situations where market conditions are forcing price reductions, timely gains are absolutely essential to maintain REM level.

Most companies concentrate nearly all of their quality- and productivity-enhancing efforts in the areas of product design, manufacturing processes, automation, and training. Important gains are both possible and necessary, however, in sales, product development, administration, management, and cencon.

To a great degree, the amount of money an organization spends in product and company development and productivity gain is discretionary. Because these expenses usually reduce today's profit, policy management has to decide between making explicit short-term choices and those that will benefit the company in the long term. If the company is to sustain consistency in REM growth and in operating profit growth, it is essential that these decisions be made with care and wisdom. REM growth has to be sufficiently large to allow for enough ongoing investment in development to perpetuate a positive feedback loop. Managers must also work steadily to find ways of raising the productivity of product and process development. Where and how to invest for development are critical questions without easy answers. The decisions are further complicated by the fact that these expenses usually must be committed in advance over a long time span, while future REM is uncertain and difficult to forecast. The best decisions come from a mix of ambition on the part of the company's managers, a perceptive and judicious view of market opportunities, and the ability to tolerate risk.

The investment decisions ultimately come down to deciding what specific projects will have priority, and what, if any, projects will be dropped. Few management decisions are as critical as these. Market-position strength for several years ahead depends on making accurate choices. Well-informed intuition is the only real guide, and carefully monitoring development progress is vital. Merely spending more money hardly assures that the choices being made are good ones, or that, even if they are, the desired result will be forthcoming.

A RISING BAR

In the Momentum Era of the late 1990s, most companies are acting to improve their market-position strength. As a business sets ever-higher standards for marketplace performance, however, it must continuously raise the bar for its overall performance if it is to grow. To stand out from the others in its marketplace, every company must concentrate on attaining more acute market strategy, shorter cycle time for new-product development, productivity gains, and expanding customer benefits in products and services as ongoing necessities.

The need for market-position strength may seem obvious, but its prime importance may become submerged in the sea of everyday company activities. Top managers sometimes unconsciously encourage this submersion by the nature of the priorities they set for themselves. Unless they pay close attention to the company's market-position strength, others will not do so either. For market-position strength to remain visible and vital, it has to be a part of a company's unity of cause, and every employee has to act on this cause. All the company's people must be involved; policy managers, by what they say as well as what they do, must lead the way. If top management pays too little attention to sustaining market-position strength, the company will pay a high price.

By focusing on superior competency, an enviable reputation, product strength, an appropriate marketplace presence, and leading-edge customer services, a company can establish a marketplace posture that is difficult for others to compete against, an advantage that usually permits firmer and more profitable pricing. This kind of market-position strength is only achieved and sustained with high organizational vitality and ongoing building of company momentum.

NOTES

1. Irwin Gross, executive director of the Institute for the Study of Business Markets at Pennsylvania State University, in "The Perils of Customer Satisfaction," *Across the Board*, April 1994.

## CHAPTER 7

Operations Strategy

The Basis for Performance Capability

STRATEGIC POSITIONING

E very successful business is positioned so its market strategy takes advantage of core competencies while its operations strategy is aimed at strengthening those competencies and adding new ones that will open new opportunities in the marketplace.

Market strategy and operations strategy are really two sides of the same coin. Once set, market strategy defines how the company will reach the market position that is necessary to fulfill its established mission and ambition. Operations strategy defines how the company will position its performance capability to reach and continuously strengthen its targeted market position. Market and operations strategy have to be synergistically reinforcing. The purpose is to secure specific marketplace advantages, stay flexible enough to meet changing future requirements, and continuously accelerate the rate of accomplishment within every part of the company. Pursuing these three guidelines—marketplace advantage, flexibility, and momentum building—sets the foundation for daily activities in all the company's capabilities areas. Market and operations strategy are always works in progress, and it is an ongoing management task to revise them as external and internal situations fluctuate and change. When clearly and concisely expressed, these strategies should guide the company's people toward building an enduring and prosperous future for the company. While poor decisions about strategic positioning can produce second-rate status or even disaster for the company, imaginative positioning can lead to dramatic company achievement, as the Compaq example in chapter 1 clearly demonstrates. One of Compaq's directors, Kenneth Roman, described the impact of the company's revised strategy as "awesome."[1]

PERFORMANCE CAPABILITY

Every growing stand-alone product company has in place a range of basic capabilities and essential resources, listed below, that in combination are sufficient to provide growth in market-position strength. The extent to which a company is able to achieve strength in each of these areas determines its competitive standing in the marketplace and its long-term financial performance. As used below, the term *sales* encompasses all aspects of selling, marketing, distributing, and customer services.

BASIC CAPABILITIES	ESSENTIAL RESOURCES
■ Company management	■ Satisfied, loyal customers
■ Sales	■ Creative, competent people
■ Manufacturing	■ Marketplace-advantaged products
■ Product development	■ Supportive infrastructure
■ Administration	■ Sufficient financing

It takes constant skill and ingenuity to obtain high performance from company operations within a changing external and internal environment, and the spotlight is on top managers to continuously improve every facet of operational capability. Along with superior performance in operations, there is the continuing need to keep control of operating costs and to earn sufficient and growing profit. As we have noted, this requires continuous productivity gain in every area of the business. For policy managers, the basic challenge is to achieve these results without involving themselves in daily activities. The only way to meet this is to establish a high level of accountability and competency throughout the company.

Figure 7-1 shows the interdependent and interactive relationships between operations and market strategy, organizational vitality, and company infrastructure. Working together, they influence the performance capability that builds market-position strength.

THE DYNAMICS OF OPERATIONS STRATEGY

Historically, a company's formally defined operations strategy has typically consisted of a bland mission statement, an authority-based organization chart, and policies-and-practices manuals. This approach hardly encourages an organization that supports involvement and creativity. To develop a company's full potential, the CEO and other policy managers must carefully construct a strategic framework focused on actual needs and must act to support it. Otherwise, both company innovation and productivity will suffer, and the result, if not dysfunction, will be an organization that is mediocre, regardless of the caliber of its people.

The absence of a helpful and well-communicated operations strategy can also cause managers and other employees to waste a vast amount of time. Strategy is always an interesting subject to talk about, so the vacuum invites frequent formal and informal debates and discussions, most of them unproductive, about what is of importance to the company. When operations strategy is vague or conflicting, individual managers have to set their own direction on a case-by-case basis; even if their decisions are in the company's best interests, they will certainly not dovetail with other decisions being made throughout the company.

Articulating management's views on operations strategy in a concise, unified way usually takes a good deal of strategic thinking and dialogue. Each manager probably will have somewhat different perspectives on critical issues, particularly those relating to company strategy for management, mission, values, ethics, employee loyalty, organization structure, compensation, growth, and profit. Yet they must arrive at a common understanding if management is going to be effective as a team in the ongoing campaign to secure lasting company strength. Establishing sound strategy takes time, but once done, the hard part can begin: translating operations strategy into innovative and effective performance capability throughout the company.

To promote growing market strength, a well-conceived, well-defined, and

Figure 7-1: Operational Interdependencies

carefully implemented operations strategy should create and sustain the following conditions:

- a practical and effective strategy for company management
- the routine use of relevant momentum indicators
- managers' efficacy in performing their primary responsibility
- a company culture in which anchorpoint objectives, accountability, and momentum drivers are firmly ingrained
- company people who are capable, creative, committed, and enthusiastic
- synergy within and between sales, manufacturing, and product development
- a high level of innovation with judicious and productive risk-taking
- the infrastructure necessary to carry out management's ambition
- a stable and strengthening financial position

Setting operations strategy means considering all the company's operating systems—revenue generation, value creation, administration, and management—together with the company's cencon system. People-related issues should be at the top of the list to generate the highest level of organizational vitality.

Are sales people accurately aware of what is happening in the marketplace and able to guide the company through the complexities of securing desirable orders? They must have the means for acquiring and assimilating information from customers that fortifies them with important, useful knowledge. For example, this means might consist of a communications-linked notebook computer containing up-to-the minute customer order-trend history, the status of their current projects, their organization structure, and their customers' markets. Is the coordination between product management, field sales, customer services, and production control simple and effective enough to solve customer problems in minutes or hours, as opposed to days or weeks?

Just as quick, accurate response to customer orders and fast throughput time in production are essential simply to stay competitive, in manufacturing the norm should be small in-process inventories, low overhead, the absence of quality problems, and sophisticated, simple scheduling. To assure the least possible delay in order delivery, the ongoing availability of sufficient raw material and finished inventory should be confirmed. Setting manufacturing strategy also means resolving the conflicts between volume, quality, cost, and time, as well as issues of make-or-buy and supplier relations.

Product development and company development each require well-focused value-creation activities. Product and process development programs have to be carefully structured to ensure timely achievements as well as cost effectiveness if they are to contribute to market leadership. Company development programs should strengthen the competency of people and fortify the infrastructure they work within.

STRATEGIC THINKING

In a small business, operations and market strategy often exist only in the mind of the CEO. As a business grows, however, it becomes important that the explicit elements of strategic positioning be established by policy managers working as a team, whose joint efforts are likely to create a strategy that is both more perceptive and capable of being better implemented. Michel Robert has observed that there is a distinction between strategic planning and strategic thinking; in most companies strategic planning is not sufficiently based on strategic thinking. Robert describes strategic thinking as a process that enables the management team to sit together and think through the qualitative aspects of its business and the environment it faces. The team can then decide on a common and shared vision and a strategy for the future of its company. Most traditional strategy planning, he believes, depends on projection of numbers more than it does on real strategic thinking.[2]

The clear distinction between strategic planning and strategic thinking is also noted by Henry Mintzberg. He describes the causes of failure in traditional strategic planning:

> Strategic planning, as it has been practiced, has really been strategic programming, the articulation and elaboration of strategies or visions that already exist. When companies understand the difference between planning and strategic thinking, they can get back to what the strategy-making process should be: capturing what the manager learns from all sources (both the soft insights from his or her personal experiences and the experiences of others throughout the organization and the hard data from market research and the like) and then synthesizing that learning into a vision of the direction that the business should pursue.[3]

Because virtually all product companies operate in an open, competitive market, their market position is vulnerable to ongoing changes in customer needs or competitor behavior. It is therefore essential for them either to take advantage of or defend against those changing external conditions that the company does not control. Frequently overlooked, however, is another vulnerability: the risk to market position that develops when company capabilities slowly become obsolete, or diminish through complacency or the loss of key people. To minimize these risks, managers need a comprehensive and objective understanding of how changes in the company's capabilities and competencies, its internal problems, and limitations in other resources have an impact on the company's existing market situation. It is vital to promptly correct the company's internal weaknesses before they cause acute problems in the marketplace.

The company's strategic positioning should be flexible and reviewed frequently, as future circumstances, both in the marketplace and within the company, will invariably change in ways that are not easily anticipated. If the strategy is too rigid, too vague, or assumed to be foolproof because things are going well, problems invariably arise.

SETTING AN OPERATIONS STRATEGY

Setting operations strategy is the process of (1) understanding in detail the company's current operational situation and relating this to trends in its market-position strength and internal performance capability; (2) defining management's ambition for the company's future and clarifying how it will operate to fulfill that ambition; (3) defining a strategy for company management that will guide all decisions and actions, by everyone, toward lasting company strength; and (4) defining the kind of company culture and infrastructure that will foster organizational vitality and generate sustained market-position strength.

This process requires developing a number of strategic elements, which the remainder of this chapter describes in detail, offering guidelines for setting them in motion in ways that enable the highest degree of company momentum.

■ *Mission, ambition, and values*

What is our mission? What is our ambition? What are our values? What is our unity of cause, and how do we enlist everyone's enthusiasm for it? Does our compensation program reinforce our unity of cause?

■ *Growth and profit expectation*

What are our specific growth and profit expectations? What are the key factors that limit our growth and profit? What are our core competencies, and do they provide sufficient marketplace advantages? Do we have sufficient company momentum? Is there a company-wide focus on the anchorpoint objectives? Does everyone understand the role of momentum drivers?

■ *Organization*

What organizational structure shall we use? Do our people have the required attitudes and competencies? How effective is our communication, coordination, and cooperation, internally and with our customers and suppliers? How do we get "stretch" and "breakthrough" into our goals and performance? Does our informal communications network support our strategic objectives? Are we adequately developing our people? Are we fostering organizational learning?

■ *Cencon System*

Do our cencon processes form a clearly articulated system? Are we using the right performance indicators? Do we deliver the right information into the right hands at the right time? Do we use meetings efficiently? Are we turning information into useful knowledge?

■ *Operational infrastructure needs*

Are our assets and resources able to support our ambitions? Where do we need to reinforce our operational infrastructure?

■ *Operational policies and processes*

What are our core business processes, and how well are they working? Is our profit planning effective? Do our operational policies and practices contribute to organizational vitality? Do we over- or undercontrol? Do we emphasize mistake prevention over innovation? Are we routinely achieving sufficient gains in productivity? Does our policy on compensation support organizational vitality?

MISSION, AMBITION, AND VALUES: DESIGNING AN MAV STATEMENT

A mission statement defines the boundaries within which a company operates, and a vision statement, more accurately called an *ambition* statement, specifies what management wants the company to accomplish within the framework of its mission. Describing mission, ambition, and the basic values that management believes in should effectively communicate the fundamental character of the company.

A mission, ambition, and values (MAV) statement is intended to succinctly inform employees and others about the nature of the company. It should answer such questions as: What gives us an identity? What can we take pride in? What do we stand for? What can we rely on? The MAV statement should reflect the deep-rooted beliefs held by the CEO and board of directors that they wish to be ingrained in the organization. It should specify what management sets as policy and is willing to act on. As deeds are more powerful than words, what managers do (or do not do) is what will be communicated to others. When managerial actions differ from beliefs conveyed in the MAV statement, the company spawns employee cynicism and mistrust of management.

Preparing an MAV statement that is telling, brief (ideally, confined to a single page), and free of platitudes is a challenging task, as attested to by the abundance of inadequate ones. Yet the time and energy spent in arriving at an MAV statement that clarifies the nature and character of the company is well worth the effort, because it helps guide everyone toward the same long-term objectives. Figure 7-2 shows an example MAV for the company I call Multi-Med.

Mission

What business are we in? What is our scope of involvement in that business? Why are we successful in pursuing our mission? Drucker points out that

THE MISSION, AMBITION, AND VALUES OF MULTI-MED, INC.

OUR MISSION

Multi-Med is a growth-oriented product development and manufacturing company whose business is to convert ideas, competency, and technology into products and services that satisfy and retain customers who use noninvasive medical instruments.

Our *unity of cause* for every employee—manager, professional, and associate—is to build sufficient momentum from company-wide accomplishments to continuously strengthen our market position and performance capability, and thereby obtain and retain leadership in our chosen market niches. Every employee with us for more than one year will share in our growth in profit resulting from company-wide momentum-building efforts.

OUR AMBITION

We strive, by exceptional performance, to earn a reputation with our customers that is second to none in our chosen markets. This is essential for company strength. We intend to be an important long-term participant and a performance and value leader in carefully chosen, specific market niches to which we bring unique competency. Size, as measured by market share or sales, is not our first consideration. We intend, however, to lead in enough niches to be a significant, well-respected, and important contributor to the medical field.

OUR CORE VALUES

Customers provide the money for our operations and for all our jobs. We will prosper only as long as we provide imaginative, high-quality products, exceptional service, and meaningful value to customers, both existing and new. While producing customer value, we must also produce value for our employees and shareholders.

To grow and endure in our markets, to be a stable and dependable employer, and to be an attractive business to sources of capital, we must be financially strong by routinely earning sufficient profit. We believe the company's strength in the marketplace is the key to profitability and the only assurance of employment opportunity. Profit is the prime source of funds to further strengthen and grow the company. Profit does not take precedence, however, when problems arise that affect our reputation or customer confidence in us.

Our relationships are based on trust, mutual respect, individual accountability, fairness, and pride in accomplishment. We expect each person to treat others as he or she wants to be treated. Honesty, law compliance, and courtesy are fundamental requirements. We will always hold to the highest ethical standards and will take corrective action when these standards are not upheld.

To provide exceptional service and high value to our customers, we need a performance-focused company culture that is socially attractive and promotes open communication, cooperation, initiative, creativity, learning, and growth in competency. Loyalty from our employees is important to us; so is company loyalty to our employees. We cannot assure permanent employment to anyone who works with us, but we will encourage and help our employees to develop competencies that will help them advance in their careers.

Figure 7-2: Example of an MAV Statement

the answer to the "what is our business" question is never obvious, and that there is never one correct answer. For every company, the answer comes from a specific decision by top management and the board of directors; that decision then defines the boundaries for the allocation of company resources.[4]

Including unity of cause within the mission statement is a new concept I believe to be an important foundation for momentum building. In one short statement, it should convey to all employees how they can contribute to the company's mission and overall success.

As we have observed, unity of cause is the shared purpose that everyone in a company must be able to identify with and rally around. All the company's people must authentically believe that the cause is vital both to the company and to their own personal interests. At a minimum, they should believe in the purpose of the cause, and ideally they should be able to develop genuine enthusiasm for it. Describing the quality of businesses that do this successfully, Robert H. Waterman has said:

> Renewing organizations seem to run on causes....Renewers seem to be able to pick causes and communicate them in a way that conveys an element of risk or challenge but not foolishly so....They seem to be able to turn tedious issues into noble causes. With effort, they do so in ways that enhance the dignity of the people they employ.[5]

For Three Dimensional Management, the singular and unwavering cause is to *build company momentum toward strengthening market position*; how it is expressed can vary, but that is the message. It is a cause that everyone should be able to accept, for company market strength is at the core of job opportunity and security. If people can be made to believe that strengthening the company's market position by strengthening its performance capability is in their best interests, the potential for high organizational vitality is great. Communicating the unity of cause in a manner that is not prosaic and that is understood and accepted by all employees will probably take persistence and patience.

Above all, the cause must be made a part of every job in the company so that each person knows that he or she is expected to contribute to it. Momentum building is the one responsibility every job in the company has in common. It ties individual job result to a company-wide purpose. For unity of cause to be actually accepted and acted on, every employee must understand and believe that a strong market position for the company is essential for future job opportunities and job security, and that performing one's job in a superior way is a vital contribution to company-wide momentum. As we have noted, establishing a company-wide profit-sharing program, in which everyone shares in the growth in company profit from momentum building, is a key element for acceptance of momentum building.

Ambition

A company's ambition is established by its CEO and board of directors. An ambition statement qualitatively defines the nature and scope of the company's future operations. It answers the question of where the company is going in the foreseeable, long-range future. This view of the company's future helps establish operational and market-position objectives and guides resource allocation, strategy development, plans, and actions. An ambition statement communicates a succinct picture of the company's future so all employees can visualize clearly the work that must take place between today and that point in the future. Without a sharply focused ambition, a company is shaped by random forces, both external and internal, rather than by management direction. The level of ambition needs to be based on marketplace knowledge, essential company competencies, and available resources, but it should also call for important accomplishment that will stimulate imagination and enthusiasm.

A verbal picture of management's ambition can be expressed as the kind of marketplace leadership it is seeking, and how large the company would like to become. It could also convey operational ambition, such as how the company will grow geographically or in reputation. The quantitative aspects of growth that define ambition more specifically will change more frequently than the "big picture," and normally should be defined separately from the ambition statement.

Values

Company values are established by clearly communicating and enforcing those management's beliefs, set forth as policy, that everyone in the company is expected to accept and live by in conducting business affairs. Ethical and moral values are a binding force that can make most people feel good about their company. The level of organizational vitality in a business depends on widespread belief in company values that all employees can rely on and take pride in. Achieving trust in relationships is the value that underpins all others. Drucker cites the Hippocratic Oath—"Above all, not knowingly to do harm"—as the essential basis for trust, and the basic rule of professional ethics.[6]

Trust within the company and among the company's people and its important constituencies—customers, suppliers, shareholders, and community—is what opens, or when lacking closes down, communications and thereby meaningful relationships. With "Swiss cheese" trust, company achievements are limited by serious barriers, because the company's people lack the interest or motivation to do anything beyond the minimum to get by. Honesty and keeping one's word are obvious values that are essential to trust, as is complying with laws. "Treating others as you would like to be treated" is the golden rule variant that implies fairness, respect, consideration, and courtesy. These are behavioral qualities that every person within or otherwise involved with the company should practice and be able to rely on from others.

Many business decisions and actions involve ethical choices, and what is right or wrong is not always clear. Tough choices abound, and they can mean personal or economic loss or gain. Few people follow a rigid ethical line. Behaving as ethically as possible appears to be a common pragmatic guideline, and situational context determines the degree of "bending" from an absolute standard, often without conscious consideration. As ethical bending seems to be a part of human nature, the issue is where to draw the line. According to Jay Halfond: "In the almost 30 years that Louis Harris has been polling Americans on their confidence in different institutions, none has declined so precipitously as U.S. corporations, in which only 16 percent of the public places its trust."[7]

It would appear that business as an entity is failing to hold to a standard that warrants public trust. Since the public includes a company's employees and customers, all managers must recognize the importance of ethics, for their job is to build trust with these constituencies. While not part of a MAV statement, clarifying the gray zone of ethical behavior is an essential area for policy definition, communicated in the form of a written code of conduct, but most clearly demonstrated by managerial behavior.

Along with general ethical values, specific business values must also guide decisions and actions that help strengthen the company. Concern for employee welfare, for example, is an important value, as is the loyalty that extends from the company to its employees and from the employees to the company. All the momentum drivers are important business values. Another is protecting the environment.

One business value which applies to every business is that a company prospers only as long as it continuously brings economic value and satisfaction to its customers. Employees and shareholders can receive no long-term value, economic or personal, if the company fails to acquire and keep customers while at the same time being sufficiently profitable to permit future company growth. Probably the most fundamental business value is profit. Without enough profit, a business will not survive. People throughout the company must believe their own personal careers and opportunities with the company depend first on company prosperity. Without it, there are limited opportunities and few permanent jobs.

Unfortunately, in our society, the word *profit* is often linked to exploitation. It is neither well understood nor widely accepted that sufficient profit is a business necessity, essential for company growth, strength, and job opportunity. Perhaps this is because so many companies engage in short-term exploitation to achieve profits that are well above reasonable. Finding ways to reverse this perception of profit, which is probably held by many employees, should be a constant managerial concern. Avoiding exploitation is one way; another is to make certain all the company's people genuinely profit from their contributions.

Another medium for communicating the company's core values is the employment policy booklet. A comprehensive review of employment policies should be part of the process of defining and communicating the company's ethical and business values.

GROWTH AND PROFIT EXPECTATIONS

The words *growth* and *profit* are so commonly used in business it would seem unnecessary to think twice about them, but it is worthwhile to do so. Most managers think of growth in financial terms, such as revenue or net earnings (or earnings per share). Certainly every manager should have explicit expectations for company performance in these areas and in other financial areas as well, including REM, operating profit, cash flow, and return on net assets. But growth also refers to nonfinancial areas such as market-position strength, performance capability, organizational vitality, productivity, core competencies, and company reputation. Growth in these nonfinancial areas usually drives every aspect of financial growth. Defining growth goals only in financial terms without linking them to short- and long-term operational actions is largely wishful thinking.

For most companies, revenue growth is highly coveted. But revenue growth without growth in revenue margin indicates a problem with pricing, product performance, production or sales costs, customer services, or a combination of these factors. A company can have sound reasons for pursuing revenue growth without commensurate growth in revenue margin, but such a direction needs an explicit strategy that will eventually provide increased REM. A growth rate in REM at least equal to growth in revenues is the minimum necessary to provide adequate funds for ongoing momentum-building efforts and to simultaneously maintain profit growth.

Referring to revenues, some people believe in the saw "grow or die," without taking into account the other side, "grow and die." The distinction between the two is in REM level and the time span in which revenue growth takes place. Rapid revenue growth might or might not lead to higher profit, but it always leads to increased cash needs for working capital. Revenue growth can also exert short-term strains in company operations that could cause problems with product quality or productivity, late deliveries, poor customer support, and excessive costs. While fast growth in sales orders is normally an important opportunity, managers should be vigilant for the internal problems that can arise. If REM grows sufficiently, and acute quality or production problems do not derail demand or reputation, the growth experience can be exhilarating as well as raise the company's profile in the marketplace.

Where, how, and when to grow in revenue are key considerations in establishing a strategic approach to both growth and profit. Sometimes a narrow-minded sales-order push can inhibit long-term operating profit if better marketplace opportunities are sidetracked by the effort. The only road to long-term profit growth is sorting out revenue opportunities and staying within a well-thought-out strategy that provides opportunity for long-term growth in revenue margin, not just revenues.

Seeking financial growth of any kind usually entails risk, with more risk involved for greater ambition. In the absence of market-forced growth, assessing what degree of risk is tolerable is a prerequisite to setting growth objectives. The parameters for risk can range from defensive (least risk) to highly aggressive (highest risk); the latter might cut short-term profit and require significant capital investment.

Undertaking a highly aggressive strategy is also likely to produce a big disturbance in company operations. As an example, when IBM was at a strategic crossroad in 1960, the decision was made to undertake a massive change in technology and manufacturing processes in order to launch a new computer generation the System 360. If this strategy succeeded, IBM would have a commanding lead in the burgeoning computer industry. If it failed, the company might go bankrupt. Billions of dollars were pumped into the program at a time when it was unclear whether the effort would succeed. The company had many technological hurdles to overcome. Young engineers with limited managerial experience were given budgets of millions of dollars to complete small but essential pieces of this huge effort. The undertaking, of course, did succeed, and the decision launched IBM into a thirty-year position of dominance in mainframe computing, going from $2 billion in sales in 1960 to $65 billion by 1992. Few companies have the resources or the will to undertake this kind of risk.

Company-Critical Size

There is usually a minimum size at which most small-to-medium product companies can best sustain leadership in their chosen market niche(s). Until this size is reached, the company may have fewer potential customers than its competitors, even though it has better products, value, quality, or services. Once a company has reached its critical size, the question for it then shifts to: What is our optimum size? The idea that bigger is better, as defined by revenues, is a frequent conclusion, but not necessarily a correct one. When the company is at the point where it is no longer disadvantaged by its size, revenue growth should become secondary to growth in REM and operating profit. This does not imply that continued revenue growth is no longer important. It is, but the parameter for evaluating growth has shifted to revenue margin.

Market share is a common measure of success for some companies, but pursuing sales for the sake of share can be hazardous. Sometimes high market share does translate into higher and more stable REM. In general, however, the company that narrowly pursues share by aggressive pricing forces a price restructuring in that market, within which lower prices then become the norm for all competitors. The net effect is little improvement in share and reduced REM unless the company can achieve concurrent productivity gains. The most advantageous route to market share increase, accompanied by a commensurate gain in REM, is to redefine a market segment or niche by way of new products, services, and increased marketplace presence. Occasionally the weakness of competitors also provides an opportunity to increase share.

Diversification

Many companies embark on diversification as a way of growing faster or reducing market risks. Sometimes they diversify to diminish cyclical market problems or to better invest their financial resources. These are sound reasons if the company has the people and the other resources available to diversify without slighting the existing business. Other companies diversify when their current profit position is under pressure and no acceptable way to change the situation is apparent; moving into a new market niche with a different customer base and perhaps greater potential for profit is a tempting possibility. Diversifying is a bad idea, however, when it is primarily a defensive move that will divert management time from the existing business. The best path for solving the company's existing problem is likely to be tackling the core problem in the existing business with a fresh creative approach.

Assuming that the question, why diversify? has been carefully examined, the next question is: what form will our diversification take? The two basic choices, related or unrelated, pose polar opposite approaches. If the diversification is to be related to the company's current competencies and products, it can use current in-house expertise to pursue new market niches, either through acquisition or in-house development. Although this form of diversification entails the least risk, it still poses substantial risk of failure and may demand valuable time and resources from the existing business activities. Looking carefully at this distraction issue before proceeding can help avert potentially serious problems.

The most risky form of diversification is the unrelated, purely financial approach, in which a company buys a patent, product line, or another company, and the specific competency necessary to insure success does not reside with the acquirer. This means that the acquiring company has to rely on others of unknown compatibility for management competency and market knowledge. The frequency of failure in unrelated diversification is high, primarily because the acquirer often lacks understanding of the specific success factors and future market opportunities for an unfamiliar business, even after engaging in extensive "due diligence." Merely having the money, along with the general management capability, to undertake diversification is no assurance of success, even when the acquirer's pockets are deep.

Both related and unrelated forms of diversification through acquisition have to address the attitude changes that inevitably take place in the company being acquired. Cultural conflicts or other problems of morale are likely to occur, and these lower organizational vitality and sometimes cause the loss of key people. Employment contracts are helpful, but they do not have any effect on underlying attitudes. A "father knows best" demeanor on the part of the acquiring company is a notoriously damaging factor that exacerbates negative attitudes, and it is essential that the acquirer move quickly to establish trust by the people in the acquired company. This means the acquirer is committed to help them and create greater opportunities for them, a task that is accomplished by working closely with the acquired management team to develop new operational and market strategies that both managements can be enthusiastic about.

Profit

The imperative, maximize the bottom line, has long been an implicit and often explicit tenet in the management of most businesses. It was reinforced in the early 1960s when computers began to radically change the way financial information was gathered, analyzed, and used. In the following decades, data-processing sophistication delivered new power, and often too much confidence, into the hands of managers at every level. Top management was now able to examine the cost-center impact on bottom-line company performance quickly and in detail. In turn, top managers applied greater pressure to improve short-term earnings through cost reduction, often because of stock market considerations. Even without pressure from above, many managers frequently looked to improving short-term profit, if that would maximize their current year bonus. Automated data processing, along with pressure from the investment community, converged with other factors to shift management thinking away from a year-to-year perspective toward quarter-to-quarter financial performance. This emphasis on short-term performance has brought about precarious roller-coaster variations for many companies, as projects that are important to long-term performance have often been underfunded.

If management is focused primarily on seeking good quarterly numbers and bases its priorities, decisions, and actions on what is good or bad for those numbers, then momentum building will normally suffer, and so will long-term profit. Managers must look ahead in making decisions on expenditures, not backward, and rely as much on qualitative information as they do on numbers. If a numbers approach to management is applied too narrowly and without adequate regard to company strengthening, it can damage or undermine the operational activities necessary to sustain and build momentum, and thereby deplete the source of strength that delivers the net income result over the long term. During periods of marketplace stability, decisions that ignore operational strengthening are usually a recipe for company-performance mediocrity, and perhaps company failure during periods when the marketplace is undergoing rapid change.

Many board members and CEOs cite shareholder interests when they press for short-term reported profit. The stock market is fickle, of course, and share price can drop if short-term earnings do not meet the expectations of traders and analysts. But what investor shareholders really want is consistent growth in long-term profit, without surprises, and they usually will have considerable patience if they have confidence that management's approach to strengthening the company will achieve that end. The only route to consistent short- and long-term profit performance is building sufficient company momentum.

ORGANIZATION: FLATTENING THE COMPANY PYRAMID

The traditional organization for product companies has been based on a control-oriented pyramid structure that compartmentalizes function and competency under a rigid management hierarchy. With this approach, company-wide needs are usually relegated to second place, beneath functional group interests. This hierarchy commonly produces communication barriers, function-interface problems, too many middle managers, and a decidedly inhospitable atmosphere for an authentic unity of cause. Although exercising management authority is essential at times, a company's performance is far better when the people actually involved in its daily activities are responsible for most recurring decisions and actions, under a "flat" structure. Simply moving "boxes" in the pyramid structure and expecting important results from the exercise is a lot like trying to change the color of flowers by replanting them in another part of the same garden. Constructive change for improved company performance requires different thinking, different strategies, and different processes.

An involvement-oriented organizational structure that will forge higher company performance depends on individual accountability and the freedom and authority for all the company's people to act on their own within a performance-focused culture. Cooperation within a unity of cause is critical to creating this atmosphere. Such a flexible structure eliminates functional barriers, opens horizontal and vertical communications, and uses the smallest possible number of middle managers. The goal is to simplify the process of everyday decision and action processes to produce fast, appropriate results, eliminating the impediments that delay and complicate getting things done. An organization's everyday business issues and problems are usually complex enough by themselves without immersing them in a stifling procedural quagmire.

To move from a pyramid to an involvement-oriented structure requires policy managers to believe that most people, most of the time, will make decisions and take actions that are in the company's best interests, provided they know what those best interests are.

The most useful organizational structure draws on the strengths of the company's operating people, without confining them to some status-bounded "box" arrangement. What strengthens companies is the motivation, creativity, decisions, and initiatives of their people, and the operational processes they work within, not the structure itself. Managerial authority should be in the background, not the basis for structuring. The structure exists only to facilitate communications, coordination, and cooperation, and to bring together the necessary competencies.

In a radical restructuring, a company can move into its new structure rapidly or slowly, depending on its current needs. Once a flat, involvement-oriented structure is in place, managers will be able to revise structure easily in an ongoing, amoebalike manner as changing conditions may require. When this has been achieved, radical restructuring in the future should never again be necessary.

CREATING AN I-BEAM STRUCTURE

One possibility to replace the pyramid is a flexible and virtually universal organizational approach that I call the I-beam, which defines capability centers and communication paths, not management hierarchy. Figure 7-3 is an example of the I-beam for Multi-Med.

In this structure, functional work centers are referred to as capability centers (CCs). Groupings of related CCs are called capability areas (CAs), and are often in physical proximity to promote easy, informal communications. Multi-Med's eight CAs are customer service, field sales, product management, manufacturing A, manufacturing B, product development, administration, and diverse teams. Product development broadly encompasses the areas of product improvement and new product design and development, manufacturing process development, technology development, and product technical support. The diverse teams CA includes team-based activities for planning, problem solving, special projects, or any other permanent or ad hoc activity that may arise.

Extending vertically (up and down) from the company's central communication pathway are the branch pathways to and from the individual CCs. All CCs communicate, cooperate, and coordinate with each other directly without in-between managerial hierarchy. Instead of promoting policy management control of operational detail, the aim is to ensure customer focus, fast reaction time, and flexibility. The central and branch pathways provide an uninterrupted, two-way communications channel, with customers at one end and manage-

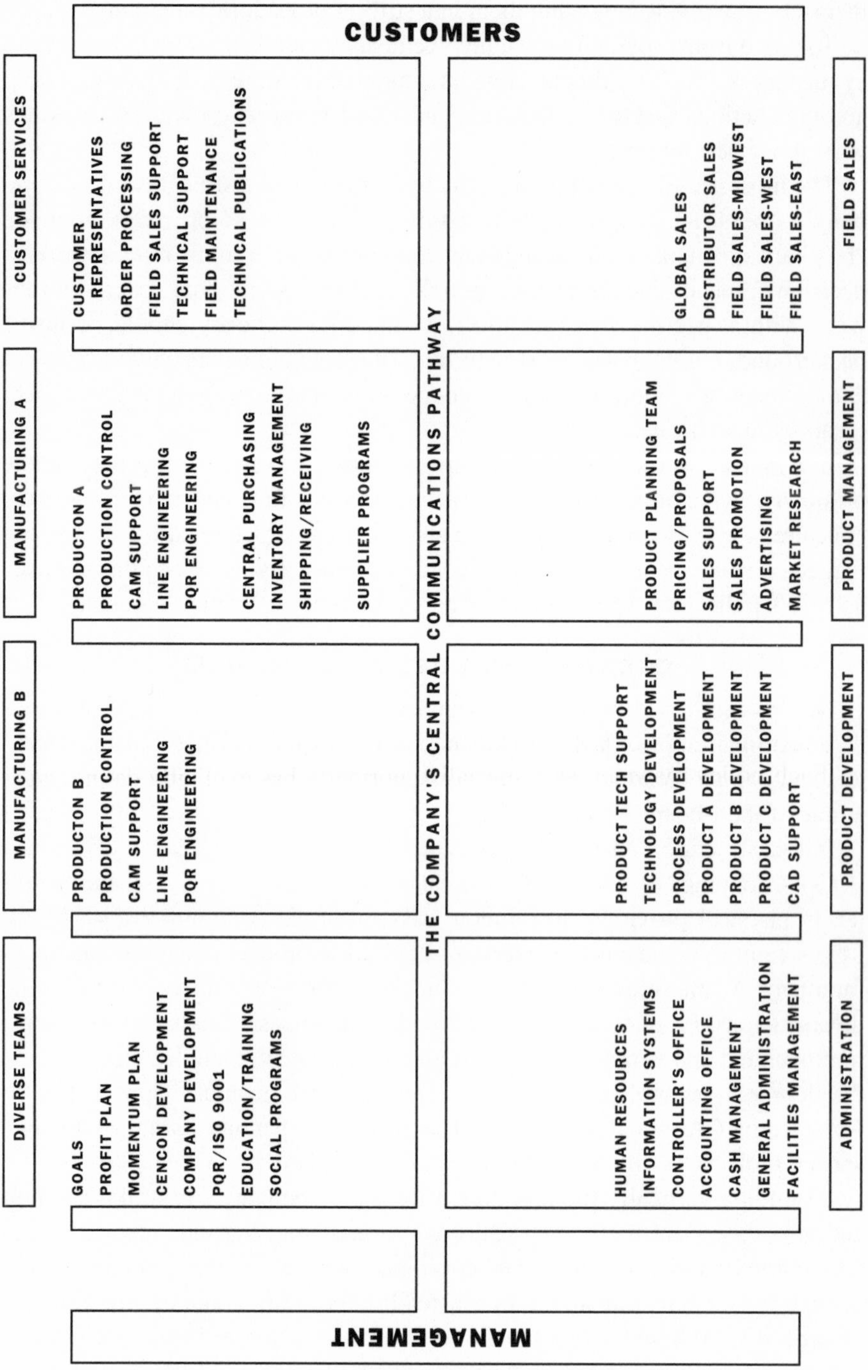

CUSTOMERS

MANAGEMENT

THE COMPANY'S CENTRAL COMMUNICATIONS PATHWAY

CUSTOMER SERVICES

CUSTOMER REPRESENTATIVES
ORDER PROCESSING
FIELD SALES SUPPORT
TECHNICAL SUPPORT
FIELD MAINTENANCE
TECHNICAL PUBLICATIONS

FIELD SALES

GLOBAL SALES
DISTRIBUTOR SALES
FIELD SALES-MIDWEST
FIELD SALES-WEST
FIELD SALES-EAST

MANUFACTURING A

PRODUCTON A
PRODUCTION CONTROL
CAM SUPPORT
LINE ENGINEERING
PQR ENGINEERING

CENTRAL PURCHASING
INVENTORY MANAGEMENT
SHIPPING/RECEIVING

SUPPLIER PROGRAMS

PRODUCT MANAGEMENT

PRODUCT PLANNING TEAM
PRICING/PROPOSALS
SALES SUPPORT
SALES PROMOTION
ADVERTISING
MARKET RESEARCH

MANUFACTURING B

PRODUCTON B
PRODUCTION CONTROL
CAM SUPPORT
LINE ENGINEERING
PQR ENGINEERING

PRODUCT DEVELOPMENT

PRODUCT TECH SUPPORT
TECHNOLOGY DEVELOPMENT
PROCESS DEVELOPMENT
PRODUCT A DEVELOPMENT
PRODUCT B DEVELOPMENT
PRODUCT C DEVELOPMENT
CAD SUPPORT

DIVERSE TEAMS

GOALS
PROFIT PLAN
MOMENTUM PLAN
CENCON DEVELOPMENT
COMPANY DEVELOPMENT
PQR/ISO 9001
EDUCATION/TRAINING
SOCIAL PROGRAMS

ADMINISTRATION

HUMAN RESOURCES
INFORMATION SYSTEMS
CONTROLLER'S OFFICE
ACCOUNTING OFFICE
CASH MANAGEMENT
GENERAL ADMINISTRATION
FACILITIES MANAGEMENT

Figure 7-3: I-Beam Capabilities Chart, Multi-Med, Inc.

ment at the other. Customers are shown on the chart as a reminder that the common denominator for all company everyday activities is customer focus.

At the other end of the channel, management is shown on the I-beam as a single block that is identical to the customer's delineation; this shows the direct access the company offers its customers and its operating people to its strategy and policy decision makers.

No constraints limit either the number of CCs or the manner in which they carry out their work. A CC can be composed of either a team or a unit under an operating manager; both approaches can be used side by side. CCs can be either permanent or temporary. The intent is to become flexible enough to rapidly create or dissolve CCs as circumstances dictate. Each CC is organized to achieve a particular result by carrying out an explicit project or an ongoing operational process (or processes). Working together, the CCs are responsible for their own everyday activities, including coordination, inter-CC and intra-CC communication, problem solving, and task initiatives, without upper management involvement except when it is necessary to resolve conflicts or clarify policy and strategy. The basic foundation for all decisions and actions within and between CCs is individual accountability. Each CC has its own well-defined mission, process(es), budget, and momentum plan. The momentum plan, developed by the center's people, outlines its goals and its approach for center strengthening. There are no middle managers between CCs and policy management, and operations people's easy, nonthreatening access to policy management is essential.

Each policy manager, as a specialist, normally has explicitly defined oversight accountability for one or more of the company capability areas. There is no span-of-control limit for policy managers. They are accountable as a team for the company's overall operating performance, and each is separately accountable for the quality of the results that the CAs under his or her aegis delivers. All policy managers are jointly accountable for ensuring that all CCs work cooperatively together, with minimum policy managerial intervention. Each CC team leader or operating manager is accountable to a single policy manager. The policy manager's role is to develop CC capability and competency; provide guidance, support, and training to CC people as needed; evaluate CC performance; set compensation plans; and initiate promotions, transfers, hirings, and terminations.

The I-beam eliminates the intrinsic flaws of the pyramid structure while retaining policy manager oversight. It is intended to optimize company performance by giving operating people the authority to run all recurring daily activities. While the I-beam poses a higher risk of mistakes from reduced supervision, it offers far greater opportunity for creative innovation and productivity gain if there is sufficient organizational vitality. It is up to policy managers to build this vitality.

ESTABLISHING CAPABILITY CENTERS

A CC can be a group of people with different competencies working for a particular purpose, such as product development, or a group with similar competency, such as field sales. Those competencies that historically have been concentrated within a single pyramid-function group may be dispersed among more than one CC. The company needs to accommodate people who are loners and give them the room to be creative. There is no status difference between CC team leaders and operating managers. Job titles should describe function rather than status.

The CCs that are teams can include people from other CCs, policy managers wearing their "expert" hats, or even temporary people. Their composition can be fluid, which means people can join or leave the group depending on situational needs for their particular expertise. One person may be in more than one CC, either permanently or temporarily. Assignments should be based not on status or seniority, but on getting the work of the CC done promptly and correctly. Policy managers must be able to deal easily with this kind of structural flexibility and personnel fluidity. The CC members must also be comfortable in the arrangement. For example, they should be able to view multiple CC involvements as learning opportunities.

To the greatest extent possible, each CC should include all competencies needed to perform a complete operational process. For example, order processing people should be able to answer questions about product availability; to approve, process, and acknowledge orders; to schedule delivery; to keep track of internal progress on order preparation; and to arrange and confirm delivery. In-house or regional field sales support people should be sufficiently broad-based to be able to quickly assess customer needs and ensure that the company is immediately responsive to them.

Capability centers work because each of their members has the competency, motivation, and diligence, along with the authority, to carry out their tasks with minimum management control. Top management has to be vigilant against the development of "functional walls" or "turf barriers." The point is to ensure an environment of seamless, fast communication, coordination, and cooperation, in which people's knowledge and competency can flourish.

DESIGNING A CENCON SYSTEM

A cencon system is the infrastructure for communicating, coordinating, and cooperating within a company. It encompasses all information that is collected, analyzed, exchanged, and disseminated, and is the source of data on momentum-indicator trends, financial results, nonfinancial operating results, trends in the marketplace, the effectiveness and behavior of competitors, trends in technology, political considerations, and other areas of importance to the company. As a mechanism for moving formal information as well as a tool for keeping people well informed and interactive, the cencon system must be carefully thought out because it is the means by which information is integrated, converted to knowledge, and put to use. Each company must customize this system to fill its own unique needs.

As the company's information infrastructure, cencon is an essential mechanism for management control, and designing it raises the issue of balancing the tension between innovation and control. Robert Simons has spent many years researching the question, "How do managers balance innovation and control?"[8] He has concluded there are four systems involved, which he calls *levers of control*:

- *Belief systems* that set core values
- *Boundary systems* that define risks to be avoided
- *Diagnostic control systems* that report on critical performance variables
- *Interactive control systems* that address strategic uncertainties

Simons's first three "levers" are in common use by most companies under a variety of different names and with varying levels of effectiveness. The fourth, interactive control systems, has not been in common use; it addresses the need to develop new strategies based on formal and informal information flow, and the techniques by which to do so. Simons provides many worthwhile examples of such techniques, developed by senior managers to obtain and use information in their own particular situations. He perceives each lever as part of a broader theory of control in business, and his insights in the design of a cencon system are well worth considering. One essential component of every company's cencon system is a data-processing-based information system. How this system is designed will either materially aid or hinder long-term company performance. State-of-the-art technology is not nearly as important as a system's flexibility and its ability to accommodate the company's future growth needs. The trend today is toward open systems in which all components, regardless of supplier, work compatibly together. The case is compelling for using a system that is technologically versatile as a means of promoting company growth, as opposed to choking it. *Change Management and the Momentum of Open Systems*, a book by Christopher Jacobs and Mike Plako, provides a highly informed analysis of the value of open systems.[9]

ANALYZING INFRASTRUCTURE NEEDS

A company's infrastructure consists of the nonhuman assets and resources that provide its capability for operational performance. The assets are the property recorded in the company's balance sheet, and any unrecorded intellectual property, intangible assets, and leases, as well as the money available from an established but unused line of credit. The resources include customers, products, operational and technological processes, facilities, organizational structure, and suppliers of goods and services. The nature and extent of these assets and resources set boundaries on a company's competitive strength. Policy managers need to know clearly what assets and resources are important for their company to succeed in its core business strategy and to make sure they have what is needed when it is needed. They must also be able to obtain these assets and resources in as cost-effective a fashion as possible.

Financial needs are uniquely set by each company according to its ambition, mission, and ownership interests. Some businesses are thinly capitalized and depend on cash flow and bank loans for their operations. Others that are more securely capitalized have the financial leverage to undertake more ambitious plans. When significant growth is expected, it is essential to minimize future money constraints in advance. If a high debt-to-equity ratio is adopted as a financial strategy, future growth could be severely restricted unless sufficient cash flow is available. A heavy debt-service burden could also limit the investment needed in internal programs if the company is to act promptly on competitive threats or new market opportunities. Another consideration is whether the company's facilities should be owned or leased. Owning offers a more stable long-term environment, but it also reduces flexibility for the future. How management chooses to finance its company will in part set the bounds on its operations and market strategy.

What is the company's policy toward its suppliers? Some companies seek to exploit their suppliers by slow payment or strong-arm tactics to lower prices; these actions invariably alienate the supplier, and in times of short supply or when special efforts are needed, an alienated supplier is likely to be relatively uncooperative. On the other hand, prompt payment and a positive approach toward getting prices down engenders supplier loyalty. One company, for example, established a reputation for reliable and prompt payment with its overseas suppliers and was then able to dispense with letters of credit and move to open account payment status. This greatly simplified the customs entry procedures and also put a higher responsibility for product quality on the suppliers, because they would not be paid until after the received product was inspected.

ESTABLISHING OPERATIONAL POLICIES AND PROCESSES

Policies are management decisions that define the conditions and boundaries within which the business must operate. They are the do's and don'ts for operating activities. Operational policies encompass a broad spectrum of areas and situations. Managerial controls, in part established by policies and processes, are necessary to keep the company's activities within prescribed limits, and to comply with legal conditions as well as tax, insurance, lender, and other externally imposed requirements.

All the recurring work done in every company, both formal and informal, is usually performed within two kinds of explicit processes, operational or technological. Operational (business) processes relate to flow of work, information, communications, use of materials, and many other such matters; the time required to get things done, the kind of result obtained, and the cost of the operations are all affected by the quality of the operational processes in use. How these processes enhance work performance is of importance to the people involved. Unnecessarily burdensome operational processes are demoralizing, and they gravely dilute organizational vitality.

The company must be particularly sensitive in setting its people-related policies and processes: this means being specific and detailed about employment conditions, benefits, pay, performance reviews, code of conduct, and other such areas. It requires considerable creativity to make these matters easy for everyone to understand, without ambiguity and onerousness, while balancing the need to contain company legal liability. The people-related policies should be frequently reviewed to strengthen their contribution to organizational vitality.

Another key task is preparing the operational profit (budget) plan. This process begins by sales forecasting, and then every other area of the company develops its budget to conform to the needs of the forecasts. This is the most important vehicle for bringing financial information together and communicating the company's overall operational picture. This process has to be flexible enough to allow for important undertakings that emerge after the plan has been completed and approved.

Technological processes establish how certain specialized work is performed—for example, in product manufacturing or in mechanical, electrical, chemical or metallurgical transformations or tests. A company's technological processes are of a very specific nature, and they are often considered to be company resources. Nearly every product company wants to achieve marketplace advantage by developing unique technological processes that provide products or services of higher performance, lower cost, higher quality, greater uniformity, or other such advantages. Intel Corporation's chip-design methodology and photolithographic processes, for example, have set state-of-the-art levels for the integrated circuit industry. These processes provide Intel with exceptional market-position strength.

Virtually all policies and processes are control mechanisms. Each policy manager is responsible for maintaining effective controls while at the same time keeping the control mechanisms from burdening operating activity, organizational vitality, or innovation. Historically, controls in most companies have been both burdens and "handcuffs" because they are so easy to impose. Being organized seems to encourage this. Too often, companies focus on avoiding mistakes instead of promoting creative, timely accomplishment. These types of controls account for why most companies fail to achieve a very high level of organizational vitality. A certain degree of control is always necessary, but operating people should have as much freedom as possible for discretionary action.

SETTING POLICY ON EMPLOYEE COMPENSATION

Compensation comes in different forms. Salary is the most common form of base pay for all except those who are paid hourly, on commission, or within other individually defined arrangements. Salary is compensation for time, not performance; it is paid as long as one holds the job. The use of variable pay as a supplement to salary is growing because it can substitute, entirely or in part, for routine annual salary increases and thereby more closely links payroll expense to company performance. Under certain circumstances, variable pay, in the form of pay-for-performance, can be an incentive for improving individual or team performance.

The trend toward variable pay is partly based on the perception that merit salary increases, a common practice in most companies, have no incentive value and are usually not actually merit-based but made routinely as time-based annual salary increases. One convincing argument to replace routine salary increases with variable pay is that in an environment of global competition, a company must have productivity gains before it can afford higher payroll costs. Through compounding, a 5 percent "routine" annual salary increase raises base salary by 28 percent in five years, by 62 percent in ten years, and by over 100 percent in fifteen years. A paradox is that most recipients are generally unhappy most of the time with the size of their annual increases.

When a variable pay plan replaces routine salary increases, the company can adjust compensation in two ways: either on the basis of improved company performance, or by increasing salary through promotion or rewarding growth in individual job performance. Total pay can fluctuate, up and down, and therefore involves more employee risk. Psychologically, variable pay cuts two ways. Morale can be raised when the company is doing well and employees get large payouts; it is usually depressed when payouts fall or disappear. This morale problem, however, is generally less severe than the one that occurs from salary freezes or employment cutbacks (downsizing). Quite another issue arises when some individuals think they did their share toward meeting the group performance goals and were therefore not responsible for poorer group or company performance. This situation is normally ameliorated, case by case, by recognizing team or individual performance with one-time bonuses, as appropriate.

The extent to which variable pay is a motivational force is the subject of some controversy. Some managers think variable pay is a wasted expense because people should perform up to their capacity as a normal part of everyday job performance, and that pay in itself is not an incentive. Others think variable pay is a significant incentive and is crucial in achieving the highest level of performance. Perhaps transcending this difference of viewpoints is the fact that to have a genuine partnership culture, offering variable pay is not only the fair thing to do but a company obligation.

A company demonstrates its desire for fairness in compensation when all employees share in the fruits of improvement. Variable pay makes visible, in a tangible way, the rewarding of all employees for their contributions toward strengthening the company. One potentially useful form of variable pay is a company-wide gain-sharing plan. Usually these plans pay out directly in cash to all employees a defined fraction of company profit above a preset threshold. This can encourage employees to be more conscientious in learning, innovation, and overall job performance. Company-wide gain sharing also encourages peer pressure for the company's unity of cause. If managed effectively, variable pay can simultaneously benefit both employees and the business, enabling the company's people to believe they are indeed partners in the company's operations, and sharing in both risk and reward. Putting in place an attractive stock purchase plan for all employees also reinforces a partner relationship.

The benefits of variable pay will be elusive, however, until a company-wide team esprit develops and each person feels accountable for improving company performance and converging around the company's unity of cause. When these two conditions are present, people appreciate the benefits of variable pay and become challenged by the opportunity. Increasingly, managers are realizing that when part of a company's payroll cost is variable rather than fixed, the dynamic created minimizes profit fluctuations and reduces the need for future employment downsizing. Substituting variable pay for time-based salary increases may also be an essential ingredient for maintaining long-term employment stability.

Compensating Policy Managers

The discussion above applies to all company employees, but policy management compensation needs additional consideration. The CEO and other policy-level managers are the core group on whose decisions and actions the company's performance primarily depends. Their compensation is therefore at a substantially higher level than that of other employees. Managerial compensation normally consists of salary, variable pay, and some form of equity participation. The variable pay is usually in the form of pay-for-performance, issued annually in cash or in a combination of cash and company stock. The amount paid is directly related to company performance. Equity participation is in the form of stock options, restricted stock, or occasionally some form of phantom stock.

The compensation package for a CEO is established by the board of directors, and the package for the other policy managers is usually similar in components but on a smaller scale. The salary considerations for policy managers are relatively straightforward; the only real question is usually at what level to set the CEO's salary. Once that is set, the salary for the others is normally established by ratio and qualitative adjustments. As a means of keeping the company's fixed costs as low as possible, the most important component of cash compensation for policy managers should be pay-for-performance. Salaries should be kept on the low end of a competitive scale, and any annual increases should be in line percentage-wise with those given nonmanagers.

Designing Variable Pay Plans for Policy Managers

Historically, variable-pay plans for policy managers were simple annual bonus plans, often tied to their function, not company, performance. This arrangement encourages self-centered short-term thinking. Variable pay for *all* policy managers should be determined in large part by a formula that measures company, not function, financial performance. This pay should range from nothing for minimum acceptable company performance to an amount that can well exceed base salary for exceptional performance. Some part of variable pay should be devoted to compensate for specific individual accomplishments that are not easily measurable by company financial performance. The time frame for determining variable pay should be several years, not annually, but a payment should be made annually.

The first step, in consultation with other policy executives and the compensation committee of the board of directors, is for the CEO to articulate a clear and concise written pay-for-performance plan for managers. This plan should also specify the philosophy that underlies it. It should be acceptable to the executives involved and should reflect the need for important company performance before there is a large payout.

The formula used to calculate performance pay should be as simple as possible, with the intent to pay in relation to consistent growth in company financial performance over several years. Without consistency, management efficacy cannot be confirmed. One way to incorporate consistency into annual payments is through the use of a three-year rolling average of the formula calculation. Performance averaging discourages short-term thinking; it also discourages executives who plan to stay with a company for only a short period. Obviously, even a three-year period is only near term, not long term. The long-term aspect of compensation is equity participation, not variable pay.

It is impossible to define an ideal plan and formula; each company's plan has to be tailored to its own size and operational circumstances. However, all policy executives, including the CEO, should be paid using the same performance parameters to encourage team thinking and actions. Here are some guidelines for an approach that offers both a carrot and a stick.

- Simplicity should be the keynote, with no more than two performance parameters
- One parameter should measure company growth, perhaps revenue margin
- The other parameter should measure profitability, perhaps return on net assets
- Payout should be averaged over a rolling three-year performance period
- A penalty should be incurred for inconsistent year-to-year growth

The pool of funds available to compensate managers in this fashion is best determined by setting a corporate maximum for cash compensation (salary plus variable pay) as a percentage of operating profit. This structure keeps the total compensation within reasonable bounds and encourages managers to produce growth in operating profit. The pool should be divided into two portions, with the principal portion paid according to the formula and paid pro rata to salary to each person. The balance of the pool should be paid according to the exceptional contributions of each manager.

Equity Participation

The equity component of managerial compensation is intended to sustain a long-term horizon for management decisions and actions. To keep management interests aligned with those of shareholders, probably the most important form of executive compensation is providing key top executives the opportunity to make a relative large amount of money though equity participation in the company. Each company's board of directors has to decide on the nature of an equity participation plan and the intrinsic value of the plan to the executives. The board is responsible for making sure that management's focus is on long-term company strength, and that they gain personally only when this strength has been demonstrated. Mediocre company performance should not be rewarded in large payouts either from variable pay or equity plans.

Few if any management compensation plans will please all participants. The best that can be hoped for is to develop a fair and reasonable plan that will keep most people satisfied most of the time. While the principles of variable pay and equity compensation plans can stay relatively constant, changing circumstances both within and outside the company usually require occasional revision of the plan's details. One issue in all variable pay and equity plans is that people often consider salary as an entitlement and want incentive pay to compensate them for routine rather than superior performance. Another issue is that sometimes managers work to optimize their personal pay rather than the company's long-term performance. All executive compensation programs carry the potential for abuse if substantial payouts are available without commensurate growth in value for shareholders. Only the board of directors can ensure that the magnitude of executives' gains is kept relative to the growth of the company's financial performance. The board does this by setting specific terms and conditions that prevent abuse.

It is helpful to keep in mind that variable pay and equity plans cannot make people more intelligent or more creative or change their ethos or demeanor. The incentives can, however, inspire them to work harder, more cooperatively, and more diligently.

PRODUCTIVITY

A crucial part of a company's operations strategy should be to achieve regular productivity gains in its operations and its use of resources. This aspect of operational strategy is the subject of the next chapter.

NOTES

1. The comment was made at a meeting of the American Electronics Association on April 20, 1995, in Burlington, Mass.

2. Michel Robert, *Strategy Pure and Simple*. New York: McGraw-Hill, 1993, p. 19.

3. Henry Mintzberg, "The Fall and Rise of Strategic Planning," *Harvard Business Review*, January-February 1994.

4. Peter F. Drucker, *Management: Tasks, Responsibilities and Practices*. New York: Harper & Row, 1973, p. 77.

5. Robert H. Waterman, Jr., *The Renewal Factor*. New York: Bantam, 1987, p. 12.

6. Peter F. Drucker, *Management: Tasks, Responsibilities, Practices*. New York: Harper & Row, 1973, p. 368.

7. Jay Halfond, associate dean of the College of Business Administration at Northeastern University, in "Facing Up to Ethical Decisions," *Boston Globe,* October 14, 1993.

8. Robert Simons, *Levers of Control: How Managers Use Innovative Control Systems to Drive Strategic Renewal*. Cambridge, Mass.: Harvard Business School Press, 1995.

9. Christopher Jacobs and Mike Placko, *Change Management and the Momentum of Open Systems*. X/Open Company Ltd. (Reading RG1 1AX, U.K.), 1995. Prentice Hall, Upper Saddle River, N.J., is the U.S. distributor.

## CHAPTER 8

Productivity Gain

An Ongoing Strategic Need

THE TRANSFORMATION OF WORK

The concept of continuously improving productivity in work has been with us, in some form, since humans began using tools. Whenever something has to be done, there is a natural tendency to want to find the easiest, most effective, least expensive, and fastest way to get it done. It is commonplace for new methodologies, skills, and tools to be sought out, tried, and refined. And when a particular process is repeated often, the need to find the most productive approach to it becomes more urgent.

According to Drucker, important productivity improvement in manufacturing began in 1881, when Fredrick Winslow Taylor first applied knowledge to the study, analysis, and engineering of work. By 1930, the foundation set up by Taylor for manufacturing productivity was in common use in the developed countries. Drucker credits this productivity revolution, which was advanced dramatically by Taylor's efforts, with raising the standard of living for blue-collar workers, and thereby with the failure of Marxism in the highly developed countries. Drucker notes:

> Within a few years after Taylor began to apply knowledge to work, productivity began to rise at a rate of 3.5 to 4 percent compounded a year which means doubling every eighteen years or so. Since Taylor began, productivity has increased some fifty fold in all advanced countries. On this unprecedented expansion rests all the increases in both standard of living and quality of life in the developed countries.[1]

Taylor's approach, as expounded in his *Scientific Management*, is now largely obsolete, although some of his concepts, which call for studied methods, harmony, cooperation, training, learning, and worker prosperity, remain valid.[2]

Drucker has further pointed out that when Taylor began his work, nine of ten working people did manual labor, making or moving things, in manufacturing, farming, mining, and transportation. By 1990, this category of worker had been reduced to about one fifth of the work force. Drucker predicts that by 2010 it will form no more than one tenth. The earlier productivity revolution is over, he observes, and "from now on, what matters is the productivity of non-manual workers. And that requires applying knowledge to knowledge....In knowledge and service work, partnership with the responsible worker is the only way to improve productivity. Nothing else works at all."[3] The "non-manual workers" are those involved in intellectual activities, and they include managers, professionals, service providers, and many other employees.

THE NATURE OF PRODUCTIVITY

In business, productivity refers to an output relative to an input of resources and time consumed. It is a measure of the efficacy of a particular activity or a combination of activities. The time required to achieve a particular output is a vital factor, often more important than money. For many situations, either output or input, or both, are qualitative, and it requires judgment to assess productivity. The most complex kind of productivity to evaluate is that which applies to generating knowledge and ideas.

A classic example of attempting to increase productivity is seeking economy of scale. Investing to increase production capacity, lower unit cost, or raise quality can, in the right market situations, return enough higher revenue margin to pay the investment costs and deliver increased operating profit as well. Aerovox Incorporated did this in their Aeromet II product line of wound capacitors. By redesigning the product and using automated production, Aerovox increased its capacity and lowered its costs to the point where manufacturing in the United States could compete with similar products produced in Mexico with lower-cost labor.

Certain productivity improvement does not directly relate to cost or time. An example is improved customer service that costs more, but delivers greater customer satisfaction. That in turn can lead to higher revenue margin through a stronger competitive posture. In this case, the gain occurs in a location and at a time other than where and when the cost was incurred. I call this *transference productivity gain*. Unfortunately, this kind of productivity gain is often not sought out, because it takes a company-wide perspective and is generally not easily measurable by using standard return-on-investment (ROI) analysis techniques.

If a company's productivity is not high enough, its profit will not be high enough. To maximize financial performance, productivity gain has to be pursued alongside market-position strength and organizational vitality. Often gains in company productivity are essential just to keep cost structures in line with changing conditions in the marketplace.

PRODUCTIVITY GAIN

Every business needs routinely to raise productivity in its operations and its use of resources if it is to deliver sufficient value to customers, employees, and shareholders. The first priority is value to customers, which is essential to obtain profitable sales orders; without them the other two values cannot be achieved. Value to employees, the next priority, means interesting jobs, stable employment, and the opportunity to grow in personal competency and income. These conditions are at the heart of a company's organizational vitality. Value to shareholders is attained through growth in the company's net income and cash flow. This multiple-value outcome, the primary measure of management effectiveness, can be sustained only if revenue-margin growth is high enough and there is continuous gain in company-wide productivity.

Figure 8-1 graphically expresses the interrelationship between these values and productivity gain. If growth in value for the stakeholders is not concurrent and consistent, then the company's revenue margin is too low, or its overall costs are too high, or both. In either situation, productivity gain is called for in the company's operations. If a company is to be highly productive, its people, processes, resource use, and management need to be synergistically productive.

Activities in any part of a company that do not contribute to meeting an-

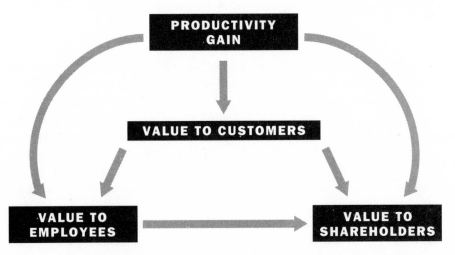

Figure 8-1: Productivity Gain Objectives

chorpoint objectives need careful scrutiny and perhaps elimination. Activities that do contribute need to be analyzed frequently to find ways of achieving productivity gain.

Achieving regular gains in company productivity is a key aspect of the policy manager's job. Yet most managers find it difficult when they are in the mainstream of daily activity to step back and look objectively at productivity, which they might regard as a somewhat abstract consideration; just getting the daily work done is often challenge enough. This shortsightedness is not necessarily the fault of the managers per se. It is the fault of the approach used in managing. When management structure is involvement oriented, the managers' direct presence in daily activity is greatly reduced, and their efforts can be concentrated on strengthening the company. One aspect of this strengthening is ongoing productivity gain. The importance of productivity gain relates not only to considerations of efficiency or cost effectiveness, although these are important, but to the basic issue of the company's performance in its marketplace. Improving market-position strength depends directly on regularly achieving productivity gain in all activities that involve revenue generation and product development.

IMPROVING PROCESS PRODUCTIVITY

All companies, regardless of structure, use operational processes to carry out daily activities. The core processes that are important to every company include:

- Sales order acquisition
- Order fulfillment
- Customer services
- Cencon system

- Product development
- Strategy development
- Company management
- Administration

In the past, under a functionally structured vertical hierarchy, work performed in function groups was not usually regarded as part of a company-wide core process. This isolation led to many operational problems and inefficiencies. Organizing essential work within a natural core process usually reveals ways to simplify the work flow and improve decisions and actions, thereby improving productivity. Organizationally, one policy manager should have oversight accountability for an entire core process area. The CEO should oversee company management and strategy development, but every policy manager has to be a team contributor to improvement of company performance in all these process areas.

Process improvement is a fertile ground for making gains in productivity, and thereby in stakeholder value growth. Every process, technological or operational, in every capability center is a candidate for improvement. Most companies place a much lower priority on improving operational processes than they do on technological processes, usually because the potential gains are not as easily measured. In addition, most smaller companies lack the staff support for analyzing and designing operational processes. These problems need to be addressed, as the collective productivity gains from improving operational processes can be substantial. Focusing on the processes and people that interface with customers is a critical area for consideration. If these processes are inadequate, or the people who perform within them are less than superior, either can cause lost marketplace opportunities and dissatisfied customers.

Resistance to making improvements in operational processes almost always occurs because the daily activities have to go on whether or not they are performed in the most effective way. NIH ("not invented here") and defense of the status quo can also be difficult to overcome. Changing a process almost always requires phasing in the new while phasing out the old. This demands redundant effort, and in the short term, more time spent by the operating people. For desired change to take place in a manner that produces permanent gain, the leadership has to be persistent, diplomatic, and sometimes tough.

Management processes are operational processes, and they too should be part of the search for productivity improvement. Company management and strategy development activities contain some of the most important core processes, as it is here that basic decisions are made and priorities for company actions determined. Unless powerful ideas emerge from these processes, management's activities will fail to generate the necessary momentum in all the company's capability centers. There are important rewards to be gained by examining how management processes, whether formal or informal, now work, their inherent strengths and weaknesses, and thinking through how the company's overall management can be changed to produce much greater accomplishment.

The operational and communication processes in a company's revenue-generation activities involve considerable cost and are therefore prime targets for creative redesign toward both lowering operating costs and raising operating effectiveness. Flexible, low-cost, fast-throughput manufacturing, when it is superior to that of competitors, can be a market-position advantage. So can a focused, highly competent sales organization. Achieving and holding such advantages means making ongoing gains in productivity that take place sooner and more consistently than gains being made by competitors.

Reaching and retaining market-position leadership by rapid product development is an essential strategic need for nearly all companies. If product development is to be a core competency, the process itself requires high productivity. In the recent past, some companies have been able to reduce by half or more the time needed from concept to market for their improved or totally new products. Attaining productivity gain in this area needs more than time reduction; however, the investments made, or to be made, in product and technology development need careful management review on the merit of each project. Marginal undertakings need to be routinely eliminated so that funds can be kept concentrated on the most important projects.

Progress on product development projects is normally neither linear nor easily predictable. While projects are underway, there is usually optimism about the outcome, but few reliable yardsticks. Throwing money at the problems, particularly by adding more people, is not usually helpful. The results of development projects depend on the creativity of the people involved and their intimate awareness of marketplace needs. The keys to development success are having the right people on each project, minimizing time to completion, and using a project management approach like concurrent engineering. Cost for development is always important, but the time taken to satisfactorily complete a project is usually even more so, for delays have great impacts on profit down the line.

Linking time and cost to complete a project with the financial benefit gained is relatively easy after the fact, when specific results are available to measure results. If the time span from project start to finish is quite long, however, there may be no meaningful interim measures of productivity. Hewlett-Packard (HP) has established a metric that helps monitor the new product development projects of interfunctional teams. HP calls it the Return Map and has been using it since 1987. The company has found it so simple and elegant that it has become a staple in the product development cycle. The Return Map graphically represents the team's forecasted achievement in terms of time and money. It shows the return or profit from the development investment, along with the time to develop the product, introduce it, and achieve the financial return in the market.

The company reports that the map's greatest virtue is not in what it says so much as in what it does. It provides a goal and measure for all functions and thus shifts the team's focus from "Who is responsible?" to "What needs to get done?" Even more important, the map forces members of the team to estimate and reestimate the time and money it will take to complete their tasks and the impact of their actions on overall project success. Giving a comprehensive picture of the common task helps create the only discipline that works, namely self-discipline.[4]

Administration processes are usually not a high priority for improvement, because on the surface they offer only modest opportunities for productivity gain. However, since they reach into every capability center in the company, these processes have an important impact on overall company productivity. Simply minimizing centrally imposed red tape is a substantial advance.

The cencon system is of critical importance to every company's operational efficacy. Most organizations will face major transitions over the next decade in how their information systems operate and integrate into their management, operational, and technological processes. As technology makes possible more effective methods of communicating, the way source data is collected, analyzed, condensed, and distributed to the appropriate people will undergo radical change. During this information revolution, holding market-position strength demands important and continuous productivity gains in knowledge development and decision making throughout the company. In certain instances, knowledge productivity may be the key to attaining marketplace advantage. A fundamental objective of cencon and intraprocess communications is to keep the information-processing technology in the background while providing easy-to-use, reliable tools for information users.

To make productivity gain a company core competency and thereby a marketplace advantage, a company needs to improve its processes more rapidly than its competitors improve theirs. Strengthening a company's competitive posture while simultaneously reducing costs means achieving regular gains in productivity in core processes. As in so many of the dynamics we are examining here, important productivity gain is often necessary just to remain competitive.

CYCLE TIME REDUCTION

The momentum drivers considered in chapter 4 are aimed at increasing the innovativeness and utility of company accomplishments. Another aspect of momentum building, shortening the time interval for accomplishment, is also relevant, particularly for companies that have not paid close attention in the past to the cycle times in their core operational or technology processes. Cycle-time reduction (time compression) in processes can usually provide large one-time productivity gains. Every company uses many such processes. Boruch B. Frusztajer has observed:

> I have found that "cycle time" is one of the best if not the best indicator of production efficiency. It is a very sensitive indicator of material control, scrap rates, machine loading, state of equipment, operator training, and even absenteeism. It is certainly very effective in monitoring and in controlling manufacturing operations. It is a simple indicator that can describe the state of the manufacturing line without a long analysis of voluminous data.[5]

Equally important is reducing cycle time for new product or process development. Success in the market often depends on being the first out with products that feature important innovation. A new or improved product introduced ahead of competition usually produces more output value (revenue margin) than if it appears later. If the time from concept to market for the new product has been kept short, the cost to develop it is also likely to be less. But even if the cost is higher, introducing it earlier still could deliver higher revenue margin.

Saving time in performing any company activity can be important in building market-position strength. One essential ingredient in seeking marketplace advantage is responsiveness to customers. If the company can compress the time necessary to perform all the activities involved in obtaining and delivering customer orders, customer satisfaction will increase and the result usually will be cost-effective for the company. According to George Stalk, Jr., and Thomas Hout, "Time-compression allows an organization to improve on all dimensions: cost, variety, speed, and innovation."[6] Their book provides many suggestions for competing effectively on responsiveness as well as on value and cost. Joseph D. Blackburn, editor of and a contributor to the book *Time-Based Competition*, provides a useful perspective on what has been learned from the Asians on the subject of time compression, principally in the processes involved in manufacturing and product development. The book focuses on "how to do it for the would-be time-focused competitor."[7]

REENGINEERING

Many of the operational processes used in today's businesses are under attack as being inefficient and hindering conscientious people from doing a good job. The early 1990s saw the popular use of an approach commonly called reengineering (or reinventing, redesigning, transforming), a technique intended to improve productivity in operations processes. A number of people believed reengineering was the way to make easy, fast, large gains in company profitability.

Reengineering calls for defining the result needed and then creatively finding the simplest way to get the job done, without regard to how it is currently being done or to traditionally accepted methodology for work organization. Activities that do not add or create value, as well as work flow that is slow and cumbersome, are modified or eliminated. Benchmark goals are a key focus. In their book about reengineering, Michael Hammer and James Champy urge companies to consider radical change, not just incremental improvement. Their message is to start over, eliminate functional structure, and redesign processes completely so they focus on serving the customer. Automating without changing existing processes is a mistake, they say; the processes first need to be reengineered.[8]

Reengineering or any other way of redesigning processes and structure can often provide important productivity gain in company operations. It can also introduce serious problems if the effort is not sensitive to the many issues that affect the people involved. Process change for improvement is frequently necessary, but it must take place in concert with actions to build organizational vitality. The most powerful success factors are still intellectual power, creativity, and élan.

Whether radical change is necessary, of course, depends on the nature of a company's existing problems. Nevertheless, except in crisis situations, it is always unwise to undertake major process reengineering programs aimed at short-term radical change, as the problems such programs cause may be worse than the solutions they provide. When productivity gain becomes a routine part of momentum plans and actions, the company should have no future need for radical reengineering programs.

PEOPLE PRODUCTIVITY

The two separate aspects of productivity gain, process and people, must be considered simultaneously for productivity gain to be maximized. Although the process issues are involved and often costly, they are usually the more straightforward to consider and act on, mostly because there are no certain methods for raising an individual's productivity, or maintaining it when it is already high. Individual attitudes, formed in part by the company culture, shape the behavior and work habits of the company's people. Because their attitudes and behaviors can change quickly as situations change inside and outside the company, managers must stay alert to their concerns.

Many employees are reluctant to take initiatives aimed at improving productivity because they believe doing so will lead to job loss for either themselves or their associates. This is a well-founded fear, as such job loss has indeed been the case in many companies. Usually it is necessary to recognize this reluctance and find ways to alleviate the employee's fear to attain serious cooperation in improving productivity.

Productivity is measured by what gets done, how well it is done, the time it takes, and the cost to do it. For all companies, payroll, which includes cost for related benefits and taxes, is a major expense, and the overall company productivity obtained from payroll cost is of critical importance. The momentum indicators described in chapter 3 provide ways to measure effectiveness and illuminate the areas needing attention.

The starting point for knowing how to raise individual productivity is to understand people's attitudes. This means paying attention, observing, asking questions, frequently evaluating performance, and providing feedback and guidance. Once attitudes are well understood, the path to raising productivity should be clearer so barriers to work performance can be eliminated. It is valuable here to offer the means for developing the competency of individuals, as well as adding useful tools to enhance their productivity. On a continuing basis, Three Dimensional Management calls for increasing individual contributions by way of greater accountability, process improvements, and competency growth.

Every manager needs to be concerned about a new employee's contribution to company performance relative to his or her payroll expense. It is no small matter to add permanent people to payroll, because it causes a ripple effect in expense: insurance and payroll taxes are added; furniture and equipment expenditures take place; supplies, telephone, and similar expenses rise; and demand is increased for internal services. The added payroll and related indirect costs become a semipermanent company expense. Again, finding the proper balance is essential; working too lean for the sake of economy can also cause serious problems in the form of reduced organizational vitality, lost marketplace opportunities, or other elusive matters that do not show up in reports.

Historically, most companies have routinely granted annual salary increases. Because the simple passage of time is not relevant to a company's capacity to take on higher payroll costs, this is not a sound policy. Instead, people who make an important and growing contribution to company performance should be properly and frequently recognized through increased compensation; those who make a consistently acceptable contribution should be encouraged to expand it before they receive an increase; and those who underperform should be firmly guided toward either improvement or departure.

IBM made a radical change in compensation priority in 1994 when they revised their salesperson compensation policy. Previously, the company paid commissions on the basis of sales-order dollar value. The new commission arrangement is based 60 percent on order profitability and 40 percent on customer satisfaction. Whether these are the right weighing factors is debatable, but the parameters of order profitability and customer satisfaction are directly on target.[9]

One major cause of the extensive downsizing undertaken by many firms starting in the 1980s was that payroll expense had become bloated by many previous years of granting routine, unproductive annual increases, and by the overhiring of both managers and nonmanagers. Given this bloating, it became painfully necessary to terminate people who had become excessively expensive relative to the value of their job contribution. If downsizing trauma is to be avoided, the only workable long-term approach for both a company and its people is to prevent payroll bloating from occurring in the first place. The fairest path for all concerned is to share operating profit as a routine compensation technique and substitute for time-based salary increases. Since the profit to be shared has to be continuously re-earned by the company, the entire organization should become more focused on the anchorpoint objectives.

People are involved in every operational process and every other aspect of operations; an essential part of productivity improvement is thus investing in the development of people and bringing in new people with new competencies where appropriate.

IMPROVING PRODUCTIVITY IN MANAGEMENT

Every CEO must ask: How productive is our management? How can we raise its effectiveness and reduce its cost as a percentage of operating profit? These are questions that are rarely asked by a board of directors and usually avoided by top management. Certainly no accounting report shows the cost of management, but to exclude it from the spotlight of productivity analysis is to hobble a company's momentum, for the direct money-cost of management is significant. An involvement-oriented organization should aim for the least possible number of people in management. As managers bear total accountability for company performance, their compensation has to be substantial, but it also must be centered on pay for performance, equity gain, and few perquisites. As a company grows, management cost should be a declining percentage of operating profit.

In the absence of a serious company problem, the process of judging effectiveness of individual policy managers, including the CEO, is often superficial. It is up to the board of directors, in conjunction with the CEO, to see that such evaluations routinely take place in a way that managers know they are expected to register real improvement in their own productivity. The first step is to look carefully at the process now in use for managerial performance evaluation.

DOWNSIZING: A PRESCRIPTION WITH DANGEROUS SIDE EFFECTS

Organizations offer a variety of explanations for employment downsizing. This drastic measure to reduce costs is usually necessary in situations where structural changes occur in a marketplace, a prime example of which is the defense spending cutbacks that began following the end of the cold war. Downsizing may also be necessary because of the redundancy sometimes produced when two companies merge. In most other situations, however, although employment downsizing can be a fast route to short-term profit improvement, it can also be the source of a serious long-term setback. Almost always, once downsizing is announced, a company's organizational vitality takes a nose dive, its productivity declines, and the company's momentum drops. When this happens, the only important long-term path to success, cost control through productivity gain, becomes entirely sidetracked. In business, cost control is fundamentally an issue of productivity, not payroll. Rarely do top managers perceive a current need for urgent cost-cutting as a prior failure on their part to obtain timely gains in productivity, yet this is usually the case.

When cost reduction is necessary, the first concern should be retaining the company's core competencies. These competencies are the source of future revenue margin, and they need to be protected and expanded. The managerial challenge is how to retain market-position strength and an overall company cost structure that supports the right people and infrastructure to create value for customers, employees, and shareholders. The only route that protects the company's long-term capabilities is not simply removing costs, but designing them out.

BIG STEPS, SMALL STEPS

Using what he called Pareto's principle, Juran has long been an advocate of separating action priorities into two categories: the *vital few* and the *secondary (trivial) many*. The vital few, the few actions that will make the most difference, are the primary targets for breakthrough undertakings, those that require important innovation. The secondary many, individually less important but collectively significant, become the targets of routine, everyday improvement efforts.[10]

Big productivity gains generally come from fresh ideas, and the source of these ideas is creative people in key positions. To nourish this kind of creativity, managers must simplify organizational structure, information flow, policies, and all the other techniques that promote higher organizational vitality. Fresh ideas can lead to vital redesign of product and process, creating more appropriate tools and raised competency levels. Some companies have experienced dramatic reductions in product throughput time and inventories after changing to a JIT (just-in-time) manufacturing approach. Others have achieved gains when they redesigned their order fulfillment processes, which included order scheduling and tracking, production management and flow, purchasing, and inventory control. Still others have redesigned their sales processes, including selling, product management, and customer services, as the path to major steps in operational improvements.

The kind of small steps Juran refers to are gains made by routinely improving the way daily work is conducted. When they are taken frequently and routinely, small steps over time can add up to important gains, even though each step individually might not be very important or even measurable. Masaaki Imai credits the Japanese concept of *kaizen*, "improvement," as a primary factor in the immense progress Japanese manufacturers have made toward building global markets for their products. The culture within these companies both embodies and practices ongoing improvement, which involves everyone—top management, managers, and workers. Imai points out that *kaizen* starts with the recognition that every corporation has problems, and that the *kaizen* culture is one in which everyone can freely admit to them. Once the problems are acknowledged, solutions become more apparent; the company culture encourages high productivity coupled with high quality and low cost.[11]

Three Dimensional Management assumes that every policy, process, and procedure is subject to improvement by making changes that raise performance or quality, reduce time, or lower cost. The gains made rely on a company culture in which all people are constructively critical of the things they do and look for improved ways of doing them. Each policy manager and capability center manager or team leader has the task of instilling the value of continuous improvement, making it a part of the company culture. Keeping track of specific improvements in each capability center will take different forms, as will the rewards to those who make the improvements. One vital part of encouraging the right mindset for everyone is recognizing team and individual achievements in financial and nonfinancial ways, particularly the latter. This includes regularly preparing a summary of achievements in each capability center and the company as a whole, and communicating these widely. They reinforce support for the company's unity of cause as well as commend those who are outstanding contributors to it.

Managers must routinely encourage people to look at how they do things with an eye toward improving quality, quantity, time, or cost. This kind of guidance usually falls on deaf ears, however, unless a high level of organizational vitality is in force. Even then, each person's sense of accountability needs to be high; making improvements means making changes which, at least temporarily, may impose added burdens while the transition in work methods takes place.

RESOURCE PRODUCTIVITY

Other than people, such resources as money, facilities, and equipment all have an ongoing cost, which collectively can be sizable. Utilization of these resources needs periodic examination against tough standards to find if there are ways to make them more productive.

Companies generally use a capital budgeting process to guide them in investing money in leases and physical assets. The usual basis for capital budget approval is return on investment analysis (ROI). Relying narrowly on ROI, which is often inaccurate, can obscure the real issue, however: the underlying assumptions that are creating the need. Carefully analyzing these factors, which are often more qualitative than quantitative, can sometimes lead to alternative approaches that are less expensive, more flexible, or more effective. In the same way, relying heavily on any formula approach obscures the possibility of many worthwhile investments from which return is not easily quantified.

Careful decisions about automating are of particular importance in analyzing resource productivity. Some companies look only at the gain to be made by automation and neglect to consider the loss of flexibility. The extensively automated approach for auto production that General Motors undertook in the 1980s to reduce costs proved to be far more expensive than anticipated because of the inflexibility of the new production modes. New car designs that required different facilities and equipment for market competitiveness rendered many of the company's previous investments obsolete. In contrast, Toyota pioneered "lean production," which, while automated in part, was based not on producing a particular vehicle at the lowest cost, but on flexible use of facilities and equipment for producing many different car models.[12]

A human factor is also involved in deciding how to invest in and utilize non-human resources. Modern, clean, and pleasant surroundings influence how people think about the company and the attractiveness of their jobs. Inadequate or unattractive facilities and equipment can cause low morale, difficulty in hiring highly competent people, and the departure of valued employees. The attractiveness of the working environment affects people's productivity as well as reflecting on the company's image and reputation with customers, suppliers, and others.

OUTSOURCING

Sometimes the most effective path for achieving higher company productivity is finding alternative approaches to operations, such as outsourcing. The facilities and people necessary when work is performed in-house are unnecessary when the work is put outside under contract. In manufacturing, subassemblies or sometimes complete products can be effectively outsourced. Some administrative functions such as payroll, insurance, and benefits are also prime areas for outsourcing. Managers should explicitly review the company's operations for outsourcing possibilities on a routine basis, especially before leases come up for renewal.

Every company depends on outside suppliers for materials and services of various kinds. These organizations and their people are essential to a company's smooth operations, and often to the quality and availability of its product. In spite of the critical role suppliers play, most companies do not treat them very well. Delaying payments to suppliers is commonplace, for example. Treating suppliers as friends has genuine benefits. Suppliers who enjoy a personal relationship with a company usually put out much more effort to ensure quality and on-time deliveries. When supply shortages occur, the friendly customers get priority. A strong buyer/seller relationship, also offers the possibility of "partnering."

CASH PRODUCTIVITY: MANAGERS AND SPENDING

A well-established axiom of management is that *cash flow equals survival.* A corollary could be: *maximizing cash flow is essential for company strengthening.* Some very successful executives consider cash flow a key measure of company performance. Dennis Dammerman, CFO of General Electric, has observed, "If I could have only two measurements, the two I would choose would be customer satisfaction and cash flow."[13]

The productive use of cash includes three critical areas: cash management, cash flow management, and spending management. Cash management describes how cash is handled once it has been received. This activity takes place under the watchful eye of the company's chief financial officer or treasurer, and it is rarely a problem. Cash flow management refers to working capital and policies for noncash expenses such as depreciation. Spending management refers to the control of expenses and investments in assets. These latter two areas have to be the concern of everyone on the policy management team.

All managers need a pragmatic understanding about how cash is generated in a business. From an accountant's viewpoint, cash flow can be a relatively complex subject, as it is affected not only by operations but also by various kinds of transactions in financial and investment accounts. Our purpose here is to consider only *free operational cash flow*, which is net income plus noncash expense less cash invested in working capital and fixed and intangible assets. Free cash is all cash generated by operations that is not required in operations.

For many companies, working capital is the largest balance-sheet asset and the principal location of their invested cash. If a company finds ways to achieve permanent reductions in inventories, particularly those in process, this can improve both cash utilization and reduce overhead costs. Receivables are a less likely area in which to reduce cash investment because of the need to grant credit to customers. Managers must be constantly sensitive to potential defaults in receivables, however, and to the possibility of inventory obsolescence.

The budgeting process in most businesses sets allowable spending levels. Managers should consider these limits only as authorization to spend, not a license to spend to the limit. Spending below budget should be a goal, not a penalty. The attitude "if you don't spend it you will lose it in the next budget plan" needs to be eliminated.

Most companies are careful with cash in nearly every area except when they decide to hire employees. Often, when things are going well, the quick solution to a short-term problem is to hire someone. When the problem passes, the employee usually remains and the payroll goes on. This syndrome is an important reason why companies become overloaded with payroll expense and are then faced with issuing pink slips during a downturn in business. An essential part of spending management is to set and abide by tough standards for justifying new permanent employees, based on long-term need, not short-term pressures.

Investing in the development of people, products, and other areas is intended to create future value for the company. Often the result of the investment will not be seen for a long time, and there is no certainty that the seeds planted will produce flowers. Cash use in any company is a risk-taking judgment call, and there has to be room in spending authorizations for intuitive and judicious actions that might lead to worthwhile strengthening, even when justification is hard to establish.

MINIMIZING PRODUCTIVITY LOSS

The other side of productivity gain is minimizing productivity loss. A company's productivity level is affected by many everyday matters; lost time from a control approach that requires many sign-offs before action takes place, for example, is a built-in loss in productivity. This kind of overcontrol reduces initiative and sends the message that costly time delay is routinely acceptable. Two other obvious examples are frequent absenteeism and personnel turnover. Other common problems that cause lost productivity are low morale, complacency, errors in operations, late shipments, equipment failures, suppliers missing delivery schedules, and defective materials.

When people who are experienced and doing well leave their jobs, whether to leave the company or to transfer within it, the area from which the departure took place suffers a loss of company competency. This loss may be alleviated in a variety of ways, but for a period of time it usually causes reduced operational productivity.

Collectively, the total productivity loss from many such problem sources can be quite high. Most are avoidable, but since their impact is not easily measured, their real cost is hidden and therefore usually ignored. When they cause a loss of customers, the company's financially measured productivity can take a deep dive.

NOTES

1. Peter F. Drucker, *Post-Capitalist Society*. New York: HarperCollins, 1993, p. 38.

2. Fredrick Winslow Taylor, *Scientific Management*. New York: Harper & Row, 1947. This book is a compilation of separate works first published in 1911.

3. Peter F. Drucker, *Post-Capitalist Society*, p. 40.

4. Charles H. House and Raymond L. Price, "The Return Map: Tracking Product Teams," *Harvard Business Review*, January-February 1991.

5. Personal correspondence, Boruch B. Frusztajer, president and CEO, BBF Corporation, Waltham, Mass.

6. George Stalk, Jr., and Thomas M. Hout, *Competing Against Time*. New York: Free Press, 1990, p. 58.

7. Joseph D. Blackburn, *Time-Based Competition*. Chicago: Richard D. Irwin, 1991, p. 22.

8. Michael Hammer and James Champy, *Reengineering the Corporation*. New York: Harper Business, 1993.

9. "IBM Leans on Its Sales Force," *Business Week*, February 7, 1994.

10. Joseph M. Juran, *Managerial Breakthrough*. New York: McGraw-Hill 1964. Juran named Pareto principle after the economist and sociologist Vilfredo Pareto. It is sometimes called the 20/80 rule, which holds that 20 percent of the items in a situation account for 80 percent of the outcome.

11. Masaaki Imai, *Kaizen*. New York: McGraw-Hill, 1986.

12. James P. Womack and Daniel T. Jones, *The Machine That Changed the World*. New York: HarperCollins, 1991.

13. "Fast Times at General Electric," *CFO*, June 1995, p. 33.

CHAPTER 9

Market Strategy

The Roadmap for Market Positioning

THINKING STRATEGICALLY
ABOUT MARKET POSITIONING

Together, market and operations strategy set a company's core business strategy. If they can be made synergistically reinforcing, they can be the basis for lasting company strength.

The purpose of market strategy is to provide a clear direction for achieving market-position strength. This strategy must set the path for achieving continuous, important, long-term growth in revenue margin. Setting a clear direction for winning market-position strength starts with knowing the company's momentum today and carefully assessing the marketplace environment the company is likely to face in the future. Some basic question to be addressed in these thinking-through sessions are:

- Is the company at or beyond the "critical mass" needed to be a leader in its chosen market areas?
- What structural or cyclical changes in market demand are likely to take place in the future? Will competition intensify? What changes in technology are likely to occur?
- Should we continue with our current market strategy? If so, how can we strengthen it?

- Should we change our strategy? If yes, why? What should our new strategy be? How can we make a step-function jump ahead in the marketplace? Can we redefine the basis for competing in our chosen market niches?*
- What changes in operations strategy are necessary to strengthen our market position? Is there a fundamental need for change in the company's cost structure, organization, capabilities, competencies, and resources?

These sessions to think through market strategy should take place as often as new ideas come forth or past assumptions change. Top management and professional and operating people should all be involved. One key aim for such a strategic thinking session is to find a seminal idea that opens the way to important new market opportunities. Airing many differing points of view helps generate ideas and expand horizons. Top managers must probe constantly to bring potentially important future marketplace needs to the surface.

Traditional market research can point out known trends; this is useful to show existing opportunities. But when trends in a segment or niche are clear enough for outside market research to point them out, it means that others too can see the opportunities. The most rewarding route to market leadership is setting trends in the marketplace, not following them. In-house market research should be sophisticated enough to look well beyond the present.

To some extent, strategic-positioning decisions have to draw on the company's past achievements and experiences, but with a wary eye on overconfidence and overreliance on the past. Setting market strategy deserves the best and most imaginative ideas available. As strategic thinking only by insiders always carries the risk of nonobjectivity and limited scope because of personal mindsets and "ownership" of existing strategy, managers should invite, when useful, outside experts to participate who can bring different points of view to the discussions. Serious mistakes become more likely when policy managers assume they always know what is best for their company, where it should be headed, and how to get there.

Once a strategic direction is set but before action begins, the strategy should be put through a reality critique by people who have not been involved in deciding the strategy. This can help identify faults in assumptions or in rationale. The people who are ultimately responsible for implementing an action plan also should be involved in the critique, because they need to have confidence that assumptions being made are realistic in terms of the necessary competencies, infrastructure, and time. If a market-positioning decision is

* *Market niches* are narrowly defined parts of a particular industry segment. This book uses four levels to describe market areas: industry, sector, segment, and niche.

flawed, it will levy a high toll in lost opportunity, time, and money. This strategic thinking phase is the most critical, as the conclusions reached there set the stage for the much more costly and time-consuming activities to be initiated in the action phase.

When strategic thinking has created an astute approach to market positioning, implementation planning can begin. This planning should be specific but flexible enough to allow adapting to the new knowledge that will invariably be obtained during the course of implementing the strategy. Objectively analyzing current situations with customers, competitors, products, selling prices, product revenue margins (PREMs), order patterns, and product mix helps identify limiting problems as well as growth opportunities. Company strengths and weaknesses need to be carefully considered, especially in the areas of core competencies, processes, and resources. The teams or capability centers involved in strategy implementation should be active participants in developing the action plan.

One common goal in a company's market strategy is incremental growth, through the improvement of existing products and services, and by locating new customers and markets. Another is step-function growth, achieved through acquiring or developing new products and services. Often these can be reached by identifying new competencies that in combination with existing ones will provide the company with important new capabilities. If competitive barriers are to be erected, an essential strategic goal is to achieve marketplace advantages through a unique combination of company core competencies.

In the context of the competing choices available to today's customers and the latent demand that is not now being addressed, providing value to customers is more central than ever to market strategic positioning. Given the difference in customers' needs, the concept of customer value can have many different meanings, and grouping customers who have similar needs in order to define market niches can help in setting strategy. Niches are based on customer-specific applications and on the products and services that satisfy those applications. Value for customers is linked to product characteristics, price, availability, and the nature of the services provided. Once niches are defined, each can be considered individually in terms of volume potential, cost, time to develop, services to be offered, and sales programs. Niche definitions need only be meaningful to the company; they do not have to be congruent with the niche definitions of others.

If the company conceives its market-position strategy carefully and if the strategy is explicit and effectively communicated, the result should bring synergy to the collective decisions and actions of all the company's people. They will see where to put their energies and ideas toward the benefit of the business as a whole, and they will tend to work more cooperatively. If market positioning is too generalized, vague, or perceived to be wrong, it will have little relation to the company's unity of cause, and people will perform far less effectively.

DEVELOPING MARKET STRATEGY

The process of developing market strategy requires insight, ingenuity, good judgment, and risk taking. Taking enough time to do a careful job is essential, for the company is betting its future on these decisions. There are no pat formulas or "correct" approaches, although a predetermined framework for thinking about market strategy can sometimes be helpful. Michael E. Porter's work in presenting concepts and principles that can guide these thinking and planning processes provides some detailed approaches; Porter takes into account the structural analysis of industries, generic competitive strategies, the principles of competitive advantage, and various approaches to achieving advantages.[1] *Strategy: Seeking and Securing Competitive Advantage*, edited by Porter with Cynthia A. Montgomery and published by the Harvard Business School Press in 1991, contains a number of useful articles about strategy development.

More recently, the work of Gary Hamel and C.K. Prahalad challenges top managers to look beyond traditional approaches to strategic planning and think about how to gain market strength by leading in producing change in their selected markets and in developing entirely new markets. In 1989, these authors presented the concepts of "strategic intent" and "core competence" as the means by which strategic thinking can lead to marketplace leadership. Their book, *Competing for the Future*, considers these strategic approaches more fully. Although it focuses on the needs of large global multibusiness companies, their work can provoke worthwhile discussions on strategy development for companies of any size.[2]

In *The Discipline of Market Leaders*, Michael Treacy and Fred Wiersema illuminate the strategic approaches of some very successful companies. Based on their examples, the authors argue that only one of three value disciplines should be chosen as a core business strategy: operations excellence, product leadership, or customer intimacy. The discipline selected should be pursued to the point of achieving market dominance, they believe.[3]

When a company's existing strategy, products, and market niche(s) no longer provide sufficient opportunity for future growth, new market opportunities have to be sought. If the current marketplace is declining in size or is competitively brutal, and if exiting is not an option, the matter of developing market strategy is more difficult, but usually it is still not impossible. Alternatives include licensing, acquiring another company, and hiring new people who bring in new expertise. Another possibility is the radical restructuring of the company to compete more effectively in the existing market. When the investment required to become adequately strong is beyond the company's resources, the sale of the company must also be considered.

THE COMPANY'S CONCENTRATION STRATEGY

Small- and medium-size businesses are usually much more limited in financial, technological, and market-access resources than the larger corporations with which they must often compete. To compensate for such limitations, successful smaller companies are entrepreneurial in character and look to ingenuity, flexibility, agility, and speed in operations; they also invariably have a well-defined concentration strategy for establishing market strength.

Drucker has said that the single most important strategic decision a company makes is on its area of concentration in the marketplace. It answers the question of what specific customers, products, and competency areas the company will confine itself to.[4]

The tightly interdependent areas, customer/product/competency, define the strategic triad to be considered in setting concentration strategy. Critical questions to be asked include: What product? For what use? Based on what competency? For what customers? With what marketplace advantages? For what expected life cycle? At what probable revenue margin? At what cost in time and money to develop?

Avoiding products or services that are not linked to the company's core competencies and limiting the number of different products will keep resources concentrated in the areas most likely to provide market success. When there are too many irons in the fire, the efforts for each are likely to be inadequate and the company's competitive posture less strong because competencies and resources are spread too thin.

ESTABLISHING MARKET LEADERSHIP

All markets are niche markets except for those that are satisfied by commodity products. Commodity products generally account for the largest part of a market segment, while differentiated products, which are sold into the niches, account for the remainder. To compete effectively, both commodity and differentiated products need dependably high product quality and reliability and excellent customer services. For commodity products, additional success factors are aggressive defense of market share, competitive price, quantity availability, and well-established customer relationships. To be profitable, the suppliers of commodity products must be able to maintain low costs in both manufacturing and sales. For differentiated products, additional success factors include unique customer benefits, technical support, and value pricing.

Within every mature market area, there are usually three categories of competitors: leaders, players, and clingers. The leaders are those companies that combine success factors in the optimal way and thereby are the suppliers most customers prefer. The players are competent competitors but have no clearcut marketplace advantages in any area; they might be past leaders that were surpassed by others, or they might have explicitly chosen to be a player to keep down expense and be profitable as a "second source." If the marginal advantage between leaders and players is small, players can have a strong ongoing market presence; as the margin widens, the players move toward a weaker market posture. The clingers are the marginal players that have not been able to keep up with the players and leaders. Clingers survive only when market conditions are sufficiently strong, or because other, stronger companies stay clear of certain parts of the market. Unless they become stronger, clingers are not in a position to influence their own destiny, and they usually disappear if market conditions toughen.

The essence of market leadership is to create and constantly redefine customer benefits and value. Leaders are usually first to market with important innovations, and they are more alert to future opportunities than others. They stay in close touch with their customers and know what is important to them. Leaders also have particular internal competencies that fortify their leadership role. A key strategy for them to retain marketplace advantage is to maintain superior competency.

Market niches are established by customers who want products and services that provide specific benefits of added value to them relative to those available from commodity suppliers. The benefits may be real or just perceived, and when they are only perceived, the supplier faces considerably higher market risk. Niches are also created, or existing ones redefined, by a supplier company that is astute enough to see opportunities that others do not. The size and importance of a niche depends on the number of customers who have a like interest and can be satisfied by the same or a closely related product.

Companies that wish to enter an established niche new to them must investigate the marketplace environment with care, including the real reasons behind the existing relationships between suppliers and customers. This includes understanding the competency and aggressiveness of present suppliers as well as their own ability to penetrate or bypass existing competitive barriers. The potential new entrant must identify the forces that drive niche demand so that the basis for entry can be unique leadership in an appropriate area. Even when the homework has been carefully done, there will be unforeseen hazards and risks. Expecting problems and being quick to solve them is always an ingredient for success when first moving into a market niche that others now control.

A more difficult but attractive way of becoming a market leader is to entirely eliminate an existing niche by establishing a new one through forward or horizontal integration. This is done by creating a new product that combines the functions of two or more interlinked products that provide the customer with a higher-value solution; a prime example is semiconductor integrated circuits. Forward, backward, or horizontal integration often presents an opportunity to raise profit margins, erect competitive barriers, and open entirely new markets.

Backward integration—eliminating a supplier—can sometimes provide a company with an edge that leads to important marketplace advantages if it solves a material availability problem, reduces costs, raises quality, or improves product performance. This is particularly useful in areas where the product's performance depends greatly on the purity or consistency of raw material.

Another resource to strengthen market position is a particularly strong distribution system. This expertise opens the possibility of acquiring rights to sell products of others that are complementary, and which can help obtain more desirable orders. Over time, building exceptionally strong channels of distribution can lead to dominant market strength.

PRODUCT LEADERSHIP

Achieving market leadership by being a product leader is the ambition of many managements. If they succeed in this strategy, companies are usually able to enjoy prestige and stable, growing profits. Product leadership can be reached and sustained by way of four basic strategies: *product performance*, *next generation*, *cost and manufacturing*, and *customization*.

The *product performance* strategy is based on producing sufficient differentiation in the value attributes of a product that a company is considered the preferred supplier by its customers. This strategy requires exceptional competence in the management of product, process, and technology development. Being ahead of competitors in the all-important factor of time-to-market is critical for this strategy to succeed. Because almost all companies need creative achievement in product and process development, management has to be willing at times to undertake some parallel projects that take different approaches toward the same specific goals. The expectation is that the initially high development expense will be recovered by higher REM derived from the future leadership position. A critical part of this strategy is a pricing approach that makes future entry by competitors more difficult.*

Using this strategy, Hewlett-Packard has built a product leadership position in data processing, medical, communications, and other areas. In a notable example, the company identified a market opportunity in laser printers for use with personal and other computers. They were not the pioneers in this product

---

* *Product performance* includes quality and physical as well as operational attributes.

area, but they saw latent demand that was not being addressed by others, took a high-momentum approach to product development in alliance with Canon, and succeeded in defining an important new market segment. The reasonable pricing at the time the product was introduced, combined with the product's exceptional reliability, propelled Hewlett-Packard to market leadership in a rapidly growing multibillion-dollar market area.

The *next-generation* strategy is based on replacing an existing product with one that has improved performance and that supersedes the early product without serious complications for the customer. For many years, Intel has used the next-generation approach to supersede its own products and thereby keep its traditional competitors at bay and retain dominant market leadership. Intel no longer promotes the product they replace, but it continues to be sold at a market-competitive price while demand shifts to their new product. For this to work well, the next-generation product should be ready for delivery before competitors make serious inroads in the existing market.

Companies that are not currently product leaders can employ a variation of this strategy, as exemplified by the following effort to displace the current leader. Digital Equipment Corporation, a past laggard in open-systems computers and currently a minor player in the computer chip market, recently developed a new computer microprocessor chip it calls "alpha," which set new performance standards. IBM, Apple, and Motorola are also taking a similar approach, but with their own unique chips. All four companies hope to replace Intel chips in newly designed hardware. Their efforts are at an early stage, and it is too early to see if they will succeed in an important way. While offering performance advantages, none of these chips are interchangeable with Intel products, because they are designed for different computer software operating systems. This drawback is a significant deterrent to early success, since mainstream applications software is not immediately usable.

The *cost and manufacturing* strategy is based on offering "acceptable" product performance, but with aggressive pricing and capacity to deliver in quantity. In entering an existing market, the first step is usually to reverse engineer the leader's product, and then develop one that meets target cost and is interchangeable and comparable in performance. Once the product is developed, low-cost manufacturing capability has to be established. This strategy's basis for competing is to underprice competitors and provide faster availability. It presents a smaller risk in product development but a larger one in the time required to achieve sufficient profitability, particularly if the existing leader feels threatened and is able to respond aggressively with lower pricing.

The *customization* strategy is based on a flexible manufacturing process that permits easy modification of a product within the production facility to meet different specifications. This approach requires a carefully thought-out product design and manufacturing process design. The product has to be programmable for adaptation in small quantities at reasonable cost to unique customer requirements.

These four strategies are not mutually exclusive; when conditions are appropriate, they can be joined. *Cost and manufacturing* can work with any of the other three. *Customization* can be linked to either *product performance* or *next-generation*, but this might mean higher cost unless the custom product's volume is sufficient. It may be necessary to employ flexible manufacturing to permit rapid movement into production of the next-generation products. To strengthen market leadership by combining strategies, the common denominators for success are appropriate core competencies, creativity in development, and short time-to-market for product development.

TWO CASE STUDIES

In the volatile battlefield of the integrated circuit industry, National Semiconductor and Advanced Micro Devices successfully (although at times traumatically) used the *cost and manufacturing* strategy for producing integrated circuits used in computers and related applications. For many years, they were able to build a growing and profitable business by entering an existing market as a second or third source competing on price and availability. Eventually they became important suppliers of memory chips. In the 1980s, however, they were challenged in the memory chip niche by several Asian companies, which lowered price and established significantly more advanced manufacturing processes. All of the U.S. companies quickly lost their basis for competing in that niche. This aggressive action by the Asian companies was so successful that the U.S. government had to step in to prevent the loss of the country's manufacturing base for these products. To recover, the affected companies, which then included Intel, shifted focus to the more profitable microprocessor chip niche and other niche areas that the Asian companies could not then easily enter.

Intel, now the long-standing product leader in the microprocessor chip segment, has prospered throughout the chip price wars by sustained and timely creative achievements in technology that continuously raised the performance bar for competition. By using the *next-generation* strategy, Intel frequently made obsolete an earlier product of its own while competitors were still buying their way into the older product area. Intel's new product always involved more complex and costly product design and manufacturing that competitors were then compelled to develop. The company accomplished this with its 8088, 286, 386, 486 and Pentium products over a span of nearly fifteen years. Intel's strategy may ultimately be less successful when semiconductor technology has reached the point of maturity, when new generations will be less frequent and product performance improvements develop more slowly. Perhaps then Intel will have to join the other two strategies, *customization and cost and manufacturing*, to its existing one to retain niche leadership in its markets. The company is already working in that direction, and is also developing products that are system solutions. These incorporate Intel's semiconductor components as well as other components that together provide a complete system function. These will open entirely new markets.

The second case study focuses on the data-processing industry, which went through frenetic change in the 1980s and early 1990s that dramatically altered its nature and its participants. Digital Equipment, IBM, Wang, Compaq, and Data General were only some of the most visible among hundreds of companies that faced great trouble because their market strategies were out of step with the structural changes occurring in their marketplaces. Dozens of new companies sprang up and led the way to open new opportunities, while many of the established companies were still trying to figure out what to do. Clones of the IBM personal computers proliferated and set much lower price levels in the marketplace. Direct marketing and catalog sales became commonplace. The general product reliability of these clones was so high that manufacturer-provided maintenance became only a minor issue for potential buyers. The importance of mainframe and minicomputers was diminished by the advent of decentralized, networked computers utilizing centralized databases. All four of the basic strategies and all their various combinations were applied by the new entrants.

The data-processing industry's structural changes were driven largely by advances in semiconductor technology that permitted millions of transistors to be included on a single chip, which combined functions that previously required many different discrete components. These advances meant that computers could now be much more powerful, smaller, and far less expensive, with corresponding improvements in work stations and peripheral equipment. These new chips also made possible parallel processing, a new technique for simultaneously handling very large data-processing needs. Many other areas drove the changes as well, including improved hard disk storage technology that provided gigabytes of capacity in small packages; flat-screen liquid-crystal displays that made notebook computers practical; high-performance dot matrix, ink jet, and laser printers that were attractively priced; and communications products such as modems, routers, and servers that permitted fast, reliable communication between computers.

Rapid software development was also a driving force. The DOS operating system, pioneered by Microsoft, became a de facto open system standard for personal computers (PCs), permitting a vast array of sophisticated application software to become available at a reasonable cost. These applications included word processing, spreadsheet, database, graphics, and many others. PCs and their peripheral components quickly replaced more expensive computers in many applications as the result of the new software, networking technologies, rapidly growing performance, and lower prices.

Apple Computer, using an operating system different from DOS, built a multibillion-dollar company from a startup and founded desktop publishing. Computer workstations from Sun Microsystems, Hewlett-Packard, Silicon Graphics, and others became a multibillion-dollar market segment by allowing designers, scientists, and engineers to break the chain that bound them to central mainframe and minicomputers. These people now had the power to perform independently complex design and analysis tasks. Computer-aided design (CAD) systems radically revised the way architects design buildings and the way engineers design products and processes. Computer-aided manufacturing (CAM) simplified many previously tedious processes for production scheduling and material control. Every small business could now afford computers for its internal business and technological processes.

The dramatic changes that took place in a relatively short span of time in the data-processing industry rippled through nearly every other business sector. Companies that were agile and not constrained by traditional structures and cultures were quick to capitalize on the market opportunities that were created. Those that did not see the opportunities unfolding or could not act in a timely way suffered. What can now be perceived as an ongoing information-processing revolution has redefined the ground rules for doing business in every company throughout the world. This revolution will have an even greater impact in the future as businesses become more adept at applying information-system strategies within their cencon systems to achieve marketplace advantages.

PRODUCT DEVELOPMENT

Deciding on the actual performance requirements for improved or totally new products is an exacting process. Before it can begin, the company must acquire a sophisticated understanding of all the trends in the market. These include the forces that are likely to change customer demand and alter competitive behavior, and the forces that are likely to change existing technology or manufacturing cost. Arriving at product specifications requires deciding on the primary strategy for creating marketplace demand. Parallel considerations are the likely behavior of competitors, existing or new, and the possibility of new market trends occurring during the development period. Once the strategy to create demand is decided on, the feature-set of the product can then be defined.

To attract orders for products, a strategic marketing approach needs to be defined to provide sales pull, customer push, or both. Sales pull relies on brand recognition, selling, promotion, services, and price more than on differentiated product performance. The primary force that "pulls" in orders is the overall sales effort. Customer push focuses on a product that significantly outperforms existing competitor products or satisfies unfilled customer needs, or both; the customer "push" to buy is the primary force that provides orders. Not surprisingly, the best results are usually achieved by combining push and pull. When a new product is introduced into a market in which there is only latent but not existing demand, the combined strategy is the only way to proceed. The most predictable product developments stem from employing known technologies; nevertheless, although they are less predictable, the most successful new products usually are created by way of major steps forward in design or technology.

The key considerations in setting product specifications are product performance, size, quality, reliability, life expectancy, and cost. Product attributes necessary for marketplace advantage must be designed in at the beginning; making any significant change after manufacturing starts is disruptive and costly. It is wise to anticipate that manufacturing might cause performance degradation of the product and incur actual costs that are higher than designed-in targets.

Once product specifications have been defined, the time has come to estimate the time and cost involved to develop the product, introduce it into the market, and ramp up production. Much of what transpires in the development process is based on estimates and best guesses, thus it is imperative to include safety factors in both development time and cost.

Risk rises if development requires that new competencies be obtained. The greatest risk, however, is if a company is depending on research to develop or apply new technology. With research, the path to finding the necessary knowledge is generally uncertain; a combination of intuitive, creative, and linear thinking, as well as serendipity, is involved, and it is usually futile to predict an outcome. Often the desired result is not achieved and the research has to be abandoned. From a financial point of view, the leading edge of technology for product development is usually the "bleeding" edge.

During development, the ideals asserted early usually run into reality. The pressure to compromise comes into play, and the critical issue becomes how to modify specifications so that the product can be developed while keeping it sufficiently differentiated by the time it arrives on the market. Sometimes companies choose to ease specifications to allow earlier market entry. At other times, it may be best to opt for a later introduction in favor of toughening specifications for greater differentiation. A two- or three-stage program might allow a product to be brought to market as soon as possible, followed soon by a second or third version that supersedes the earlier ones.

Many companies now find that reducing product-to-market development time has become essential to stay competitive. Steven C. Wheelright and Kim B. Clark have analyzed the many issues, human and other, that affect the time taken for product development and have developed a conceptual model for a multifunction team approach based on real-world situations. In doing so they examine such questions as:

> Why do some companies move quickly and efficiently to bring to market outstanding new products, while others expend tremendous resources to develop products that are late and poorly designed? What are the critical concepts, ideas, practices, and processes that lie behind truly outstanding performance in the development of new products and processes? What can managers do to bring about significant improvements in the performance of their development process?[5]

From another perspective, Preston G. Smith and Donald Reinertsen contend that product development cycles can be cut in half. Their book provides a compelling economic analysis of the financial benefits of reducing development time, along with many examples of how cycle time has actually been reduced. They note the importance of concurrent engineering, an evolving, comprehensive strategy for product development that concentrates on the factors influencing product development time and result outcomes. For example, concurrent engineering seeks to perform many projects in parallel rather than the sequenced order so routinely assumed to be natural.[6]

RELATED-PRODUCT DIVERSIFICATION

Another facet of market strategy involves the development, or acquisition, of new products that can be sold into existing or new market niches which are well understood and are within a company's realm of core competencies. Selling into multiple market niches can provide the advantages of diversification while minimizing the risks involved in a single market niche. Risk is never low in any form of diversification, however, no matter how straightforward the venture may seem. The potential for serious pitfalls and other surprises is commonplace, and it is essential to carefully develop operations strategy to ensure that sufficient resources are devoted to the new undertaking without having an adverse impact on existing business areas. The chance of succeeding in the new undertaking is greater if it can be decentralized and treated as a separate business unit which can allow greater operations focus. The most practical and fastest path may be acquiring another company already operating in a targeted niche, as compared with the risks of internal product development and the delay in market entry.

A case study offers a cautionary example. Aerovox, Incorporated, a seventy-year-old capacitor manufacturer with $120 million-plus sales in 1995, is a leader in the development and manufacture of wound capacitors used in air conditioning, fluorescent lighting, microwave ovens, and other applications. With about a 40 percent market share, Aerovox is a major factor in this market segment. The company has retained a leadership role in this mature market by concentrating on superior competency in product design and process technology in manufacturing, and, of key importance, by building close relationships with important customers. It has invested heavily in innovative product design and automation. The company considers its product quality to be a major factor in its success, as it does its product price, availability, and service.

For diversification, Aerovox entered the field of wound capacitors for telecommunications applications. It did so by purchasing an existing division of AT&T which specialized in that area. The acquired entity was initially established as a separate business unit because the particular technology, while related, differed from that of Aerovox's other products. Because the newly acquired products were sold to different customers, Aerovox also established new marketing capability. Eventually, this business unit was successfully merged into the larger wound capacitor business unit, to the benefit of both product areas.

Once this acquisition was fully digested, which took nearly two years, Aerovox took another, larger, diversification step, acquiring a long-established, domestic-based company in another related field, electrolytic capacitors. These products were used in applications that differed from the company's other two product areas, but they could be sold through the company's existing marketing channels. Within weeks of this acquisition, Aerovox purchased a British company, also in the electrolytic capacitor business. This company had better technology in some aspects of manufacture than the earlier acquisition and also provided a manufacturing base for entry into the European market for some of Aerovox's other products. The expectation was that the two acquired companies would mutually strengthen each other. Both acquisitions were financially troubled when they were acquired. The British company was turned around quickly and grew impressively. The domestic-based company was moved to Mexico to improve cost structure; over a two-year period, it encountered numerous expensive problems in manufacturing and in the marketplace before starting on a path to recovery.

THE SALES STRATEGY

All aspects of selling, distribution, and marketing are involved in sales strategy, which defines the product line boundaries within which specific products will be confined; the product line scope and mix; the company's selling channels and pricing policies; warranties and payment terms; the kind and extent of customer services and support; and advertising, brand development, and sales promotion programs. Sales strategy also encompasses information-gathering on competitors; licensing of the company's intellectual property when appropriate; the sale to others of unbranded products for resale under their own brand name; alliances; and joint ventures. The aim of a company's sales strategy is to design a comprehensive selling program that is of value to customers, provides the company with sufficient orders, and achieves a marketplace presence stronger than that of its competitors.

A performance-driven sales strategy must also address the issue of maturity in market niches. As customer applications mature, product differentiation becomes a less important advantage, and a supplier will find fewer, although more competent, competitors. The marketplace tends to become more predictable, but the pressure that sophisticated buyers exert on prices and the actions of competitors invariably reduce revenue margins. In a mature market, a company must normally hold or increase market share as a condition of survival. Finding ways to produce growth in revenue margin in this market environment is vital. If the company is to maintain a competitively advantageous market position, it must achieve higher productivity that allows lower costs in manufacturing and sales. It is essential to recognize the inevitability of revenue margin pressure and to work hard to stay in front of it.

The issue of product life cycles must be considered from the perspective of marketplace demand, not company sales. When a competitive product comes along that is interchangeable with and of higher value to customers than an existing supplier's product, that product becomes obsolete in its present form. As long as market demand remains firm, however, continuing innovation can redefine the earlier product's value to customers and restore it to a competitive posture. Success usually requires both performance improvement and productivity gain to lower cost. Of course, if shrinking demand is the driving force, the product may have the destiny of the buggy whip.

PRICING

Setting a selling price for a product is a vital strategic issue, but it is often not treated that way. Companies usually pay a great deal of attention to establishing the frontline price (price before discounts) but much less to the more complex matter of establishing actual prices for individual orders. Yet the actual price on an order is what determines revenue margin. How a price moves from frontline to actual is usually through negotiations between the buyer and the company's salespeople. It is not uncommon for sales people to discount price and to offer extras (added features to product or special services), which increase the cost to fulfill the order and are provided at no additional charge. As a consequence, the process by which actual prices are set must be strategically guided by top management if revenue margins are to be protected. From a profit viewpoint, product price is as important as the cost to manufacture, sell, and support the product. Both price and cost determine REM level.

The marketplace sets actual prices, influenced strongly by the extent and nature of competition. A supplier company can only set an asking price. The extent to which discounts and extras are employed as incentives to obtain orders depends on the seller's negotiating strength. This, of course, is directly related to its market-position strength, and the extent to which customer push is present. If the customer can walk away from the negotiation without being hurt, the seller is in a weak position. Even when the seller is in a strong negotiating position, the buyer will appeal to fairness and good future relations as a way of extracting concessions.

Most salespeople have been paid by commissions on revenues, a standard arrangement which emphasizes that orders are not to be lost because of price or any other reason. The pressure to reduce prices can be compelling, even when the company's market position is reasonably strong, because the salesperson may be uncertain of the company's relative strength with a particular customer. Quite often, prices are reduced much more than is necessary, particularly when salespeople are given broad discretion to adjust prices or add no-charge extras.

Most companies use one of two approaches to set their frontline prices. The most common is market value—what the supplier company believes customers are willing to pay relative to their alternative options. This is a judgment call by the supplier. The second approach is cost-plus, which bases price on a multiple of cost. Cost-plus is generally less useful, as it is usually marketplace factors that actually determine what customers are willing to pay. Cost analysis should always be used as a reality check, however. In many companies, cost information is inadequate and often inaccurate for individual products. Using activity-based accounting can help establish more accurate cost determination.

A third approach to pricing is to "buy" orders at whatever price is necessary. This approach is used when a company's major goal is to increase market share. Buying orders may mean sacrificing short-term revenue margin to gain sufficient volume and so to benefit ultimately from the economies of scale, thereby raising long-term revenue margin. Sometimes this approach is used simply to damage competitors under the guise of gaining economies of scale.

Top managers cannot be involved routinely in day-to-day pricing matters, of course. Nevertheless, they must be certain that the company has a strategic approach to pricing in place, and that it is explicit and realistic. The general objective of pricing is to maximize long-term REM dollars for a given production level. Product unit volume drives production costs, and these normally decline as quantities increase up to the point of full capacity in manufacturing. Pricing that keeps operations at or near optimum capacity usually returns the largest REM level. This is not normally the highest REM percentage of sales; from the point of view of profit, it is important to keep in mind that the priority is to maximize REM dollar amount, not its percentage of sales.

A strategic approach to pricing should include a method of monitoring that will quickly signal when reducing price will cause profit problems. One useful method is to establish a *company-critical price*, one beneath which REM will be at an unacceptable level, and routinely compare it against a *market-critical price*, one which an informed buyer would require to make a purchase. Above this price, the buyer will not act.

The market-critical price is set by customers and competitors; it is usually a moving target, as customers are almost always less than candid about their buy/no-buy price point. Some competitors are also likely to take a "We will not be undersold" approach in the market. The company-critical price, usually a matrix of price versus unit volume, is set by a management decision based on prevailing cost considerations and the need to obtain orders. In defining company-critical prices, linked products need to be considered together.

The reason for defining company-critical prices is twofold: to set the lowest acceptable price level, and to provide a reference to compare against the actual prices on incoming orders. As a reference, the figure is used to sound an alarm when REM is at risk. As the lowest acceptable price, it sets the point below which the company might walk away from an order. Of course, other factors besides company-critical price influence the decision of whether to take an order. These include gaining leverage to obtain other more important orders, retaining the customer over the long term, and maintaining employment continuity.

Often a competent competitor will force a drop in market price because it has a better cost structure or simply wants more sales and is willing to accept lower profits. This kind of change can cause massive profit bleeding for all the involved suppliers. If this pricing is based on a structural change, and the new market-critical price is near or below a company-critical price, some immediate management action is called for before profits move downward too far. When the situation is sufficiently serious, managers must consider reestablishing the affected product area as a separate business unit with a lower cost structure. This usually means redistributing or cutting the previously existing overhead costs so they will no longer be allocated to the newly created business unit.

ERECTING COMPETITIVE BARRIERS

A competitive barrier is anything that makes it more difficult for a competitor to take away customers. The ideal barrier is one that keeps competitors out of a market niche because of the cost or difficulty of entering it. Maintaining a lasting barrier is extremely difficult, and a persistent competitor can normally find ways over or around most of them. When no direct barrier is possible, an alternative is to create conditions that are hard for competitors to duplicate, such as a very strong marketing or distribution capability, low-cost manufacturing and marketing that is reflected in prices, exceptional product quality, faster delivery, or a more attractive product mix. Other situations that provide a preferred position are superior competence, the ownership of critical intellectual property, a towering reputation, brand recognition, and a mutually gratifying working partnership with the customer.

The only sustainable competitive barrier is for a company to be continuously more innovative through a broad-based program of momentum building that keeps competition constantly in a relatively weaker market position. The most rewarding strategic guideline to remain strong in both the marketplace and financial statements is to keep customers content, to invest in company and product development, and to work steadily on productivity gain.

NOTES

1. Michael E. Porter, *Competitive Advantage*. New York: Free Press, 1985; "Corporate Strategy: The State of Strategic Thinking," *The Economist*, May 23, 1987.

2. Gary Hamel and C.K. Prahalad, *Competing for the Future*. Cambridge, Mass.: Harvard Business School Press, 1994.

3. Michael Treacy and Fred Wiersema, *The Discipline of Market Leaders*. Boston: Addison-Wesley, 1995.

4. Peter F. Drucker, *Management: Tasks, Responsibilities, Practices*. New York: Harper & Row, 1974, p. 96.

5. Steven C. Wheelwright and Kim B. Clark, *Revolutionizing Product Development*. New York: Free Press, 1992.

6. Preston G. Smith and Donald Reinertsen, *Developing Products in Half the Time*. Van Nostrand Reinhold, 1991.

## CHAPTER 10

Building Momentum

Infusing an Entrepreneurial Mindset

THE EVOLVING COMPANY

Every existing business began as a startup. Its founding entrepreneurs had a vision for the company and set about to transform that vision into reality. They were able to bring together ideas, people, competencies, and resources with a compelling commitment to produce the results that would successfully establish the enterprise. They got through the trouble spots by persistence and confidence in their vision and in themselves, along with generous amount of ingenuity and energy. The CEO and other key people provided meaningful leadership that clarified direction and inspired loyalty.

Once a company is established and viable, a new vision of its future is normally needed. Should it circle the wagons and defend against competition, or should it move on to other frontiers? Usually the answer is to do both, but with special focus on either defending market niche or creating new routes to growth. The completion of each subsequent growth phase is cause for a review and perhaps change in the vision for the company's future. Frequently, growth-phase endings have not been very clear to management, so that periods characterized by vagueness of vision, backsliding, and false starts were likely. But the successful companies survived these setbacks and moved forward again by calling up the attributes compelling commitment, persistence, confidence, ingenuity, and energy that forged their earlier achievements.

In its early life, a company had no significant need for business controls except for money, employment policies, and law compliance. Formal controls were kept to a minimum. The overriding priority was profitable growth by strengthening the company's market position, addressing competitive threats, and building performance capability. Things had to get done within limited time, and people were expected to carry their own weight. The organization was lean, with little hierarchy. People knew what was expected of them as well as of others; they were accountable for their own performance. If someone didn't get a job done the right way, everyone else knew it, and they would usually pitch in to help. Reality, simplicity, trust, and openness prevailed. The company's unity of cause, a powerful catalyst for inspiring accountability and enthusiasm, was well known to all. Everyone had a stake in a successful outcome for the company—for some it was financial, for others career development, and for all, the satisfaction of being part of a winning team. An entrepreneurial mindset prevailed.

As a company grows, the issue of management control inevitably rises to the surface. The historical model for sound management has been authoritarian control. Authority, with both "long and short strings attached," is delegated downward by the chief executive officer and then harnessed and applied by managers at every level to get things done. Usually, without much reflective thought, this model has been adopted by most managements as the maturing adolescent company approaches adulthood. Little by little, new layers of management are added as managers take on the urgent unwritten goal of mistake prevention. Top management becomes more and more isolated, and increasingly complicated processes for decision making and actions are put in place. Costs escalate. If the company's market position remains strong enough, and if its competition generally functions in the same command-and-control way, the company may continue to grow profitably as long as changes in the marketplace are slow to take place. When change is more rapid, usually serious problems develop.

Today's rapidly changing, globally competitive marketplace requires virtually every business, even large and long-established ones, to behave in ways that resemble a successful young company. Adapting to young-company thinking and action is the only way that long-term profit growth and employee opportunity and loyalty can be sustained in a business of any size.

The essential young-company behavioral characteristics include a unity of cause; clear and appropriate objectives; accountability throughout the organization; simplicity in decision and action processes; and a rate of accomplishment that achieves and builds strength in both market position and performance capability. The company priorities are set through knowledge-based leadership that calls on the abilities of everyone in the organization. These entrepreneurial elements underpin almost all successful young companies, and they are at the foundation of Three Dimensional Management.

STRENGTHENING

Momentum is a concept that is easily understood and universally viewed as the underlying force for winning in any competitive activity. Building momentum is a proactive, exciting team effort that can bring out everyone's intellectual, creative, and energetic power. Virtually everyone wants to be associated with a growing, dynamic company. And what translates strategically set ambition into a higher level of company performance is not day-to-day operations, but the managerial action of strengthening. The *means* by which management creates value for its three key stakeholders is by building company momentum.

People at every company level have to be aware of the importance of company strengthening and enlist as enthusiastic boosters of the effort. They have to realize that the marketplace sets the required rate at which strengthening must take place to be beneficial to the company, and that it is customers who make it possible for the company to employ and pay them. These are not always easy concepts for people, including some managers, to identify with, even when they accept them intellectually. The managerial task of getting all the company's people to support and contribute to momentum building always entails helping them bridge the gap between intellectual acceptance and emotional involvement in the strengthening process.

Before meaningful strengthening can take place, the company needs a momentum plan that provides an overview of its strategy and objectives. The underview of detail should evolve from a wide range of contributions from many people involved in the teams organized for specific undertakings. Momentum indicators have to be in place so that results from ongoing changes can be seen and decisions for subsequent actions can be made.

Building momentum is an innovation process of five key steps, as shown in Figure 10-1.

The process begins with awareness of where strengthening has to take place and with the setting of specific improvement goals. The degree of urgency and therefore priority for action should also be apparent from the gap between these goals and today's situation. The next step is to develop ideas on how to accomplish the needed strengthening. The next, actually producing the change in a timely way, is often the most difficult step; while accomplishing the change, it is imperative to build in a means for ensuring that it will be retained in the future. Without this precaution, a fallback to prior ways is possible. Throughout the process, it is essential to stimulate and support widespread communication on needs, problems, and progress. People at every level must be able to be candid about issues; if effective solutions are to be found, prob-

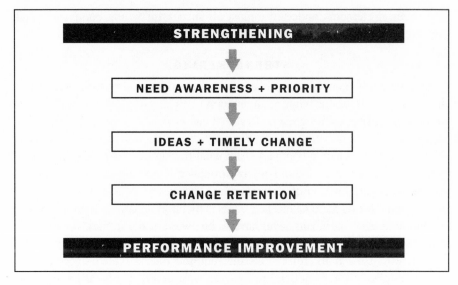

Figure 10-1: The Strengthening Process

lems must be openly stated in an atmosphere that discourages blaming and supports rather than isolates the expression of difficulties.

The current people, competencies, internal capabilities, and infrastructure of a company are in place as the cumulative result of a number of past decisions and actions that were made over a long period of time. Those responsible for them may have a personal interest in defending and retaining the present approach, but such a defense might protect mediocre performance and support complacent attitudes. To build momentum, the mindsets and attitudes of those who support and defend the status quo will have to change; until these attitudes and mindsets are truly changed, or until these people are changed, little progress will be made toward momentum building. The task of bringing about the necessary constructive attitudes that embody personal accountability for performance is a vital early critical step in attaining a momentum-building organization.

The path to strengthening lies in four managerial actions: asking an almost unending series of questions that challenge the status quo; producing wide-ranging discussions that lead to an understanding and acceptance of the reason for change; involving as "change agents" those people affected by the change; and establishing rewards and new opportunities for those people contributing to desired change. In most situations, the most dynamic approach to producing change is likely to be establishing teams. Teams share the common purpose of fulfilling the team mission—as opposed to committees, which usually consist of people whose interest is to represent a parochial point of view. Each team should be composed of the most qualified people required for the task. An adroit team leader is a critical catalyst for team success. When a team needs organizational clout, the team leader has to be a policy manager.

MANAGEMENT MINDSETS

If a company's management currently depends primarily on command and control, the company will have to adopt an explicit strategy for converting it into an involvement-oriented management. A flat and flexible structure assumes the risk that operating employees will behave accountably, and that risk is necessary if the substantial benefits of the structure are to be achieved. All policy managers have to endorse the strategy and must be able to take the initiative to put it into practice. Exactly how and over what time span this takes place will differ according to the approach taken by the CEO. If the company is currently facing trauma of some kind, the transition might be easier and faster as a result of the current malaise. If not, those who launch the conversion process will have to overcome the inertia created by management satisfaction with the status quo.

One example of a high-profile conversion from command-and-control to involvement-oriented management is John F. Welch. After he took over as CEO of General Electric Company in 1981, he methodically, and sometimes ruthlessly, restructured it. Subsequently, as he considered what the company needed for future success, he began to focus on the company's less tangible, nonfinancial aspects, factors he calls the "soft" side of management. Although some of Welch's early structural-change methods have elicited criticism, he has succeeded in raising General Electric to the top ranks of the Fortune 500 and has built substantial customer, employee, and shareholder value. Talking about his experience, he observes:

> Trying to define what will happen three to five years out, in specific, quantitative terms, is a futile exercise. The world is moving too fast for that. What should a company do instead? First of all, define its vision and its destiny in broad but clear terms. Second, maximize its own productivity. Finally, be organizationally and culturally flexible enough to meet massive change....The way to control your destiny in a global environment of change and uncertainty is simple: Be the highest-value supplier in the marketplace.
>
> To create change, direct, personal, two way communication is what seems to make the difference: exposing people without the protection of title or position to ideas from everywhere, judging ideas on their merits....You need an overarching message, something big but simple and understandable....If you are not thinking all the time about making every person more valuable, you don't have a chance. What's the alternative? Wasted minds? Uninvolved people? A labor force that's angry or bored? That doesn't make sense!...We're trying to differentiate GE competitively by raising as much intellectual capital from our workforce as we possibly can.[1]

Managers who routinely cling to command-and-control approaches are obsolete. Involvement-oriented management is a partnership approach, but it does not compromise decisions for consensus. The aim is to enable better and more imaginative decision-making and action by bringing to them all the insight and brain power available, from all sources.

STRENGTHENING MARKET POSITION

A 1995 survey of 193 North American companies by Mercer Management Consulting found that companies that were industry leaders produce as much as 50 percent of their revenue from products or services that were developed during the prior five years. The survey indicates that these companies maintain their marketplace advantage through superior project execution, market-driven portfolio management, and effective management support systems for product research and development. The top third of the surveyed companies outperformed the bottom third on revenue contribution to growth and on development productivity. One conclusion is that once a company has established the expertise, its new-product development can drive growth indefinitely, as long as the company manages the capability as a critical competency.[2]

As the earlier chapters show, a company's ambition for growth and future market position has to be clearly defined and then translated into specific projects that will successfully achieve the growth objectives. Deciding on the projects means examining all five elements of a company's market position—unique competencies, reputation, products, customer services, and marketplace presence—within the context of customer needs and competitors' market position and likely actions. Another vital consideration is the rate of change in the technology now employed in its products. The questions that need considering include:

Unique Competencies

What exactly are the competencies that we rely on for market-position strength? Are they unique, or do competitors possess competencies that equal or exceed ours? Is customer focus a real competency for us? How do we strengthen our customer/product/competency advantages?

Company Reputation

What exactly is our reputation in the marketplace? How do customers see our products and services relative to those of the competition? Is our reputation a market-position advantage and therefore an important factor in customer decision-making? How can we make our reputation a stronger advantage in the marketplace?

Products

Are our existing products providing the company with sufficient REM growth? Are there real barriers to competitors? Is our pricing strategy working? Does our product line offer enough choice? Could a broader product range raise our REM level? Are we refreshing existing products to extend their life cycle? Is our product-development capability a core competency? If not, how do we make it into one?

Customer Services

What exactly do customers think about our service? Do we handle orders and solve problems in a prompt, decisive, and customer-satisfying way? Are our relationships with customers a market-position advantage? What can we do to strengthen service to the point where it becomes a recognized benefit by customers?

Marketplace Presence

Are there markets we are underserving because we lack sales presence? Can we open new markets domestically or globally by expanding our marketing efforts into those areas? Would creating a different approach to advertising and sales promotion be more effective?

ASSESSING AND IMPROVING ORGANIZATIONAL VITALITY

Building momentum depends on vision and tenacity in managers and a unity of cause that ignites enthusiasm in everyone for company strengthening. The only means for transforming the company from what it is now to the superior momentum-driven entity that management wants it to be is ongoing strengthening. Recognizing the necessity for market-position momentum is relatively easy; thinking through what is required to raise it to a desired level is not. The availability of money, as a resource advantage, is usually not as important as promoting significant ideas, superior competencies, and high organizational vitality. The success of many small-capital companies illuminates this.

If a company moves forward more slowly than competitors in its market, it will be in trouble. If it moves forward at the same rate, it can usually cope. If it leads the pace of advancement in some important area, it will usually prosper. What makes the difference is the timely contributions of people. The primary route to building performance capability is a focused, energetic, and creative organization that consistently delivers important accomplishment. People who are enterprising get things done; organizations with many enterprising people get many things done.

Improving organizational vitality requires the following focus: What is our current level of organizational vitality? What is its direction of change? Do we have a company culture that encourages a high level of vitality? Is there widespread acceptance of our unity of cause? Is there sufficient accountability to stimulate and sustain our initiatives and achievements? Are we able to set breakthrough goals and marshal enough creativity to achieve them? Do our people stay current in their fields? Is organizational and individual learning taking place at a sufficient rate?

Momentum can be seen and felt in the words, actions, and behavior of people. As in Duke Ellington's comment, "It don't mean a thing if it ain't got that swing," momentum building has the sense of improvisational jazz, in which a group performs a single song with specific individual creativity that ultimately blends into the whole with an exciting, rewarding, and stimulating result.

PRODUCTIVITY GAIN

Market-niche leadership is based on being the highest-value supplier in the marketplace as well as being a leader in productivity. Every corner of company operations provides some potential for making productivity improvements. Operating processes must be as simple and efficient as possible, with latitude for people to exercise discretion and judgment to take actions toward continuous improvement in the processes.

Focusing on improving productivity means asking: Are we consistently creating sufficient value for our customers, employees, and shareholders? Is productivity gain in manufacturing, sales, and product development contributing adequately to REM growth? Are we finding new customers and market opportunities at a sufficient rate? Is our cencon system contributing effectively to company productivity? Should we have higher productivity in management and administrative activities?

SETTING GOALS

Because result follows expectation, an organization usually needs to set high expectations for performance in order to achieve important results. Every company must make its anchorpoint objectives and momentum drivers situation-specific by setting concisely defined goals. These goals must be described clearly enough to set direction for localized strengthening actions, and they must also provide a basis for measuring progress toward their achievement. The goals should provide for both big- and small-step change. Sometimes the goal-setting process should be one of "ratcheting up" over time; once a goal has been achieved, a higher one follows. The ratcheting-up should continue until the desired level of performance is reached.

Knowing what *kind of goal* is needed is an important aspect of goal setting. A *normal* goal defines a result attainable through a process of incremental improvement without significant risk of failure. A *stretch* goal, also reached by incremental action, is more difficult to achieve and carries some risk that it may not be met. A *breakthrough* goal calls for a much higher level of performance, cannot be met by incremental action, and requires significant creativity; failure is a distinct possibility, as are budget and schedule overruns. The kinds of goals to be set depend on each company's management ambition, the specific situation priority, the company's market position, and marketplace vicissitude.

Setting breakthrough goals and meeting schedules that deliver marketplace advantages are the most lucrative routes to achieving important financial performance results. Hewlett-Packard accomplished breakthrough in its laser printer development program, and its resulting LaserJet product series soon became the industry leader. Pharmaceutical and biotech companies set breakthrough goals for research as a primary strategy for arriving at marketplace advantage. Their approach requires both a great deal of money and a long period of time, but when they succeed, the payoff can be huge.

Unfortunately, many companies waste money and lose time in product development by targeting breakthrough goals without the sufficient underlying competency and organizational vitality to meet them. Setting the appropriate type of goal has to be based on an intimate knowledge of the company's available intellectual and creative resources and on the level of motivation of the people involved. It may be necessary to develop or seek new competencies and new approaches for higher vitality if breakthrough goals are to be set realistically.

THE SPIRIT OF CONTINUOUS IMPROVEMENT

Making continuous efforts at improvement is an essential part of momentum building. Within the company's unity of cause, all the company's people are expected to contribute to continuous improvement within their respective activity areas. When change is continuous and is produced by those who are involved in the work, the concept of change encounters little resistance. Continuous improvement should be regarded as a routine and essential part of every job in every part of the company.

Managers have to be sensitive to the fact that some people would rather not make needed changes because the impact of change is uncertain and may not be positive for them. This reluctance often produces procrastination and WIND (acronym for "why it's not done") excuses that must be overcome. "No time," the most common WIND excuse, normally translates into "It's not important for me." Such attitudes have to be converted to others that perceive momentum building as an ongoing need and opportunity. Whatever fears exist must be eliminated, which means they must be able to be expressed in a safe atmosphere that promotes trust. The comfort now derived from routine has to be replaced with the satisfaction of making things better. Change does not occur easily unless those involved want to bring it about. People must see the need for change and be able to expect some personal benefits in it for themselves.

Motorola's Robert Galvin was in the middle of the storm when the Asians took over the U.S. industries for radios, television sets, and other electronic consumer products. He ultimately conceded when he sold Motorola's troubled Quasar television business to Matsushita, who, within a year, completely re-structured it and made it a profitable, growing company. Galvin learned from this experience and went on to make Motorola a formidable force in wireless communications and in semiconductor integrated circuits. Commenting on his experience in retrospect, he observed: "Long-term success hinges more than anything on emphasis on continuous improvement of existing work processes, and continuous advancement of great ideas."[3]

Similarly, Gary Hogue, president of The Hogue Cellars, a preeminent pro-ducer of quality wines in the state of Washington, has said: "In the wine busi-ness, you've got to turn up the level of performance each year. You can't just cruise. Sit back and you'll go backwards. I find that motivating."[4]

FORMING A PARTNERSHIP
WITH THE COMPANY'S PEOPLE

Except under unusual circumstances, all of us want to do the right things and want to do them properly; usually, there is nothing but pain for those who make mistakes. Most honest mistakes occur because people lack the necessary knowledge at the time they act, or misperceive priorities. The presence of syn-ergy in company operations can only be authentic when all the company's people have an understanding of the big picture and most of them have a strong desire to contribute to it.

Momentum building requires that policy managers organize operations and influence behavior so that all the company's priorities and actions are func-tioning together synergistically: in revenue generation, administration, value creation, cencon, and management. For this to happen, all the anchorpoint ob-jectives and momentum drivers need to be fused into the fabric of managerial and nonmanagerial thinking, decisions, and actions. In concert with this fu-sion, the three C's of communicating, coordinating, and cooperating must be routine behavior for everyone. Operational synergy can build and flourish once these qualities are integrated, and all the company's work will reflect the importance of accountability, the conviction that customers come first, quality must prevail, ideas count, and time is precious.

Most current literature on promoting organizational change indicates that the most difficult problem by far is changing peoples' behavior. While this is certainly true, the root of the problem often lies with the company's managers. Addressing only the employee side of the problem may help, but until the management side is addressed, little important progress in changing attitudes will be made. If managers expect open and frank communication from others along with a genuine change in behavior, they may have to change their own personal approach to managing.

One productive approach to managerial change is a concept used by CEO Terry Ivany. He grants, openly and formally, to all employees a license to be constructively critical of company operations and to take initiatives toward improvement. The license also permits any employee to take whatever actions he or she thinks appropriate to satisfy the company's customers. This license comes with a guarantee that there will be no direct or indirect penalties to the employee—without which provision, he believes, the license would be meaningless.[5]

Whether Ivany's approach or another is adopted, it is essential to create some kind of formal charter for all employees, including managers, to open two-way communication with top management and to encourage employee initiatives. The CEO and other policy managers must be prepared to accept reality and not punish the messenger. This is a difficult task for some managers, since some of the information they may learn will not reflect well on their past decisions and actions. Another issue is also ego related; some managers are not happy taking advice from someone they consider to be subordinate. A third issue relates to power. Certain managers feel their own authority is eroded if they are expected to treat employees as partners instead of subordinates. All these barriers have to be overcome.

MAKING JOBS MORE INTERESTING

Within every company, the people involved in revenue generation and administration perform the everyday recurring activities which provide the company's revenue margin. The repetitive nature of these activities and the frequent lack of intellectual challenge mean that these jobs are often boring, and that the people who perform them are vulnerable to making mistakes and suffering low morale as well. Several measures can help. The first is to build into the job some worthwhile quality checks that will minimize errors and break up the job routine. The second is to automate some of the repetitive tasks so that other, more challenging ones can be undertaken. A third is to rotate the job among several people so that each works only a half day or less at one job and the remainder of the time on one or two others. The rotation breaks up the repetition and also provides people with cross-training. Another helpful intervention is to ask the worker to think about how to improve productivity while actually performing the job, and then later to give him or her time to work on the improvement.

Some jobs are by nature so dull or repetitious that none of these relieves the boredom. In this circumstance, the company usually must resort to putting the job on some form of incentive pay, so that the worker has an opportunity to earn more by performing more conscientiously. Lincoln Electric, more than fifty years ago, took this approach by putting virtually all their production employees on an incentive pay system that proved to work extremely well for both the company and the employees. The system considered both the quantity and quality of output. If there were quality problems, the person responsible was expected to take the necessary corrective actions without additional pay. The workers were paid for what they produced, which could be quite substantial, and in addition they were given bonuses from company profit. Bonus payments could be quite large, up to 70 percent of their regular pay.

FOUR MAJOR STEPS TOWARD CREATING COMPANY-WIDE MOMENTUM

■ Based on the perspective outlined in chapter 2, establish a managerial job plan that redefines management's essential role and ultimate aim, primary responsibilities, and accountability. Reissue all management position descriptions to incorporate this perspective. Measure, evaluate, and widely communicate the ensuing company momentum performance.

■ Introduce and apply an involvement-oriented approach to management, in which the role of policy managers is to strengthen, not run, the operations under their oversight. Use a flat and flexible, communications-based organization structure like the I-beam. Adopt a company-wide unity of cause that has credibility and permanence. Design and employ meaningful performance appraisal standards for everyone including the CEO and the company's directors. Issue an employee charter to every person who works for the company.

■ Phase out routine annual salary increases and designate growth in competency as the standard for attaining salary increases. Establish gain sharing for all employees based on company performance, not individual contribution or success by function area. Where appropriate use one-time bonuses for exceptional individual contributions.

■ Build organizational vitality to the point that it becomes a market-position advantage for the company.

Be aware that unless there is trauma in a company, some people will resist these changes, sometimes openly, often subtly. Management must take leadership to build support and enthusiasm and to overcome the sometimes intangible obstructionism that holds back progress.

MANAGING CHANGE

There are two kinds of performance growth—the kind measurable in dollars on financial statements, and the kind that strengthens capabilities, competencies, and company infrastructure. The two are rarely synchronized. Strengthening performance capability is virtually always the predecessor to financial growth.

In its most basic sense, building momentum is a process of both producing and preventing change. Lance A. Berger and Martin J. Sikora have offered a comprehensive guide to the process; more than forty people contribute their views on the various aspects of changing a corporation to become more productive.[6] In another book, Daryl Conner focuses on the importance of both time and resilience as vital ingredients to achieve successful change.[7]

Genuine constructive change is not a one-time or infrequent event but an ongoing necessity that should be made a routine part of everyone's activities. But if change is to be easily accepted, people cannot fear it, and managers must be aware that periodic downsizing is organizationally destabilizing and creates fear of job loss. This understanding must be balanced with the knowledge that it is crucial to achieve sufficient profit levels, even during cyclic business downturns, to maintain a consistent, stable, and constructive internal culture. Without reasonable employment stability, the company's organizational vitality and unity of cause will be difficult to attain or retain.

Most successful managers who intuitively build momentum welcome change. They prepare well; move cautiously but confidently; expect the unexpected; compromise toward perfectionism, not mediocrity, even when it takes more time and money; and perform even the little things according to high standards. They also select people who are doers and who demonstrate resourcefulness and ingenuity. These managers are both toughminded and patient. They make sure that mistakes become learning experiences and provide frequent feedback to others on job performance. Any successful manager will testify that producing and preventing change is not easy. Only if managing change becomes a responsibility elevated in status to that of managing money and becomes a part of each manager's personal resource bank will momentum building become a routine company activity. Building momentum means winning the constant duel between making progressive change while keeping operations consistent. This dynamic was eloquently described by the British philosopher Alfred North Whitehead: "The art of progress is to preserve order amid change and to preserve change amid order."

CHANGE AGENTS

If exceptional results are to flow within a reasonable time frame, all policy managers must view themselves as change agents for company strengthening, starting with the CEO. Being a change agent begins with the basics of trust, respect, fairness, and a plan. Prompt, insightful managerial decision-making is also essential. Controlling the company's purse strings carries with it the obligation to understand the priorities that will contribute to building company momentum. This includes having appropriate situation-specific knowledge. Bringing to bear all the necessary intellectual talent from within and outside the company is also vital to generate the creative ideas needed to move forward.

Each undertaking requires the participation of operating managers, team leaders, and nonmanagers at early levels of decision making and action planning. They too need to view themselves as change agents. They must know how they can help and what specifically they can do to strengthen the company. Each must be able to perceive herself or himself as a momentum builder. Most of the actions required will be taken by these people, not by policy-level managers, and involving them early and obtaining their commitment for strengthening will greatly improve the momentum-building program outcome. It will also alleviate some of the uncertainty and concern about future change in current work patterns, job assignments, and operational processes. Perhaps more importantly, it will help assure all the company's people of future opportunities.

A CHALLENGE FOR SMALL- AND MEDIUM-SIZED BUSINESSES

The past lethargic nature of many large corporations has bestowed numerous market opportunities on agile small- to medium-sized businesses, but as more and more large companies restructure for improved market strength, lethargy and inertia are now giving way to momentum. Commenting about the Xerox Corporation's market problems in the 1980s, its chairman and CEO, Paul Allaire, has said:

> Xerox grew from a high-tech startup to one of the country's biggest corporations in large part because we were the only game in town. Then in the 1980s, we faced our first serious competition from the Japanese. This posed a real threat to the company, but thanks to our quality process, we have responded to that threat extremely well. However, the competitive challenges don't stop there. Xerox is now in the midst of a technological transformation that is revolutionizing our business. It is changing the skills our employees need, the competitors we face and indeed, the very nature of the business we are in....We are trying to break the bonds that tie up energy and commitment in a big company. Our goal is to make this $17 billion company more entrepreneurial, more innovative, and more responsive to the marketplace. In fact, we intend to create a company that combines the best of both worlds—the speed, flexibility, accountability, and creativity that comes from being part of a small, highly focused organization, and the economies of scale, the access to resources and the strategic vision that a large company can provide.[8]

The following comments were made by John F. Welch, Jr., chairman and CEO of General Electric, in the company's 1992 annual report to stockholders:

> Most small companies are uncluttered, simple, informal. They need everyone, involve everyone, and reward or remove people based on their contribution to winning. Small

companies dream big dreams and set the bar high—increments and fractions don't interest them....What we are trying relentlessly to do is get that small-company soul and small-company speed inside our big-company body.

And so the newly sought-after momentum in well-established, larger companies is now adding yet another facet to the forces of change in the marketplace. Once business units of large companies become more competent and aggressive, serious future problems will develop for small and medium-sized companies. This will be particularly troublesome to those smaller enterprises that are too slow in moving forward because of insufficient company momentum.

NOTES

1. "Jack Welch's Lessons for Success," *Fortune*, January 25, 1993. Excerpted from Noel M. Tichy and Stratford Sherman, *Control Your Destiny or Someone Else Will*. New York: Doubleday, 1993.

2. Barbera Ettore, "A Little Well-Managed R&D Goes a Long Way," *The President*, May 1995, a publication of the American Management Association.

3. Robert W. Galvin, chairman of Motorola, Inc., in an interview with *Boardroom Reports*, September 1, 1993.

4. From a Hogue Winery advertisement in *Decanter*, June 1995.

5. Terry Ivany, president and CEO of Marine Atlantic, Inc., a company that runs ferry services in Eastern Canada. Mr. Ivany outlined his management approach at the Cambridge Forum on Executive Leadership, held April 15 and 16, 1993 in Cambridge, Mass., by the Cambridge Center for Behavioral Studies.

6. Lance A. Berger and Martin J. Sikora, *The Change Management Handbook*. Chicago: Irwin Professional Publishing, 1994.

7. Daryl R. Conner, *Managing at the Speed of Change*. New York: Villard, 1994.

8. Robert Howard, "The CEO as Organizational Architect: An Interview with Xerox's Paul Allaire," *Harvard Business Review*, September-October 1992.

## CHAPTER 11

Lasting Company Strength

The Ultimate Aim

COMPANY LIFE CYCLES

Since the beginning of the industrial revolution, a nearly all companies have risen, prospered, and declined. Their life cycles have ranged from a few years to many decades. Not many have passed the century mark; few leading companies at the turn of the 20th century are as important today as they were then. Some lost rank through slow growth; some were absorbed through acquisition or merger; and some failed.

There are many explanations for the declining fortunes of previously successful businesses, but there can be only one basic reason: management inadequacy. Most companies that eventually falter do so because their management is not up to the demands of the job, frequently because they lose sight of their own accountability while the company drifts into dangerous waters. These managers miss important market trends and pay too little attention to their companies' declining momentum, both internally and in their market-position strength. When adverse change is rapid, the need to act is clear; slow change is easier to miss entirely, by ignoring it or simply wishing away a fatal mistake.

The truth is that changing market demand, together with changing technological, economic, and political forces, continuously and relentlessly alter the external environment within which companies operate. Existing market segments/niches routinely expand, diminish, or disappear, while new segments/

niches are created. This is a normal market environment. Without timely and innovative management actions, these forces will invariably push a company toward mediocrity and weakness. Companies that do not learn to adapt to their changing environment inevitably fade away. Every company's management has sole accountability for seeing early opportunities and problems in the marketplace. Then management must take appropriate action to ensure the company's capability to succeed within its continuously changing environment.

Being at ease with change—indeed, thriving on it—is probably what most successful companies have in common over the long haul. IBM, one of the most admired growth companies for many decades, has shown especially great endurance. The company began before World War I, reaching $2 billion in sales by 1962 and $65 billion by 1992. In addition to the company's being in the right place at the right time, its most dramatic performance was the result of superior management by its two early CEOs, Thomas J. Watson, Sr., and his son, Thomas J. Watson, Jr. Over the course of the company's life, IBM's products have ranged from butcher scales, typewriters, and punched card tabulators to its present highly sophisticated data-processing equipment. It has been profitable in nearly every year of operation and a highly rated blue chip until its marketplace changed faster than the top management that followed Thomas Watson, Jr., could grasp. In 1993, the company began painful restructuring under a new CEO. It returned to profitability in 1994.

Commenting in the early 1960s about the company's qualities, Thomas Watson, Jr., observed:

> I believe the real difference between success and failure in a corporation can very often be traced to the question of how well the organization brings out the great energies and talents of its people. What does it do to help these people find common cause with each other? How does it keep them pointed in the right direction despite the rivalries and differences which may exist among them? And how can it sustain this common cause and sense of direction through the many changes which take place from one generation to another?...This then is my thesis: I firmly believe that any organization, in order to survive and achieve success, must have a sound set of beliefs on which it premises all its policies and actions....Next, I believe that the most important single factor in corporate success is faithful adherence to those beliefs....And finally, I believe that if an organization is to meet the challenges of a changing world, it must be prepared to change everything about itself except those beliefs as it moves through corporate life.[1]

The pertinent beliefs at IBM, which Watson attributed to his father, were: respect the individual; give the best customer service of any company in the world; and pursue all tasks with the idea that they can be accomplished in a superior fashion.

The predatory aspect of nature and its unforgiving principle of survival of the fittest has its counterpart in the realm of business. No business organization is granted any particular life expectancy: the life term of every company depends on its market-position strength, the rate and nature of the changes in its operating environment, and the manner in which its management takes advantage of change, or fails to do so. A company's life expectancy and prosperity are tied tightly to management's ongoing capacity to *create value more rapidly than the forces for change reduce it.* As long as its managers continue to accomplish this, a company's life expectancy can be unlimited—for its age is not defined by its years, but by its vitality in adapting to new situations and opportunities.

CREATING VALUE: THE ETERNAL QUEST

The overriding aim for the CEO and the policy-management team has to be lasting company strength, achieved by creating value for the company's customers, employees, and shareholders. At the heart of value creation is the company's organizational vitality. All the company's people, manager and nonmanagers, provide the energy, creativity, and persistence that together produce growing market-position strength and thereby growth in the company's financial performance. In a culture where value is continually being created for customers and employees, both the company and the shareholders benefit. No other environment works very well for very long.

Creating value for employees reaches beyond simply offering financial rewards to ensuring them psychological benefits from their work. The company's managers must combine the financial and psychological benefits in a way that galvanizes the company's people to be self-motivated and to want to contribute to company strength. There are no long-term or sure-fire formulas that create value for employees, but trust, fairness, and opportunity must be present in every effort, as well as a sense of faith on the part of the employees in the company's future potential for growth. As noted, critical to this enterprise are a company-wide unity of cause, and a culture that expects accountability and superiority in job performance by everyone.

Company accomplishment is driven by organizational vitality, but this is not enough. The process of creating value is a complex array of many different decisions, activities, and undertakings, all of which must mesh into tangible, timely results in each of the company's anchorpoint objectives. Value is not created by strategy alone; it is the combination of both setting a clear direction and bringing the strategy into working reality within a deliberate time frame that provides marketplace strength.

Because change, external and internal, will continuously produce situations that reduce the company's value-producing capability, creating value is an eternal and unending quest. Managers pursue this quest by acting under their three essential responsibilities—strategic positioning, performance-capability positioning, and momentum building—while keeping their focus on attaining lasting company strength. Management's only path to making important achievements is to look to the future and constantly seek to shape it to the company's advantage. Opportunities invariably come to those who are prepared and earnestly pursue them.

THE NATURE OF SUPERIOR MANAGEMENT

This book has outlined two routes to long-term growth in business: economic-franchised market strength and superior management. The crucial importance of seeking both simultaneously has been noted. An economic franchise is normally built, as Gillette has done, through long-term superior management that sustains the company over time, drawing for its energy on a continually generated supply of company momentum. Products can come and go, and market niches can shift like the desert sands, but with superior management a company will adapt, retain a leadership role in the marketplace, and continue to grow and prosper. This ability to adapt is what separates superior companies from others over the long term.

Policy managers are the integrators of knowledge and ideas who decide on what is important for the company and thereby shape its future. For a company's management to be superior, individual policy managers must perform in a superior manner. Many businesses depend on specialty expertise as the primary criterion for managerial qualification, neglecting the need for competence in management. Although specialty expertise is a critical need, unless managers can work together as a team guided by the principles of lasting company strength and momentum building, the company's performance will be undermined by many of the forces that silently work toward producing operational mediocrity.

Managing a company can be likened to the creation of a multipatterned, multicolored collage by a team of artists. All must be devoted to a design and pictorial story beforehand, and the team must have the resources to get the job done. Nevertheless, the capability, talent, and creativity of each team member determines the value of the finished product. Superior management does not evolve by following a recipe, but by creating an overarching strategy for management that keeps the door open for unique individual contributions.

To achieve consistent long-term performance, a company has to pass through a sequence of "short terms," each of which must provide secure footing on the trip to the long term, a constantly moving target. The capacity to perform in the marketplace today is determined by yesterday's strategy and today's current company strengths. Tomorrow's capacity to perform will be determined by today's strategy and the new strengths the company has gained from momentum building. The synergy from the accomplishments, yesterday and today, will determine the level of the company's future success. If sufficient momentum has been created and sustained along the way, company performance can indeed be superior.

SIMPLICITY

The ultimate message of this book is that policy managers must revise their role, cast out old stereotypes, and perceive themselves as change agents within a company-wide unity of cause. The parallel to the "center" at which Emerson found simplicity and unity of cause is management's steady concentration on forging lasting company strength through momentum building. The framework of principles and paths for Three Dimensional Management offered here provides a strategy for management that can generate company performance growth year after year—the principal management challenge now and into the 21st century. The paths to building a high-momentum company require both time and money; even in a very small company, the complexities involved in building strong capabilities and competencies are formidable and challenging. There are few shortcuts and many potholes in the road to building company value, but if the journey is enthusiastically taken, with one eye on the future and one on the paths toward it, the process will be gratifying and productive.

Business success is fragile and easily shattered. Regardless of its past achievements, every business has to re-earn its reputation and enhance its strengths every business day. If it rests on its laurels even briefly, its momentum will begin to fade. Will Rogers said it clearly: "Even if you are on the right track, you'll get run over if you just sit there."

Management is not yet a science, and perhaps it never will be, but a strategic approach to management focused on momentum building is a prerequisite today for every company. With a sound and explicit strategy for management, a clear view for tomorrow, enough competency and resources, and an abundance of ingenuity and persistence, the potential for accomplishment is without limit.

NOTES

1. Thomas Watson, Jr., *A Business and Its Beliefs*. New York: McGraw-Hill, 1963, p. 4.

APPENDIX A

Glossary

Activity-based Accounting (ABC): A method of cost accounting useful in situations where multiple products or services share labor, materials, supplies, or internal services. Costs are allocated based on the extent to which a product or service causes resources to be consumed in the activity.

Aim: A broadly defined target, end result, or outcome.

Anchorpoint: An important point of reference. The word is defined in Webster's 3rd International Dictionary as a point in an archer's face (as the chin) up to which he brings his drawing hand to stabilize his aim before release of the arrow.

Anchorpoint Objectives: Universal critical success factors for every business, which are: astute core strategy; market-position strength, organizational vitality; productivity gain; and financial performance. These anchorpoints set the aim for managerial efforts in momentum building.

Ambition: The future that management is striving to attain for its company.

Assets (Company): The company's property recorded in its balance sheet accounts, and any unrecorded intellectual property, intangible assets, leases, or money available from established but unused lines of credit.

Business (Company): A social system with the purpose of producing economic value.

Capability: The people and infrastructure that are committed for a specific purpose.

Capability Areas (CAs): Organizational groupings of related capability centers (CCs). Typical CAs in a product company are customer services, field sales, product management, manufacturing, product development, administration, and diverse (an eclectic group of teams).

Capability Centers (CCs): Work centers or groups, archaically called cost centers, supervised by operating managers or team leaders; or self-directed teams that perform work within an explicit operational process(es). All CCs communicate, cooperate, and coordinate with each other directly without in-between managerial hierarchy.

Cash Flow, Operating: The gross cash generated by company operations before adjusting for working capital changes.

Cash Flow, Free: Operating cash flow adjusted for working capital changes.

Cencon System: A company's central information and control system. The term describes a company-wide comprehensive and interactive system for information gathering and dissemination and operations control, including regularly scheduled meetings. Cencon includes the company's financial statements, momentum indicators, internal and external information processes, policies and practices documents, and its network of personal computers, including e-mail. Cencon encompasses all the formal processes by which the company's people interact, communicate, and coordinate.

Competency: Refers to both people and company. People competency is the competency attributed to specific persons and that exists only with them. Company competency combines people and institutionalized competencies those based on such resources as patents, documentation, and processes that exist independent of any individual.

Control: To exercise authority, regulate, verify, measure, or set boundaries. *Internal controls* are the explicit policies and processes that provide for the accuracy and trustworthiness of all information, used internally or externally, and for safeguarding company assets and resources. *Operational controls* are the explicit policies and processes that provide for efficacy and operating consistency throughout the company.

Core Competencies: The specific and unique operational competencies of a company that constitute its ability to compete in the marketplace.

Cost: A broad, general term that refers to the amount of time, money, or effort spent on something.

Critical Success Factors: The key factors that determine a successful outcome in any undertaking.

Culture: The characteristic features of a social group, including its beliefs, values, traditions, habits, and behaviors. A company's culture is shaped in large part by its social and work environment.

Customer Focus: The quality of both satisfying customers and learning from them about their current and future needs.

Cycle Time: In work flow, the time required from start to finish to complete an undertaking, operation, or transaction.

D&A Expense: Development and administration expense. Development expenses are in three categories: manufacturing, product, and company. Administrative expenses are the company-basic, recurring costs that are fixed or semi-fixed, such as rent, insurance, administrative salaries, and management salaries.

Demotivate: To behave or act in a fashion that reduces the level of motivation in another person.

Economic profit: A broad, overall measure of effectiveness in the use of company capital that refers to the net profit of a company after "cost" of capital has been subtracted from net income.

Efficacy: A combination of *effectiveness* and *efficiency* as defined by Peter F. Drucker. Effectiveness means doing the right things; efficiency means doing things right. Efficacy means doing both the right things and doing them right.

Executive: A general term that refers to any high-level manager.

Expenditure: The amount of time, money, or effort spent on something. The term is often used to describe money spent that is not an expense as formally defined in accounting terminology.

Expense: As in GAAP accounting, a period cost for income statement reporting.

GAAP: An accounting profession acronym for generally accepted accounting principles.

Goal: A desired, specifically defined result that contributes toward meeting an objective. There are typically three kinds of goals: a *normal* goal is attainable through a process of incremental action without a significant risk of failure; a *stretch* goal, also reached by incremental action, requires greater effort to achieve and carries some risk that it will not be met; a *breakthrough* goal demands a much higher level of result that cannot be met by incremental action and requires significant creativity; failure is a distinct possibility, as are budget and schedule overruns.

Innovation: Change that creates a new dimension of performance (Drucker).

Infrastructure: Assets and nonhuman resources that provide a company's capability for operational performance.

Intellectual Power: The capacity to develop ideas, strategies, decisions, and actions that provide performance results of value to a company. Intellectual power is derived from individual and group knowledge, ability, judgment, competency, creativity, and continuous learning. Along with human energy, intellectual power is the basis of organizational vitality.

Knowledge: The result of a person or persons translating information into a useful context. There are three levels: explicit, tacit, and intuitive. *Organizational knowledge* is institutionalized in documents, in processes, or within the context of two or more people.

Learning: Study to gain new knowledge, insights, and abilities. Experiential learning is derived from experience.

Management: Most commonly, the group of people in charge of and with the authority to direct the affairs of a business. Another meaning refers to the *process of managing*, by which managers carry out their responsibilities.

Management's Purpose: To provide leadership, oversight, clarity, coherence, and control so all company operations work interactively and synergistically together to add to and create value for the company's key stakeholders.

Management's Essential Role: To bring together ideas, people, competencies, and resources, shaping them into a unified creative force that will achieve the company's anchorpoint objectives.

Management's Primary Responsibility: To establish, as a team under CEO leadership, the company's core business strategies and relevant performance capabilities, and to build and hold the company's marketplace and operations momentum to a level that ensures lasting company strength.

Managing Process: A closed-loop process of making decisions, taking actions, solving problems, and analyzing results, each step of which is shaped by learning, communicating, and involving others.

Manufacturing: A broad term that encompasses all functions and processes associated with the production, inventory, and movement into sales channels of a company's product.

Marketing: Part of a company's sales capability. Usually marketing includes product management, advertising and sales promotion, customer prospecting, brand development, and related activities that are not a part of face-to-face selling to customers.

Marketplace Advantage: A differentiated product attribute or service that provides the supplier with a preferred position for obtaining orders.

Market-position Strengthpoints: The five elements of market-position strength—reputation, products, customer services, marketplace presence, and the unique competencies on which a company's capability to perform in the marketplace depends.

Market Strategy: The approach taken to establish market strength within the bounds set by the company's mission, ambition, and values.

Mission: The business of the company, the nature and scope of its involvement, and its *unity of cause* for carrying out the business activities that will fulfill its mission.

Momentum: The force for growth that results from the rate of company accomplishment. Market-position momentum is the rate at which market-position strengthening is taking place. Operations momentum is the rate at which company performance capability strengthening is taking place.

Momentum Building: Enhancing the rate of company strengthening.

Momentum Drivers: A group of interrelated factors that are the fundamental contributors to momentum in every business. *Core drivers* are unity of cause, accountability, and learning. *Key drivers* are organizational vitality, risk taking, creativity, quality, and control. *Momentum catalysts* are communication, coordination, and cooperation.

Momentum indicators: A group of qualitative and quantitative business performance measures in the broad areas of market-position strength, organizational vitality, productivity gain, financial performance, and stakeholder value produced.

Objective: A qualitatively defined, sought-after overall result for which specific goals need to be set. The word *goal* is used as a subcategory of an objective and can be either qualitative or quantitative. The words *aim, outcome, end, endpoint, target, destination,* and *payoff* are used similarly to *objective,* but they do not imply specific subcategory goals.

Operating managers: Managers responsible for daily operations.

Operating profit: The amount that remains after all non-revenue-generation operating expenses are deducted from revenue margin.

Operations strategy: The planned approach taken to internal operations that establishes and strengthens the company's performance capability. Its aim is to carry out operations in a manner that provides growth in market-position strength and achieves regular gains in company productivity.

Organizational Development: The selection and involvement of people, their nurtured growth in individual capability, and the establishment and maintenance of a constructive, energizing company culture.

Organizational Learning: The process by which an organization obtains new knowledge and competency through the initiatives and interaction of its people.

Organizational Vitality: The intellectual power and human energy of a business.

Performance-capability Positioning: Putting in place the right people and infrastructure to effectively conduct the affairs of the company. This involves the establishment of essential operating activities and their oversight, guidance, and support, but not routine supervision or direction of daily affairs by top management except in exceptional circumstances.

Performance Indicators: The full range of specific measures, quantitative and qualitative, used by a company to comprehend the status and effectiveness of its overall activity.

Policy: Those management decisions that set conditions and boundaries for company operations; the do's and don'ts of operations.

Policy-based Expenses (PBE): Nonoperations expenses—such as debt expense, goodwill amortization, and other charges shown on an internal operations financial statement—that are determined by top management policies.

Policy Managers: The CEO and managers who report to the CEO.

Practices: Specific actions or procedures for policy implementation.

PREM: An acronym for product revenue margin. This is the aggregate revenue margin produced by a specific product or product line.

Processes: The components of a system. A process is composed of a cohesive group of steps or operations in which related activity takes place. There are two broad categories of processes: operational (business) and technological. *Process* is sometimes used synonymously with *system*.

Productivity: An output relative to an input of resources and time; a measure of the efficacy of a particular activity or a combination of activities. Output and input can be defined either qualitatively or quantitatively.

Productivity Gain: An anchorpoint objective for improvement in company-wide productivity.

Renewal: Developing new competencies and capabilities to fit current and future needs.

Resources (company): Customers, employees, products, organizational structure, operational and technological processes, money, and suppliers of goods and services.

Revenues: The monetary value of products or services of which a customer has taken ownership.

Revenue Margin (REM): The profit from a company's revenue generation system, calculated by subtracting all costs of sales and manufacturing from revenues.

REM: An acronym for revenue margin.

Sales: A basic capability area within a company's revenue generation system; as used here it encompasses all aspects of selling, marketing, and distribution. In a narrower context, sales refers to the orders received by a company. The word is sometimes also used informally to refer to revenues.

Stand-alone Entity: A business that is able to sell, fulfill orders, and develop products or services; it can be an independent company or a subsidiary, division, or business unit of a larger corporation.

Strategy: An approach or path toward, or perspective on, achieving an end result. *Core business strategy* describes a company's operations and market strategies; *management strategy*, a part of operations strategy, is the approach to company management as set by the CEO and the board of directors.

Strategic Positioning: Defining, and redefining as needed, the company's specific core strategy for achieving market position and operations strength. Its aim is to set and communicate, clearly and concisely, the long-term view of where the company is going and how it will get there.

Strengthpoints: The elements of a company's market-position strength, which include reputation, products, customer services, marketplace presence, and the core competencies that underlie company performance in the marketplace.

System: A complex unit formed of many often diverse components subject to a common plan or serving a common purpose; a collection of parts that interact with each other to function as a whole. Systems can be nested within a higher-order system. A system is normally composed of processes made up of cohesive groups of steps or operations in which related activity takes place.

Tactics: The specific near-term actions taken to implement a strategy. The actions are usually guided by a situation-specific strategy that is tied into a higher level strategy.

Time Compression: Minimizing the time taken to complete an undertaking or an operational or technological process. Reduction of cycle time.

Unity of Cause: The explicitly stated company-wide purpose to which all employees are expected to contribute.

Vision: A view of the future, not a forecast of it. Closely related to *ambition* and *strategy*.

Values (Company): The beliefs, ethical and business, about behavior and company operations that influence the company's growth and long-term strength.

Value Added: A company's revenue margin (REM) from current operations. Also, in another context, an incremental increase in financial value resulting from a contribution of work or knowledge or the addition of materials.

Value Attribute: A feature of a product or service of identifiable value to a buyer.

Value Created: New sources of revenue margin, or productivity gain, or a reduction in cost.

Value Produced: The combination of value added and value created.

VAREM: An acronym for variable product revenue margin, the incremental revenue margin, up or down, produced by changes in unit volume of a particular product or product line.

APPENDIX B

A Company Profile of Multi-Med, Inc.

As a means for putting guidelines in this book into a real-world context, I have sometimes used a hypothetical company, Multi-Med, Inc., as an example to elaborate on particular points. The characteristics of this company are formed by an amalgam of the successful management practices that have been a part of my business experience or that I have observed in other situations.

The following documents for Multi-Med are found at the end of this appendix:

- B-1. Mission, Ambition, and Values Statement
- B-2. Organizational Capabilities Chart
- B-3. Perspective of Management Accountability
- B-4. CEO Job Description and Performance Accountability
- B-5. Multi-Med, Inc. Operating Financial Statement

COMPANY CHARACTERISTICS

Multi-Med is a manufacturer of medical instruments and a leader in product performance in carefully selected niche markets. It has a well- established reputation in the marketplace. Reference B-1 shows its Mission, Ambition, and Values Statement. The company has adopted Three Dimensional Management as its strategy for management and has made the transition from a traditional pyramid to the I-beam organizational structure. Multi-Med's Capabilities Chart is shown in Reference B-2.

The company does not have seasonality cycles except for a small amount of government business, which is impacted by government budgeting cycles. Its products are capital-asset purchases by its customers, so that economic cycles have some impact on order levels. Because of short cycle time in manufacturing, product delivery to customers is also short. The company does not normally have a large order backlog. Its payment period for customer receivables is forty-five to sixty days. An Operating Financial Statement (reference B-5) provides information on the current year actual results to date and the profit plan for the remainder of the year.

PRODUCTS

Product reliability is a prime consideration for Multi-Med, because its products are used in situations where a patient's life may be at risk. The company does not undertake original scientific research, but creatively applies existing science and engineering knowledge for its specific product and technology process needs. It employs patents, copyrights, and trade secrets as mechanisms for establishing competitive barriers.

Multi-Med currently has two distinct product lines with manufacturing in separate areas. A third line is under development. Product line A is a family of standard instruments that do not offer the option for customizing. These products compete in a relatively mature market segment. Their manufacturing is extensively automated and based on tightly controlled, rigidly structured processes. The company maintains a continuous-improvement program under a process-engineering group that seeks tighter performance tolerances, higher reliability, and lower costs. Product line B provides instruments for several low-volume niche markets. Using a basic modular design, these instruments can be readily custom produced for particular customer needs. The operating mode is flexible production with fast order-response time.

Because of the different operating modes for the two product lines, their manufacturing is situated in separate areas within the same building. Both product lines, however, use technology unique to Multi-Med, from which the company gains marketplace advantages. Both areas maintain reasonable inventories for source materials and modular subassemblies. Production throughput-time is short, and there is minimal in-process inventory. Line A has a small amount of finished product on hand for instant delivery. Line B keeps no finished product inventory.

The quality principles of Crosby, Deming, and Juran are well ingrained in the thinking of Multi-Med's management and operation people. The company uses ISO 9001, an international standard for quality assurance in design/development, production, installation, and servicing in product companies. Management has now gone beyond the TQM movement to an approach that is broader in scope, which it calls the PQR standard, shorthand for performance, quality, and reliability of products and associated processes. This standard, unique to Multi-Med, sets tough criteria for the four key attributes of the company's products and processes: performance, quality, reliability, and productivity.

MANAGEMENT

The company's policy managers own 15 percent of its stock plus stock options; all are corporate officers. There are a president (CEO) and seven vice-presidents; there is no chief operating officer. An outsider chairman leads a seven-person board of directors, and the president is the only insider director. The board holds six regularly scheduled meetings each year, two of which have an appended executive session for only outside directors. The company's chief financial officer attends all board meetings, and the other VPs participate frequently.

The president and VPs have offices in near proximity so that meeting informally is frequent and easy; they are located near but not in the operating areas. All the VPs carry only capability area titles, and no "senior" or "assistant" or other rank distinctions are used. Policy managers receive no significant perquisites, such as company cars or reserved parking. The Perspective on Management Accountability (reference B-3) provides the basic guideline for company management. The CEO's position description (reference B-4) incorporates a performance-appraisal process. The other policy managers' positions are briefly described.

Compensation

All employees are salaried; there are no automatic or merit salary increases. Salary increases are granted when employees either take on increased responsibility or demonstrate increased performance capability. A separate company-wide gain-sharing program, for all employees except policy managers, has a pool size of 40 percent of operating profit above a pretax 12 percent return on net assets. This is paid quarterly in proportion to base salary.

All policy managers' compensation has three components: salary, variable pay, and stock options. Salaries are kept to the low side of the industry average to emphasize the role of variable pay in cash compensation. One half of the variable pay for all managers is determined by company financial performance, using a formula with two variables, revenue margin and return on net assets; individual payout is proportional to base salary. The other half is qualitatively determined, based on individual performance. The formula-derived variable pay, averaged over a three-year period with a penalty applied for inconsistent year-to-year growth, is paid annually. The payout pool size is 10 percent of operating profit above 12 percent return on net assets.

Ownership-linked stock options provide the equity-based compensation; these are granted at the time of initial employment and on a discretionary basis thereafter. The options are intended to provide financial gain that is much larger than salary and variable pay combined if company financial performance is consistently good to exceptional. Options vest in the fourth through the eighth year and expire after ten years. At least 40 percent of the prior vested shares must be purchased and retained for the recipient to benefit from future options. The size of the options is determined by the CEO in consultation with, and with the approval of, the compensation committee of the board of directors.

Reference B-1

THE MISSION, AMBITION, AND VALUES OF MULTI-MED, INC.

OUR MISSION

Multi-Med is a growth-oriented product development and manufacturing company whose business is to convert ideas, competency, and technology into products and services that satisfy and retain customers who use noninvasive medical instruments.

Our *unity of cause* for every employee—manager, professional, and associate—is to build sufficient momentum from company-wide accomplishments to continuously strengthen our market position and performance capability, and thereby obtain and retain leadership in our chosen market niches. Every employee with us for more than one year will share in our growth in profit resulting from company-wide momentum-building efforts.

OUR AMBITION

We strive, by exceptional performance, to earn a reputation with our customers that is second to none in our chosen markets. This is essential for company strength. We intend to be an important long-term participant and a performance and value leader in carefully chosen, specific market niches to which we bring unique competency. Size, as measured by market share or sales, is not our first consideration. We intend, however, to lead in enough niches to be a significant, well-respected, and important contributor to the medical field.

OUR CORE VALUES

Customers provide the money for our operations and for all our jobs. We will prosper only as long as we provide imaginative, high-quality products, exceptional service, and meaningful value to customers, both existing and new. While producing customer value, we must also produce value for our employees and shareholders.

To grow and endure in our markets, to be a stable and dependable employer, and to be an attractive business to sources of capital, we must be financially strong by routinely earning sufficient profit. We believe the company's strength in the marketplace is the key to profitability and the only assurance of employment opportunity. Profit is the prime source of funds to further strengthen and grow the company. Profit does not take precedence, however, when problems arise that affect our reputation or customer confidence in us.

Our relationships are based on trust, mutual respect, individual accountability, fairness, and pride in accomplishment. We expect each person to treat others as he or she wants to be treated. Honesty, law compliance, and courtesy are fundamental requirements. We will always hold to the highest ethical standards and will take corrective action when these standards are not upheld.

To provide exceptional service and high value to our customers, we need a performance-focused company culture that is socially attractive and promotes open communication, cooperation, initiative, creativity, learning, and growth in competency. Loyalty from our employees is important to us; so is company loyalty to our employees. We cannot assure permanent employment to anyone who works with us, but we will encourage and help our employees to develop competencies that will help them advance in their careers.

Reference B-2: Organizational Capabilities Chart

CUSTOMERS

CUSTOMER SERVICES

- CUSTOMER REPRESENTATIVES
- ORDER PROCESSING
- FIELD SALES SUPPORT
- TECHNICAL SUPPORT
- FIELD MAINTENANCE
- TECHNICAL PUBLICATIONS

MANUFACTURING A

- PRODUCTON A
- PRODUCTION CONTROL
- CAM SUPPORT
- LINE ENGINEERING
- PQR ENGINEERING
- CENTRAL PURCHASING
- INVENTORY MANAGEMENT
- SHIPPING/RECEIVING
- SUPPLIER PROGRAMS

MANUFACTURING B

- PRODUCTON B
- PRODUCTION CONTROL
- CAM SUPPORT
- LINE ENGINEERING
- PQR ENGINEERING

DIVERSE TEAMS

- GOALS
- PROFIT PLAN
- MOMENTUM PLAN
- CENCON DEVELOPMENT
- COMPANY DEVELOPMENT
- PQR/ISO 9001
- EDUCATION/TRAINING
- SOCIAL PROGRAMS

THE COMPANY'S CENTRAL COMMUNICATIONS PATHWAY

FIELD SALES

- GLOBAL SALES
- DISTRIBUTOR SALES
- FIELD SALES-MIDWEST
- FIELD SALES-WEST
- FIELD SALES-EAST

PRODUCT MANAGEMENT

- PRODUCT PLANNING TEAM
- PRICING/PROPOSALS
- SALES SUPPORT
- SALES PROMOTION
- ADVERTISING
- MARKET RESEARCH

PRODUCT DEVELOPMENT

- PRODUCT TECH SUPPORT
- TECHNOLOGY DEVELOPMENT
- PROCESS DEVELOPMENT
- PRODUCT A DEVELOPMENT
- PRODUCT B DEVELOPMENT
- PRODUCT C DEVELOPMENT
- CAD SUPPORT

ADMINISTRATION

- HUMAN RESOURCES
- INFORMATION SYSTEMS
- CONTROLLER'S OFFICE
- ACCOUNTING OFFICE
- CASH MANAGEMENT
- GENERAL ADMINISTRATION
- FACILITIES MANAGEMENT

MANAGEMENT

Reference B-3: Perspective on Management Accountability

PERSPECTIVE ON MANAGEMENT ACCOUNTABILITY

Management's purpose is to provide leadership, oversight, clarity, coherence, and control so that all company operations work interactively and synergistically together to add and create value for the company's key stakeholders. The essential role of managers is to bring together ideas, people, competencies, and resources and shape them into a unified creative force that will achieve the company's anchorpoint objectives.

Management's primary responsibility, as a team under CEO leadership, is to establish the company's core business strategies and relevant performance capabilities, and to build and hold the company's marketplace and operations momentum to a level that will ensure lasting company strength.

ULTIMATE AIM

● Lasting company strength

THREE DIMENSIONAL MANAGEMENT

■ Strategic positioning   ■ Performance-capability positioning
● Momentum building

MANAGERIAL FOCUS

◆ Anchorpoint objectives   ◆ Accountability
◆ Momentum drivers   ◆ Momentum indicators
◆ Infrastructure

APPROACH TO OPERATIONS

■ Company-wide unity of cause   ■ Involvement-oriented operations
■ Meaningful performance appraisal ■ Performance-based compensation

MANAGERIAL ACCOUNTABILITY

■ Astute core strategy   ■ Market-position strength
■ Organizational vitality   ■ Productivity gain
■ Financial performance   ■ Protection of resources and assets
■ Value: for customers, employees,
   and shareholders.

● The two principles and ◆ five paths of Three Dimensional Management

Reference B-4 CEO Job Description and Performance Accountability

POSITION: CHIEF EXECUTIVE OFFICER (CEO)

JOB OVERVIEW

The CEO's role is to define the company's mission, ambition, and values; to provide overall direction and leadership for the company; and to bring together ideas, people, competencies, and resources, shaping them into a unified creative force that will achieve the company's fundamental objectives and goals. The CEO selects, involves, and leads a policy management team that guides all the company's affairs. The CEO decides on corporate policies and operational processes, sets performance standards and evaluates company and individual performance, interprets and applies the policies of the board of directors, and represents the company to outside people and organizations.

PRIMARY RESPONSIBILITY

Top management's primary responsibility, as a team under CEO leadership, is to establish the company's core business strategies and relevant performance capabilities, and to build and hold marketplace and operational momentum to a level that will ensure lasting company strength. This includes:

- Deciding the company's operations and market strategic positioning
- Providing the people and infrastructure for the company's performance capability
- Continuously strengthening the company's market position and operations

AUTHORITY

The CEO has the full authority, except as specifically limited by the board of directors and law, to conduct all the affairs of the company.

ACCOUNTABILITY

The CEO's ultimate accountability to the company's customers, employees, and owners is for company

1. growth, as evidenced primarily by financial performance
2. character, as evidenced by the favorable reputation the company has earned
3. perpetuation, as evidenced by the company's capacity for self-renewal and sustained momentum.

The CEO is accountable to the board of directors for the efficacy of all aspects of the company's plans, people, operations, and control. The CEO's job performance will be evaluated based on company and personal performance in the following accountability areas:

- Core strategy
- Market-position strength
- Productivity gain
- Value creation for customers, employees, and shareholders
- Organizational vitality
- Financial performance
- Protection of resources and assets

CEO PERFORMANCE EVALUATION

Separate from the corporate annual profit plan, which is intended to be a conservative communication and control instrument, a momentum plan (MP) is to be submitted to the board of directors prior to the beginning of each fiscal year and updated quarterly. The MP is the road map by which policy management carries out its essential responsibility for company strengthening. The plan is to specify the "stretch" and/or "breakthrough" goals, under each of the above seven areas of accountability, that the corporation will undertake. The strategy, target schedules, and costs to meet these goals should be outlined.

The board's expectation is that the CEO will build significant company strengths while simultaneously creating sufficient value for its customers, employees, and shareholders. A designated committee of the board will formally evaluate the CEO's performance annually, and do so informally on an interim basis. The MP establishes a common understanding beforehand between the committee and the CEO on the actions to be taken and levels of momentum to be sought. This understanding will form the basis for subsequent performance evaluation.

The first consideration in the evaluation will be the actual strengthening achieved under each of the seven areas of accountability. The CEO's personal effectiveness in carrying out his or her job and the extent of "ambition" in the goals will also be considered. Evaluation will be based, not necessarily on whether goals were or were not met, but on the real gains made in corporate strengths, The intent is for the goals to target major progress, not small increments.

The corporation's cencon system is to be structured to gather pertinent momentum indicator information that is regularly made available to the directors. This information and any outside studies initiated by the company or board committees will be the basis for determining actual performance results. At the end of each quarter, the specific results achieved, qualitative and quantitative, for each MP preset goal are to be given the committee in the context of an informal progress report. At the end of the year, and before the formal review takes place, the CEO is to summarize for the committee the impact on the company of the results achieved. He or she should also provide a self-evaluation of his or her own performance. Enough time should be allowed for this introspection.

When the actual review takes place, the committee's agenda will be to examine corporate performance results in the seven accountability areas; consider the impact of these results on corporate strength relative to its mission, ambition, and values; take into account pertinent issues not related to the preset goals; consider the CEO's personal effectiveness; and summarize its overall conclusions while offering guidance for future actions to be taken by the CEO. The CEO's self-evaluation will be an important aspect of the discussions. Specific steps toward CEO self-improvement should be agreed on.

The board committee's basic role is to become fully aware of all corporate and CEO performance-related issues and help the CEO remain objective in self-evaluation. The committee should take into account both the nature and the importance of the goals and the methods by which they were achieved. The committee's aim is to come to agreement with the CEO in a way that is helpful for future decisions and action.

CORPORATE VICE-PRESIDENTS (VPS)

The position descriptions for corporate vice-presidents follow the content and general format of that of the CEO. Each policy manager is accountable to the CEO for company performance in his or her assigned capability area(s) or capability centers, and for meeting company-wide goals set by policy management as a team; the extent to which the company's unity of cause is effective; and the expenditures involved in meeting job responsibilities.

The CEO, with the chairman of the compensation committee occasionally sitting in, evaluates the performance of each VP. A VP's individual performance evaluation follows the same process and criteria as established for the CEO, except that the scope is focused on a particular capability area. The company expects good to excellent performance from all its managers, professionals, and associates. It will be supportive, helpful, and patient with those who are making progress in self-development but will not long tolerate performance that is less than good from anyone.

The role of each VP is briefly as follows:

VP, Treasurer, and CFO

The vice-president, treasurer, and chief financial officer is responsible for the company's administrative system, including all the normal treasurer and CFO functions, and all risk management, legal, and other company-central administrative activities that are not within the scope of the VP for human relations. The CFO is team leader of the team responsible for the cencon system.

He or she is accountable to the CEO, and to the board of directors where applicable, for the efficacy of internal controls, including internal auditing; the availability of cash to meet operational needs; cash-control processes; the development and control of all reports issued under the cencon system; compliance with all applicable laws and regulations; the adequacy of insurance coverage; and providing support services to others in data processing and in operations process design.

VP, Human Relations

The vice-president for human relations is responsible for routine human relations (HR) functions, including the company's employment policies and benefits, employee education programs, and the development of specific programs for measuring and raising the level of organizational vitality.

He or she is accountable to the CEO for ensuring that employee matters are handled smoothly and fairly, and that employment policies, benefits, and HR processes support the need for high organizational vitality.

VP, Business Development

The vice-president for business development is responsible for developing strategy for long-term company growth, including possible acquisitions, locating and characterizing new market opportunities that can be undertaken using existing company competencies, and, when needed, identifying and guiding the development of specific new company competencies that can synergistically combine with existing competencies to open totally new market opportunities.

He or she is accountable to the CEO for the effectiveness of the growth strategies developed, the vitality of the programs that undertake product and market development or acquisitions, and for the extent, nature, and analytical insight of the research to identify market and technology trends.

VP, Sales

The vice-president for sales is responsible for the company's worldwide sales, which includes direct sales and distributor channels, all marketing activities, development and execution of market strategy to provide continuing growth within existing markets, identifying new market opportunities linked to existing company competencies, achieving customer satisfaction and loyalty by providing superior customer services and after-sale support, developing information on the future needs of existing and potential new customers, and analyzing the current and expected future behavior of competitors.

He or she is accountable to the CEO for the efficacy of the sales operations, setting and meeting specific performance goals for short- and long-term growth rate in REM, the usefulness of nonfinancial momentum indicators developed for monitoring market-position strength, and controlling accounts receivable defaults.

VP, Manufacturing

The vice-president for manufacturing is responsible for timely manufacture and order fulfillment, to PQR and ISO 9001 standards, for his or her manufacturing areas. He or she is accountable to the CEO for the cost, efficacy and productivity gain of the manufacturing unit, the usefulness of nonfinancial momentum indicators developed for monitoring performance in manufacturing, the employment of outsourcing and partnering when advantageous, and the losses incurred from inventory writeoffs.

VP, Product Development

The vice-president for product development is responsible for the development of cost-effective product improvements and new products that will provide high value to customers and high REM levels, and that will extend both the performance range and the life expectancy of the company's existing products.

She or he is accountable to the CEO for the efficacy of the product and technology development processes, for setting and meeting PQR standards that provide ongoing product position advantages in the marketplace, and for defining and meeting a cycle time from concept-to-market for product improvements and new products that maintain and strengthen the company's marketplace leadership. A key goal for product and technology process development is proprietary technology that will establish competitive barriers to market entry.

Reference B5, Multi-Med, Inc. Operational Financial Statement

OPERATIONS FINANCIAL STATEMENT   JUNE 1996,

| OPFIN 7/3/96 | | | ACTUAL | | | | PLAN | |
$ in Thousands	Jan	Feb	Mar	Apr	May	Jun	Jul	Aug
# NET NEW ORDERS (NNO)	5930.2	6225.6	6466.1	6384.3	6559.9	6921.5	5600.0	5600.0
NET REVENUES (NR)	6108.3	6192.8	6378.2	6290.7	6566.7	6809.1	5800.0	5800.0
Std Cost to Manufacture	2321.2	2353.3	2423.7	2390.5	2495.3	2587.5	2204.0	2204.0
Manufacturing Cost Variance	91.6	61.9	76.5	56.6	118.2	129.4	87.0	87.0
Cost to Sell *	549.7	532.6	593.2	610.2	682.9	646.9	551.0	568.4
Sales Commission	366.5	371.6	382.7	377.4	394.0	408.5	348.0	348.0
Write Offs: AR & Inv.	30.5	31.0	31.9	31.5	32.8	34.0	29.0	29.0
Cost of Revenues Total	3,359.6	3,350.3	3,508.0	3,466.2	3,723.3	3,806.3	3,219.0	3,236.4
# REVENUE MARGIN (REM)	2748.7	2842.5	2870.2	2824.5	2843.4	3002.8	2581.0	2563.6
% of NR	45.0%	45.9%	45.0%	44.9%	43.3%	44.1%	44.5%	44.2
Manufacturing Develop't Expense	333.3	316.7	336.7	323.3	326.7	340.0	306.7	300.0
Product Development Expense	533.3	506.7	538.7	517.3	522.7	544.0	490.7	480.0
Company Development Expense	133.3	126.7	134.7	129.3	130.7	136.0	122.7	120.0
Admin & Mgmt Expense	466.7	443.3	471.3	452.7	457.3	476.0	429.3	420.0
Variable Pay Expense	244.3	247.7	255.1	251.6	262.7	272.4	232.0	232.0
Dev & Admin (D&A) Exp Total	1711.0	1641.0	1736.5	1674.3	1700.0	1768.4	1581.3	1552.0
# D&A EXPENSE % of REM	62.2%	57.7%	60.5%	59.3%	59.8%	58.9%	61.3%	60.5
# OPERATING PROFIT (OP)	1037.7	1201.4	1133.7	1150.2	1143.4	1234.4	999.7	1011.0
% of NR	17.0%	19.4%	17.8%	18.3%	17.4%	18.1%	17.2%	17.4
Debt Expense	50.0	50.0	50.0	50.0	50.0	50.0	50.0	50.0
Goodwill Amortization	25.0	25.0	25.0	25.0	25.0	25.0	25.0	25.0
Other (Income) Expense	-4.0	-4.0	-4.0	-4.0	-4.0	-4.0	-4.0	-4.0
Policy-Based Exp. (PBE) Total	71.0	71.0	71.0	71.0	71.0	71.0	71.0	71.0
INCOME PRE-TAX (IPT)	966.7	1130.4	1062.7	1079.2	1072.4	1163.4	928.7	940.6
Income Taxes	386.7	452.2	425.1	431.7	429.0	465.4	371.5	376.2
NET INCOME	580.0	678.3	637.6	647.5	643.4	698.1	557.2	564.4
% of NR	9.5%	11.0%	10.0%	10.3%	9.8%	10.3%	9.6%	9.7
Non-Cash Expense	119.0	119.0	119.0	119.0	119.0	119.0	119.0	119.0
Capital Asset Expenditures	100.0	95.0	101.0	97.0	98.0	102.0	100.0	100.0
# OPERATING CASH FLOW	599.0	702.3	655.6	669.5	664.4	715.1	576.2	583.4
FREE OPNG CASH FLOW	437.7	540.0	491.1	506.0	497.6	545.4	418.6	425.8
# Sales Cost % of Revenue	10.8%	9.5%	10.4%	10.4%	12.2%	11.2%	11.4%	11.7
# Payroll % of Revenue (PPR)	58.9%	58.1%	56.4%	57.2%	54.8%	52.9%	62.1%	62.1
# Return on Net Assets (RONA)	14.2%	16.6%	15.6%	15.9%	15.8%	17.1%	13.6%	13.8
# Working Captl Turnover (WCT)	5.1	5.1	4.9	5.0	4.8	4.6	5.4	5.4
Net Receivables > 60 days	1246.1	1263.3	1301.2	1283.3	1339.6	1389.1	1183.2	1183.2
Inventory < 3 Turns	1600.0	1520.0	1616.0	1552.0	1568.0	1632.0	1472.0	1440.0

# Denotes that the line item is a momentum indicator.

* Includes all sales costs except sales commissions.

and FORECAST FOR YEAR 1996

| | | | | QUARTER ENDING | | | | YEAR PLAN | | |
| | | | | ACTUAL | | PLAN | | | % up from | |
Sep	Oct	Nov	Dec	MAR	JUN	SEP	DEC	YEAR	PLAN	LAST YR
7000.0	7500.0	8200.0	7300.0	18621.9	19865.7	18200.0	23000.0	79687.6	-5.0%	9.2%
6600.0	7000.0	7400.0	7300.0	18679.3	19666.5	18200.0	21700.0	78245.8	-5.4%	8.8%
2508.0	2660.0	2812.0	2774.0	7098.1	7473.3	6916.0	8246.0	29733.4	-7.0%	-8.6%
99.0	105.0	111.0	109.5	230.1	304.2	273.0	325.5	1132.8	-10.0%	-1.9%
646.8	693.0	740.0	730.0	1675.5	1940.0	1766.2	2163.0	7544.7	9.0%	6.6%
396.0	420.0	444.0	438.0	1120.8	1180.0	1092.0	1302.0	4694.7	-5.0%	8.8%
33.0	35.0	37.0	36.5	93.4	98.3	91.0	108.5	391.2	-10.0%	0.0%
3,682.8	3,913.0	4,144.0	4,088.0	10217.9	10995.8	10138.2	12145.0	43496.9		
2917.2	3087.0	3256.0	3212.0	8461.4	8670.7	8061.8	9555.0	34748.9	-5.5%	9.1%
44.2%	44.1%	44.0%	44.0%	45.3%	44.1%	44.3%	44.0%	44.4%	-	-
346.7	343.3	336.7	306.7	986.7	990.0	953.3	986.7	3916.7	1.5%	8.7%
554.7	549.3	538.7	490.7	1578.7	1584.0	1525.3	1578.7	6266.7	-3.2%	5.5%
138.7	137.3	134.7	122.7	394.7	396.0	381.3	394.7	1566.7	3.5%	7.9%
485.3	480.7	471.3	429.3	1381.3	1386.0	1334.7	1381.3	5483.3	-4.0%	4.3%
264.0	280.0	296.0	292.0	747.2	786.7	728.0	868.0	3129.8	-13.4%	12.1%
1789.3	1790.7	1777.3	1641.3	5088.5	5142.7	4922.7	5209.3	20363.2	-0.2%	7.8%
61.3%	58.0%	54.6%	51.1%	60.1%	59.3%	61.1%	54.5%	58.6%	-	-
1127.9	1296.3	1478.7	1570.7	3372.9	3528.1	3139.1	4345.7	14385.8	-3.5%	11.0%
17.1%	18.5%	20.0%	21.5%	18.1%	17.9%	17.2%	20.0%	18.4%	-	-
50.0	50.0	50.0	50.0	150.0	150.0	150.0	150.0	600.0	0.0%	-9.0%
25.0	25.0	25.0	25.0	75.0	75.0	75.0	75.0	300.0	0.0%	0.0%
-4.0	-4.0	-4.0	-4.0	-12.0	-12.0	-12.0	-12.0	-48.0	-	-
71.0	71.0	71.0	71.0	213.0	213.0	213.0	213.0	852.0	0.0%	-6.5%
1056.9	1225.3	1407.7	1499.7	3159.9	3315.1	2926.1	4132.7	13533.8	-1.9%	12.8%
422.7	490.1	563.1	599.9	1264.0	1326.0	1170.5	1653.1	5413.5	-	-
634.1	735.2	844.6	899.8	1895.9	1989.0	1755.7	2479.6	8120.3	-1.9%	12.8%
9.6%	10.5%	11.4%	12.3%	10.1%	10.1%	9.6%	11.4%	10.4%	-	-
=====	=====	=====	=====	=====	=====	=====	=====	======	====	=====
119.0	119.0	119.0	119.0	357.0	357.0	357.0	357.0	1428.0	0.0%	-8.5%
100.0	100.0	100.0	100.0	296.0	297.0	300.0	300.0	1193.0	0.0%	7.0%
653.1	754.2	863.6	918.8	1956.9	2049.0	1812.7	2536.6	8355.3	-1.8%	9.2%
485.9	582.2	686.8	743.2	1468.8	1549.0	1330.3	2012.2	6360.3	-1.8%	9.4%
10.7%	10.6%	10.4%	11.5%	10.2%	11.3%	11.2%	10.8%	10.9%	10.0%	-12.3%
54.5%	51.4%	48.6%	49.3%	57.8%	54.9%	59.3%	49.8%	55.2%	-7.4%	-5.5%
15.5%	18.0%	20.7%	22.0%	15.5%	16.2%	14.3%	20.2%	16.6%	-1.2%	9.5%
4.7	4.5	4.8	4.3	5.0	4.8	5.2	4.3	4.8	-3.5%	6.9%
1346.4	1428.0	1509.6	1489.2	1301.2	1389.1	1346.4	1489.2	1489.2	-8.2%	-7.6%
1664.0	1648.0	1616.0	1472.0	1616.0	1632.0	1664.0	1472.0	1472.0	-10.1%	-8.4%

INDEX